KW-467-035

SCOTLAND

AND THE

FRENCH REVOLUTION

SCOTLAND

AND THE

FRENCH REVOLUTION

BY

HENRY W. MEIKLE

[1912]

FRANK CASS & CO LTD
LONDON *1969*

S B N 7146 1503 X

First Edition 1912

(Edinburgh: James Maclehose and Sons, Publishers to the University, 1912)

Published in the United Kingdom by

FRANK CASS & CO LTD

67 Great Russell Street, London W C 1

PRINTED IN THE UNITED STATES OF AMERICA

by SENTRY PRESS, NEW YORK, N. Y. 10019

SCOTLAND AND THE FRENCH REVOLUTION

SCOTLAND

AND THE

FRENCH REVOLUTION

BY

HENRY W. MEIKLE

M.A., D.LITT.

LECTURER IN SCOTTISH HISTORY IN THE UNIVERSITY OF EDINBURGH

GLASGOW

JAMES MACLEHOSE AND SONS

PUBLISHERS TO THE UNIVERSITY

1912

TO MY WIFE

PREFACE

THIS study of the influence of the French Revolution on Scotland was accepted by the University of Edinburgh as a thesis for the degree of Doctor of Letters. Its main theme is the political awakening of Scotland. I have therefore devoted considerable attention to the various reform movements which either originated in the political upheaval of the period or were stimulated by it. I have tried to show, more briefly, that although the dread of innovation suspended the activity of the reformers for a time, the Reform Bill of 1832 was due, in part at least, to the agitation engendered forty years before. An attempt has also been made to trace the effects of the French Revolution in other departments of the national life, chiefly social and ecclesiastical, and to describe the rôle assigned to Scotland in French schemes for invading the British Isles. Though I am indebted to the recent works of Professor Hume Brown, and Dr. W. Law Mathieson, the ampler space at my disposal has enabled me to draw largely on unpublished material, and to give a fuller account of a somewhat neglected aspect of Scottish history than has hitherto been possible.

I take this opportunity of acknowledging the courtesy of the officials of the British Museum, London, and of the University, Advocates', Signet, and S.S.C. Libraries, Edinburgh. In examining the Scottish manuscripts in the Public Record Office, London, I was greatly assisted by Mr.

Hubert Hall; and the same kindness was extended to me by M. le Sous-Directeur des Archives and his colleagues at the Foreign Office, Paris. My heartiest thanks are due to my friends, Dr. W. Law Mathieson, and Mr. Alexander Robertson, M.A., B.Litt., New College, Oxford, for their careful and suggestive reading of the proofs. In connection with the whole work, Professor Hume Brown has been to me an unfailing source of help and encouragement.

Finally, I have to record the generosity of the Carnegie Trust for the Universities of Scotland. The research was begun during the tenure of a Carnegie Scholarship, which was supplemented by successive grants; and the publication of the results has been facilitated by a further grant from the same Trust.

University of Edinburgh,
October, 1912.

CONTENTS

INTRODUCTION

CHAPTER I

SIGNS OF POLITICAL AWAKENING

CHAPTER II

BURGH AND ECCLESIASTICAL REFORM

CHAPTER V

"THE FRIENDS OF THE PEOPLE"

CHAPTER VI

THE STATE TRIALS

CHAPTER VII

THE BRITISH CONVENTION

CHAPTER VIII

FRENCH PROJECTS OF INVASION

CHAPTER IX

THE MILITIA RIOTS AND THE UNITED SCOTSMEN

CHAPTER X

THE CHURCH AND THE FRENCH REVOLUTION

CHAPTER XI

CONCLUSION. 1802-1832

APPENDICES

Erratum. Page 127, *line* 9, *for* '*Dundas*' *read* '*Montgomery.*'

INTRODUCTION

Scotland in the eighteenth century is characterised by a variety of interests not to be found in any other period of its history. The poverty of the country had hitherto hindered the growth of a rich civilisation such as was to be found in England or France; but after the Union of 1707, and more especially after the 'Forty-Five, its material prosperity advanced by leaps and bounds. The linen and woollen manufactures received a fresh lease of life; coal and iron mines were opened up; "Gothish methods" in agriculture gave place to a system which included the rotation of crops and the use of manures; the modern plough and the threshing-machine were invented; new roads, canals, and bridges increased the means of communication.

This material prosperity was accompanied by the long delayed Renaissance of Letters. The intellect of the country, freed from the turmoil of dynastic and ecclesiastical disputes, turned to the more liberal studies of literature and science. It was in this connection, indeed, that Scotland made its special contribution to the history of civilisation; for, while industrial progress was a feature of Great Britain as a whole, in Scotland there was also a conspicuous literary activity, which, within a comparatively brief period, produced a series of works destined to enjoy a vogue not only at home but abroad. Hume and Reid in philosophy, Adam

Smith in political economy, Black and Hutton in science, Macpherson in poetry, Hume and Robertson in history, all won European fame, and Edinburgh almost outrivalled Paris as the intellectual capital of the world.[1]

While industrially and intellectually Scotland by 1780 was thus an awakened country, politically it was still asleep. This was largely due to the lack of a constitutional element in its history. A small country with but a scanty population, divided by racial hatred, and clan and family rivalries, scarcely afforded an opportunity for such development. The Scottish Parliament, for example, remained to the end of its existence a feudal assembly. It had little influence on the national history. In its earlier stages it was a baron court registering the decrees of whatever party happened to be in power. Later, as from 1640 to 1651, it endeavoured to emulate the Parliament of England, but such spasmodic efforts were revolutionary rather than evolutionary, and the changes then introduced were quickly reversed. Even during this period it was much less influential than the General Assembly of the Kirk. Under the new conditions of the Revolution Settlement, it had barely time to show its capacity as a legislative and deliberative body, when it was merged in the Parliament of Great Britain.

Local institutions might still have served to arouse an interest in public affairs, but these were wanting in all but name. The freedom of the burghs had been early crushed. In 1469 it had been enacted that the old town council should choose the new, and that the two together should appoint the officers of the burgh. This Act rendered impossible any healthy political life in the towns since even the Scottish burgh representatives at Westminster were chosen

[1] Hume Brown, *Hist. of Scot.* iii. 371 ; v. *The Learning of the Scots in the Eighteenth Century*, an article by the present writer in the *Scot. Hist. Rev.* April 1910. It is mainly a reprint of a contemporary pamphlet.

by delegates from the town councils. In the counties, the franchise was of such a restricted nature that in 1788 there were only 2662 voters on the freeholders' roll. The issues at stake in the elections were mainly personal, and Wilkes is reported to have refused to interfere in a Scottish election petition on the ground that he could discern no principle in the strife of "Goth against Goth."

There was little in such family politics to commend them to the nation at large. Some of the better minds of the age had welcomed the Union for the very reason that place-hunting and its attendant evils would be abolished, and that, in the language of Mar, Scotsmen would be at liberty "to live at peace and ease, and mind their affairs and the improvement of their country—a much better employment than the politics."[1] This improvement, as the Jacobite Risings had shown, was bound up with the Hanoverian succession; so that public opinion, as reflected in the pulpit, in the teaching of the universities, and in the newspapers of the time, was strongly Revolution Whig. Politics were dynastic rather than party, and opposition to the Administration in London was denounced as disloyalty to the reigning House.

The Wilkes crisis, to which some historians have traced the rise of modern political agitation, could not appeal to Scotsmen. It was against a Scot that the invective of Wilkes was directed, and the subservient Scottish members were the supporters of the prerogative that was assailed. The people of North Britain, therefore, unanimously supported the King and their fellow-countryman, Bute, his unpopular Minister. It would be a mistake, however, to assign to this incident the conscious turning away of the Scots from participation in what was regarded as English

[1] *Cromarty Correspond.* ii. 20, cited by W. L. Mathieson, *Scotland and the Union*, 159.

political life. In contemporary pamphlets and newspapers it is the industrial development of the country that is dwelt upon in answer to the sneers of Wilkes. This national pre-occupation finds a striking illustration in the proceedings of the Select Society, a club formed avowedly on the model of the French Academy. Its debates for the year 1757 are all of an economic character,[1] and when some of the same "Literati" founded the Poker Club in 1762 "to stir up the fire and spirit of the nation," it was patriotic rather than political in its aims. George Dempster of Dunnichen wrote to Dr. Carlyle of Inveresk, one of its promoters, that when they got their militia, they ought to agitate for Parliamentary reform "so as to let the industrious farmer and manufacturer share at least in a privilege now engrossed by the great lord, the drunken laird, and the drunkener baillie"; but the suggestion bore no fruit.[2]

Exactly twenty years later, in 1782, Mrs. Hamilton, the authoress of *The Cottagers of Glenburnie*, could thus describe the apathy prevailing in her native land. "The people here are not such great politicians as in Ireland," she wrote to her brother. "There, politics engross the greatest part of discourse in every county, and man, woman, and child, enter as zealously into every debate, as if they had been perfectly acquainted with all the hidden springs of government. The people here pretend to no such knowledge, but whatever changes happen, either in ministry or constitution, they seem to adopt the maxim of Mr. Pope, that 'whatever is, is right.'" She referred to a recent speech of a Scottish gentleman who had declared that "as that man was esteemed the best sportsman that brought down the most birds, so was he the best representative that brought the best pensions

[1] J. Rae, *Life of Adam Smith*, 110.

[2] *Edin. University MSS.*, *Letters of Dr. Carlyle*, No. 90; Rae, *op. cit.* 135.

and places to his countrymen." [1] Yet this very year saw the beginning of a movement, which, in the fulness of time, was to lead to a vigorous political life in Scotland, and to take away the reproach thus expressed by the *Encyclopédistes*: "L'Écosse a été redoutable tant qu'elle n'a pas été incorporée avec l'Angleterre ; mais, comme dit M. Voltaire, un état pauvre, voisin d'un riche, devient vénal à la longue ; et c'est aussi le malheur que l'Écosse éprouve." [2]

[1] Benger, *Memoirs of Mrs. E. Hamilton*, i. 89. The speech referred to was that of Boswell of Auchinleck ; v. *Cal. Mer.* Nov. 16, 1782. Hume Brown, *Hist. of Scot.* iii. 377.

[2] Diderot and d'Alembert, *Encyclopédie*, art. Écosse.

CHAPTER I.

SIGNS OF POLITICAL AWAKENING.

THE American War of Independence exercised a considerable influence on the thought and action of England, Ireland, and France. To the same source may be traced the first signs of the political awakening of Scotland. There the progress of the war was closely followed. About 1779, the ill-success of the British arms began to produce what Dr. Somerville of Jedburgh calls "a great change in the sentiments of the nation at large." "The discussion of this subject," he says, "not only engaged the attention of public bodies of men, but became a principal object of conversation in every company, and often excited angry debates which impaired the pleasures of social life, and weakened the confidence of friendship."[1] To judge by the resolutions of its public bodies, the war had hitherto been highly popular in Scotland, though little weight can be attached to such resolutions passed in meetings practically closed to free expression of opinion.[2] It is significant, therefore, that the editor of the *Caledonian Mercury*, the most widely circulated Scottish journal of the time, should have inserted in the first number for 1780 a note "To the Reader," in which he apologised for

[1] *Own Life*, 198-9.

[2] "I trust that although our county meetings and borough corporations were implicit worshippers of the Ministry, the people of Scotland, in general, thought differently." Letter in *Cal. Mer.* April 24, 1780.

having paid proper deference to the different views regarding the war prevailing "even on this side of the Tweed." "While one of the most learned and respectable societies in Scotland refused to subscribe supplies, or testify their approbation," he wrote, "it would ill become the publisher of a newspaper, however clear in his own opinion, to treat all opposition to the measures of the Government as factious and unwise." [1]

There is other evidence that the issues raised by the conflict in America were rousing an unprecedented interest in public affairs. The Edinburgh Pantheon Debating Society, for example, the membership of which was on a popular basis, discussed such questions as: "Ought the present Ministry to be dismissed His Majesty's Councils?" "Should the American War be immediately terminated?" [2] Less academic were the debates in the General Assembly of the Church. In May, 1782, the friends of the Rockingham Administration, led by Henry Erskine, the most popular advocate at the Bar, endeavoured to carry a motion congratulating His Majesty on the late change of Ministers, but their opponents were successful in defeating it. [3] In April, the Provincial Synod of Glasgow, and the Freeholders and Commissioners of Supply of Kirkcudbright, had sent up addresses approving of the plans of economy proposed by the Government. The latter added a clause eulogising

[1] The learned society was the Faculty of Advocates. They refused to vote a grant from their funds for a regiment that was being raised in Edinburgh. They, however, recommended it to the private liberality of their members. *History of the Rise, Opposition to, and Establishment of the Edinburgh Regiment*, Edin. 1778.

[2] *Cal. Mer.* Jan. 5, 12, 1782. For the history of this society, v. *The Book of the Old Edin. Club*, vol. i. Edin. 1908. The debates are not given.

[3] The debate was reported at unusual length in the *Cal. Mer.* May 29, June 1, 3, 5, 1782. Adam Smith was therefore not the "one just man in Gomorrah" to speak out for the Rockinghams. Countess of Minto, *Life and Letters of Sir G. Elliot*, i. 84.

the King for "making the parliamentary sentiments of his people the rule of his choice of ministers." "These addresses," commented the *Scots Magazine,* "are said to be the first of the kind from Scotland since the Union." [1]

The reforms of Burke, therein commended, directly affected Scotland. The Board of Police was abolished, and it was publicly affirmed that its revenues were divided into pensions to Burke and Barré. "Every gazette," says Creech, the publisher, "teemed with addresses from all quarters. The contagion . . . in a short time reached the north like the influenza which accompanied it. The first loyal address (and it was the last) from Scotland on the subject proceeded from the county nearest to England. The example was strenuously urged in Edinburgh by the friends of the new Ministry, and a meeting called by public advertisement for the purpose; and, had it carried, would probably have been followed by the counties and boroughs throughout Scotland." To prevent this, an advertisement was inserted in the local press giving a circumstantial account of a meeting in which resolutions against the Ministry were carried.[2] "These," says Creech, "created much speculation, and it was not generally known that there had been no such meeting of citizens till many months after the publication. They were the subject of much controversy in the London papers, and coinciding with the general sense of the nation, put a stop to the progress of loyal addresses." [3]

[1] *Scots Mag.* xliv. (1782), p. 277. Cf. J. Wilde: "The American War and the events which followed it, brought in names of attachment [into Scotland]; the first of the sort since those had fallen, that chieftainship consecrated, or which marked the zeal of Jacobites and Whigs. . . . I thought the Whiggism of the Rockingham connection was beginning to take root in Scotland." *An Address to the lately formed Society of the Friends of the People*, Edin. 1793.

[2] *Cal. Mer.* June 22, 1782.

[3] W. Creech, *Edinburgh Fugitive Pieces*, Edin. 1815, pp. 4-9. The Pantheon Society negatived by a majority of 123 in an audience "more

In 1783, the struggles of George III. to maintain his personal influence in the Government were represented to the inhabitants of Edinburgh in dramatic form. In that year, John Logan, better known to posterity as a minor poet, produced his *Runnamede* in the Theatre Royal, as it had been banned from the London stage by the censure of the Lord Chamberlain.[1] The parallel between King George and King John, the Whig magnates and the mediaeval barons was sufficiently clear, and the dramatist boldly announced the theme of his play as

> " One subject still a stranger to the stage,
> Fair liberty, the goddess of the Isle."

But to the ideas conveyed by such phrases as, " the rights of Britons and the rights of men," " the majesty of all the people,"[2] a Scottish audience proved as hostile as the official censor, and the piece only ran for one night.

That the citizens of the capital faithfully reflected the feelings of the vast majority of the Scottish people was

than the room could hold," a motion on " The Propriety of addressing His Majesty on the Late Change of Ministry." *Cal. Mer.* July 17, 1782. The debate, contrary to custom, extended over three different meetings of the society.

[1] J. Logan, *Poems and Runnamede, a Tragedy*, new edition, with Life of the Author, Edin. 1805. J. Rae, *Life of Adam Smith*, 396. For a contemporary criticism, v. *Scots Mag.* 1784, p. 245.

[2] Act IV.

> JOHN: The majesty of kings I will sustain
> And be a monarch, while I am a man.
>
> ---
>
> ELVINE: The rights of Britons and the rights of men,
> Which never king did give, and never king
> Can take away.
>
> ---
>
> JOHN: At whose tribunal can a king appear?
> ELVINE: At the tribunal of the kingdom.
> JOHN: Ha!
> Before whose majesty can he be brought?
> ELVINE: Before the majesty of all the people.

shown by the general satisfaction with which Pitt's accession to office in December, 1783, was hailed. It was with astonishment that they had seen Henry Erskine appointed by Fox and North to the post of Lord Advocate. That the leaders of faction should have controlled the administration of the country ran counter to all those notions of government which had prevailed in Scotland since the 'Fifteen and the 'Forty-Five. The voting of loyal addresses was at once renewed. But the Coalition was not undefended. Lively proceedings occurred at a meeting in Glasgow where John Millar, Professor of Law in the university, urged delay in addressing the Crown. For the first time, it was noted, "hissing" was heard at a public gathering in that city,[1] and when the general election took place later in the same year, the *Caledonian Mercury* reported that "never was there a period where the spirit of party ran so high."[2]

More unmistakable evidence of the awakening of the public mind, or, as a contemporary put it, that "the spirit of liberty had taken a northern turn,"[3] is to be found in the demand that arose for county and burgh reform. This demand was but an echo of the general "cry for redress of grievances," which had been raised in England owing to the disastrous course of the American War. In 1779, a committee was formed among the freeholders of Yorkshire, long the stronghold of Whig territorial influence, to agitate for administrative reforms.[4] By the beginning of 1780, it had established a committee of correspondence to promote its views throughout the country. Numerous counties and towns signified their approval of the scheme, and in March, 1780, deputies from similar associations met in conference in London, and drew up a series of resolutions pledging

[1] *Cal. Mer.* Mar. 3, 1784. [2] *Cal. Mer.* May 19, 1784.

[3] Letter in *Cal. Mer.* April 14, 1783.

[4] C. Wyvill, *Political Papers*, i. *passim.*

themselves to advocate Parliamentary reform, and to support such candidates as were in sympathy with their proposals. These methods of organisation and propaganda were deemed by many unconstitutional. Would not the delegates intimidate the legislature? Would not the associations eventually supplant Parliament? Had not the Gordon Riots shown the danger of exciting public opinion in this way? On these grounds, the Commons, in 1781, rejected the petition of the delegates, the Solicitor-General for Scotland reminding the House of the mischievous authority of such committees in his own country, during the religious upheaval of the seventeenth century.[1] These proceedings evoked much interest. In the pages of the *Scots Magazine*, prominence was given to the action of the delegates, and its legality discussed in the light of the writings of Locke and Machiavelli;[2] while the Pantheon Society debated the question, "Does the present conduct of Opposition in procuring County Associations tend to the real advantage of the British Empire?"[3] The Yorkshire Committee did not limit its operations to England. Its aim was to enlist the help of sympathisers throughout the British Isles, and its manifestoes were circulated in Scotland and Ireland. In May, 1782, Pitt, who had espoused the cause, moved for an inquiry into the state of the representation of the country. The motion was defeated, but this only stimulated the reformers to make further efforts. In November, the Yorkshire Committee issued a circular letter recommending a plan of reform embodied in four resolutions. In the last of these it was suggested that support should be extended to "the application of any county in Scotland for setting aside nominal and fictitious votes, and for regulating elections to Parliament in that part of the kingdom in a manner agree-

[1] *Parl. Hist.* xxii. 164. [2] *Scots Mag.* 1780, Jan., Feb., April.
[3] *Cal. Mer.* April 1, 1780.

able to the true intent and spirit of the Constitution."[1] This circular was forwarded to all town councils, sheriffs, and sheriff-substitutes in Scotland, and to such well-known men as Adam Ferguson, Professor of Moral Philosophy in the University of Edinburgh, and Gilbert Stuart, the historian. The Corporation of Glasgow stated in a cautious reply that it "could not sufficiently applaud the moderation and true public spirit of the Yorkshire Committee in resolving to abandon any of those propositions that shall not receive the approbation and concurrence of a decided majority of the principal Towns and Counties who support the claim of Parliamentary Reformation."[2] The Sheriff of Moray indicated the steps which were being taken by the counties to effect a change in the election laws.[3] Stuart and Ferguson were keenly alive to the opposition likely to be encountered. "My own earnest wish," wrote the latter, "has long been, that we had the same law of Parliament with you as far as relates to county elections, but I confess that I do not hope ever to obtain it."[4] "I believe," Stuart wrote to Lord Buchan in commendation of the Committee's proposals, "that there exists in Scotland an inclement faction of men who are enemies of the freedom of our constitution, and who would gladly seek for the true order of government in the dead calm of Despotism."[5]

Commenting on these letters, Wyvill observes that the communication of the Yorkshire freeholders with Ferguson and Stuart "was probably the first from any public body of men in England which evidenced a disposition to extinguish every remaining spark of those animosities which the writings of Mr. Wilkes, in opposition to Lord Bute, had

[1] Wyvill, *op. cit.* ii. 21. [2] *Ibid.* No. x. 82-5. [3] *Ibid.* 92-3.

[4] *Ibid.* iv. 215-6. Ferguson, however, was not in favour of the Committee's scheme.

[5] *Ibid.* 200.

been too successfully employed to excite. . . . The Yorkshire Committee felt the impropriety of such conduct, and with a manly frankness, held forth to their worthy fellow-citizens in Scotland the right hand of conciliation." [1] If Wyvill exaggerates the importance of the Wilkes controversy in tending to keep Scotland outside the pale of English politics, he does not over-estimate the significance of the action of those whom he represented. The example and encouragement of England lasted during the fifty years' struggle for reform. A bond of sympathy united the reformers and, to an equal degree, the anti-reformers in both countries, and a common interest in the burning question of the day rendered the Union of 1707, on its political side, complete.

County reform, to which Wyvill's circular had referred, was begun in 1782.[2] In the spring and summer of that year, the counties of Inverness, Moray, and Caithness, appointed commissioners to consider the question of nominal and fictitious votes, and, in August, a general meeting of the delegates of twenty-three counties was held in Edinburgh.[3] A committee was appointed to draft a Bill to remedy the anomalies in their representation and to raise subscriptions to meet expenses. At the same time a series of "Letters from an Old Freeholder" appeared in the press.[4] In these, the case for reform was put forward with ability and learning, and the circumstances which rendered it imperative were stated. A cloud was hanging over the constitution, and every man who loved his country was called upon to restore its original purity.[5] "Suffer me," he wrote, "to rouse you from that lethargy which has become universal." [6]

[1] Wyvill, *op. cit.* iv. 197-8.

[2] Not 1783 as in W. L. Mathieson, *The Awakening of Scotland*, 100.

[3] *Cal. Mer.* July 31, Aug. 7, 1782.

[4] *Ibid.* Aug. 31, 1782, reprinted in *Scots Mag.* Jan. and Feb. 1783.

[5] *Scots Mag.* 1783, p. 66.

[6] *Ibid.* 9.

The county franchise, to which attention was thus directed, was based on feudal tenure.[1] Originally, all persons holding land from the Crown were under obligation to attend Parliament. Since in early times this privilege was little valued and considered burdensome, a number of Acts, dating from 1427, gradually built up a system of representation of the "smaller barons." The last of these enactments, that of 1681, fixed the qualification of electors, with slight modifications, down to 1832. According to its provisions, the county electors were those who possessed either in property or superiority land, holden of the Crown, valued at forty shillings in the "auld extent"—a valuation said to have been made in the time of Alexander III. Where the old extent was not known, an elector was qualified if he held land *in capite* assessed by the Land Tax Commissioners at £400 Scots. The only change introduced at the Union was the reduction of the number of county representatives to thirty.

The abuses which had crept into this system were due to the fact that the franchise was vested, not in the land, but in the superiority. From this peculiarity a practice arose, soon after the Union, of creating "Parchment Barons," for the purpose of holding what were called "Nominal and Fictitious" votes. Peers or wealthy landowners, anxious to increase their importance in the county and with the Government, conveyed pieces of land of the necessary value, in trust only, to their friends. The title deeds were not registered, and were destroyed after they had served their purpose for an election. An Act of 1714 put an end to this by providing that every voter, when challenged, was

[1] E. and A. Porritt, *The Unreformed House of Commons*, ii. chaps. 35, 39; W. L. Mathieson, *op. cit.* 17-20; R. Bell, *Treatise on Election Laws*; A. Connell, *Treatise on Election Laws*, *passim*; C. E. Adam, *View of the Political State of Scotland in 1788*, introd.

bound to take an oath that he did not hold only in trust the land entitling him to a vote. By the ingenuity of lawyers, well versed in feudal law, another device was resorted to. The property was separated from the superiority, and the superiority of portions of land valued at £400 Scots was conveyed as before to confidants, either in naked superiority, wadset,[1] or liferent, care being taken to reserve to the disponer of the superiority, the right of revoking the grant at pleasure. To check this abuse, an oath of a more searching character was imposed by an Act of 1734. It proved no less ineffectual than the former, as did likewise a series of questions drawn up by the Court of Session for use in controverted election cases, to test the sincerity of the oath taken by an elector whose vote was challenged.[2] As a result of an appeal to the House of Lords, this method of investigation was dropped, and since few scrupled to take the oath, Parchment Barons continued to increase. In 1775, the Lord Advocate drew up a Bill to suppress nominal and fictitious votes, but it was " smothered by those powerful, though nameless beings, called the 'folks above.'"[3] By 1782 nominal voters, in many counties, outnumbered the real freeholders. In Ross and Cromarty, for example, out of 83 voters only 33 were actual proprietors.[4] In West Lothian, two years later, the proportion was given as 57 to 28.[5] In 1790, there were 2665 voters, but of these 1318 were fictitious.[6] Moreover, those landowners who were not freeholders, that is, who were technically sub-vassals, did not possess the franchise, so that it could be said without exaggeration that " the representatives of the Landed

[1] Wadset was a form of mortgage.

[2] For the questions v. Porritt, *op. cit.* ii. 151.

[3] Mathieson, *op. cit.* 100; *Scots Mag.* 1783, p. 67.

[4] *Cal. Mer.* Nov. 20, 1782. [5] *Ibid.* April 5, 1784.

[6] Mathieson, *op. cit.* 20.

Interest in Scotland might be chosen by those who had no real or beneficial interest in the land." [1]

In November, 1782, the committee appointed in August produced the draft of two Bills for the consideration of the freeholders, justices of the peace, and commissioners of supply, at their statutory meetings. The one, on the lines of the 1775 Bill, merely abolished liferenters and wadsetters.[2] The other, in addition, attached the franchise to land, as opposed to superiority, and extended it to those holding estates assessed at £200 Scots. This sum, the committee considered, was a much nearer equivalent to the forty shilling land of old extent than the £400 Scots fixed in 1681.[3] A third proposal seems to have suggested a property qualification for a Parliamentary candidate in the county which he wished to represent. These various schemes showed a lack of unanimity, and when they came to be discussed at the county meetings, they provoked a corresponding diversity of opinion. Though a Bill on the more conservative lines of 1775 seems to have been drawn up in 1785,[4] the movement made little progress. The more ardent reformers once more had recourse to test cases, and in 1790 a decision in the

[1] Reform Petition of Grey quoted in Porritt, *op. cit.* ii. 156. In 1811 the number of landowners was 7637; the number of voters never rose to 3000. *Ibid.* 157.

[2] *Observations on the Laws of Election of Members of Parliament*, Edin. 1782, gives the heads of the proposed Bills; v. also *An Address to the Landed Gentlemen of Scotland upon the subject of Nominal and Fictitious Qualifications . . . with Observations upon Two Sketches of Bills*, Edin. 1783.

[3] "The value of forty shilling land seldom rises higher than £150 or £160 Scots." *An Address to the Landed Gentlemen, etc.* In England no such difference between the nominal and the real value of forty shilling land existed, as the Act of Henry VI. made no reference to any particular valuation at the time. "Thus, whilst in England the county franchise fell automatically with the decrease in the purchasing power of money, in Scotland it rose." Mathieson, *op. cit.* 18.

[4] *Cal. Mer.* April 18, 1793.

House of Lords was hailed as a final blow to votes based on wadsets and liferents of superiority. This triumph proved delusive, and the old abuses continued, until, as we shall see, the reforming spirit, born of the French Revolution, once more stirred the counties to take joint action.

One argument advanced in favour of nominal and fictitious votes was that they enabled the Scottish peers to exert a political influence which, they complained, had been unduly diminished by the Act of 1707. The number entitled to sit in the Parliament of Great Britain had then been limited to sixteen, and even this representation had long been robbed of any real significance. In 1707, the sixteen had been selected by the Queen's Commissioner from among those who were in favour of the Treaty of Union, and this method, though expressly limited to the first election,[1] lasted in effect down to 1832. For it was the custom of the Minister in power to send to his supporters in Scotland the names of the peers whom he recommended, so that this "King's List" or "Treasury List," as it was called, rendered the election a foregone conclusion. The self-constituted champion of the independence of the Scottish nobility since 1768 had been Lord Buchan,[2] and in 1780 this eccentric brother of Henry Erskine renewed his protests. He published a characteristic letter in the press, inviting his brother peers to meet in Fortune's Tavern, Edinburgh, to discuss a scheme whereby the sixteen should be chosen in rotation.[3] Nothing came of this appeal, or of another protest he made in 1782 when he himself was a candidate in opposition to Lord Lauderdale.[4] "The Mar-

[1] Hume Brown, *Hist. of Scot.* iii. 125.

[2] Mathieson, *op. cit.* 70.

[3] *Cal. Mer.* May 24, 1780.

[4] "There is not half of our sixteen peers can afford to be independent as they call themselves: they all would take either a post or a pension could they get it." Letter in Polton MSS. quoted by A. Fergusson, *The Hon. Henry Erskine*, 200.

quis of Rockingham's express," he wrote, "arrived at Lord Lauderdale's on or about the 10th of May, when his Lordship's agents did immediately propagate everywhere the contents of the letter from the Minister, and it was presently known what risks were to be run by the peers who should vote for me on the basis of a free election." From this moment, therefore, Buchan determined "never to enter the walls of Holyrood as a Peer of Scotland."[1] Yet in 1787 we find him writing again, under the well-known name of Albanicus, to complain of the lack of interest shown in the choice of the representatives of his order, and a few days later appearing within these very walls of Holyrood to take part in an election of peers.[2]

Lord Buchan's efforts are regarded by his brother's biographer as "the marked success" of his youth.[3] Yet there is no evidence that the Treasury List was abolished. But, instead of being openly circulated as before, it was handed over in more secretive fashion to the Lord Advocate and some trusty henchman on the spot such as the Duke of Buccleuch;[4] and this plan of procedure, though "more decorous," was equally effective in rendering the sixteen peers as compact a body of supporters of the Government as the forty-five Scottish members of the House of Commons.

[1] *Cal. Mer.* July 29, 1782.

[2] *Cal. Mer.* March 26, 29, 1787.

[3] A. Fergusson, *op. cit.* 489.

[4] *Castlereagh Correspondence*, iii. 368-9, cited in Porritt, *op. cit.* ii. 30. Cf. *View of the Political State of Scotland at the Late General Election*, Edin. 1790, p. 16: "This custom, so openly dishonourable to the peerage of Scotland, was at last violently resisted, and seems now laid aside, at least is not avowed." The truth lies in the last clause, for in May, 1796, we find the Earl of Kellie inquiring of the Lord Advocate if his name is to be on the Government list of Scottish peers. *Edin. Univ. Laing MSS.* No. 500.

CHAPTER II.

BURGH AND ECCLESIASTICAL REFORM.

BURGH reform, like county reform, was due to the unrest born of the American War. It is true that Archibald Fletcher, "the father of burgh reform," declares in his *Memoir*[1] that the movement was not the result of any external influence, but was generated from within by the gross abuses that necessarily flowed from the self-election of the town councils.[2] But it must be remembered that Fletcher, writing in 1819, was anxious to free the cause he had so much at heart from the associations it had then acquired with the French Revolution. Those who started the propaganda used the political phraseology of their day. As "patriots" they spoke of "determined opposition to arbitrary establishments," they welcomed the encouragement extended to them by the Yorkshire Committee,[3] and they published Dr. Price's letter, in which he hailed their agitation as but a manifestation of that spirit of civil liberty, which, rising in America "had diffused itself into some

[1] A. Fletcher, *A Memoir concerning the Origin and Progress of the Reform proposed in the Internal Government of the Royal Burghs in Scotland*, Edin. 1819. The account which follows is based on this work and on E. and A. Porritt, *The Unreformed House of Commons*, Camb. 1903, vol. ii.

[2] Fletcher, *op. cit.* 12.

[3] *Letters of Zeno to the Citizens of Edinburgh on the Present Mode of Electing a Member of Parliament for that City*, Edin. 1783.

foreign countries and . . . was now animating Scotland";[1] while their opponents affirmed that the reformers were echoing the "ravings of political insanity imported from the republicans of the south."[2]

It is to be noted that the seed sown by the American Revolution fell on prepared ground. By 1782, the effects of the intellectual revival had spread from exclusive literary circles to the professional and middle classes, Under the guidance of Hume and Adam Smith that movement had been largely occupied with social and constitutional questions. Of the Literati of the period, none exercised a more potent influence than the author of the *Wealth of Nations*. He had been eminently successful in arousing among his students in Glasgow[3] and his friends in Edinburgh an interest in what was then termed "the mechanism of political society";[4] and his opinions gained even wider currency under the teaching of John Millar and Dugald Stewart, who both acknowledged the debt they owed to their master. The numerous translations of the French philosophers

[1] *Scots Mag.* April, 1784.

[2] Letter of Atticus, *Cal. Mer.* April 21, 1783.

[3] Rae, *Life of Adam Smith*, 59.

[4] Adam Smith's authority was acknowledged by the politicians of the day. "He now and then revisited London. The last time he was there, he had engaged to dine with Lord Melville, then Mr. Dundas, at Wimbledon; Mr. Pitt, Mr. Grenville, Mr. Addington, afterwards Lord Sidmouth, and some other of his lordship's friends were there. Dr. Smith happened to come late, and the company had sat down to dinner. The moment, however, he came into the room, the company all rose up; he made an apology for being late and entreated them to sit down. 'No,' said the gentlemen, 'we will stand till you are seated for we are all your scholars.'" Kay, *Original Portraits*, i. 75; v. also *Brit. Mus. Add. MSS.* Auckland Papers, No. 34416, ff. 470 and 472, for correspondence of Dundas with Adam Smith regarding free trade between Ireland and Great Britain. But after the French Revolution, Adam Smith's principles were regarded with suspicion. Rae, *op. cit.* 293. D. Stewart, *Memoir of Adam Smith*, *Works*, x. 87. Cf. speech of Marquis of Landsdowne in the House of Lords, Feb. 1, 1793.

published at Edinburgh, and the popularity of Adam Smith's writings, testify to the attention paid to the problems of government in its widest sense, and it is not surprising, therefore, to find the reformers, county and burgh, frequently quoting in their pamphlets and in their articles in the press, such writers as Machiavelli, Locke, Montesquieu, Blackstone, Hume, and Adam Smith.

Towards the close of the year 1782 and the beginning of 1783, there appeared in the Edinburgh newspapers a series of letters advocating reform under the signature of Zeno, the pseudonym of Thomas Macgrugar, a wealthy Edinburgh burgess.[1] About the same time, John Ewen, a citizen of Aberdeen, published a similar series.[2] To these two individuals is to be ascribed the origin of the first effective agitation for burgh reform.[3] Zeno regretted that his fellow-countrymen, though famed for their valour in the field, had not often been distinguished by their love of civil liberty.[4] The time had now come to assert their claim to freedom, and to shake off the restraints to which their ancestors had long been subjected. Though many branches of the constitution demanded reformation, there was one outstanding grievance—the manner in which the Parliamentary representatives of the burghs were chosen. In Edinburgh, for example, twenty-five persons, thirteen of whom formed a quorum, elected the member for the city. The *bourgeois* of France might, with equal propriety, lay claim to the same privileges, for they had an equal share

[1] *Cal. Mer.* Dec. 23, 28, 1782; Jan. 6, 22, Feb. 5, 1783. As previously stated, they were subsequently published in pamphlet form.

[2] Fletcher, *op. cit.* 13.

[3] As Fletcher shows (*op. cit.* pt. i. sect. 1) there had been numerous complaints in the past.

[4] Boswell of Auchinleck, in his speech at Ayr Quarter Sessions, had expressed a wish that "the sentiments of civil liberty were universally diffused among the *people* of Scotland." *Cal. Mer.* Nov. 16, 1782.

in the appointment of their governors. In his second letter, Zeno denied that " the dregs of the populace " should have votes. The franchise should be conferred on " men in the middle ranks of life who generally constitute the majority of every free community." This idea was taken from Montesquieu, and in his fifth letter Macgrugar quoted his favourite authority to rouse his fellow-burgesses to action: " Sleep in a state is always followed by servitude." The times were propitious for demanding redress. His Majesty's Ministers had declared their intention of bringing in a Reform Bill, the freeholders were considering the abolition of nominal and fictitious votes, and the gentlemen of the county of York had promised to support the cause of the burgesses of Scotland. In April, Atticus among others gave expression to the views of those opposed to change. He too could quote Montesquieu. " What was his definition of liberty ? " he asked. " Government must be such as to give no reason for one citizen to dread another." Their liberties and properties were safe, and Zeno was mistaking the means for the end. All attempts to bring about equality in the past, such as " Wat Tailor's " and Jack Cade's, had failed. " Alas! my countrymen," he concluded, " it is to *trade, industry*, and *improvement of the soil*, that poor Scotland must look for salvation, and not to the nonsense, and distraction, and the turmoil of politics." [1]

Meanwhile, on February 18, 1783, the Merchant Company of Edinburgh had met to take into consideration the representation of the people in Parliament, owing to the intimation of the Ministry that they were about to legislate on the matter. At this meeting, the anomalies existing in municipal elections were discussed, the complaint being made that " so numerous and respectable a body as the Merchant Company " had no voice in the appointment of the magistrates. A

[1] *Cal. Mer.* April 21, 1783.

committee was chosen to correspond with any individuals or societies disposed to co-operate in preparing a scheme of reform.[1] The quick response to their appeal from societies in Aberdeen, Nairn, Stirling, and other towns showed that considerable interest was being taken in the question throughout the country. But on April 23 the Merchant Company resolved to take no further action until the result of Pitt's motion in the House of Commons was known, and from that time they refused to countenance the movement.[2] Nevertheless, by suggesting a change in the election of town councils, as well as of Members of Parliament, they had widened its scope.[3] The task of giving a lead to the other Scottish burghs now devolved on a committee of Edinburgh citizens, formed on April 21, as a result of Macgrugar's letters.[4] Under its auspices, a convention of delegates was held in Edinburgh in March, 1784, thirty-three out of the sixty-six royal burghs being represented.

Though the local committees were composed chiefly of the merchant class, most of the members of the standing committee to whom was entrusted the drafting of Bills were connected with the Bar. These included such advocates as Archibald Fletcher, Henry Erskine, Adam Gillies, John Clerk of Eldin, and Lord Gardenstone, a Court of Session judge [5]—all of whom were to play a leading part in the coming struggle. This standing committee, in April, 1785, produced two Bills for the approval of the assembled delegates. One dealt with the abuses in the internal government of the burghs, the other with the election of their

[1] *Scots Mag.* 1783, p. 108.

[2] *Cal. Mer.* April 23, 1783; A. Heron, *Rise and Progress of the Company of Merchants of the City of Edinburgh, 1681-1902*, Edin. 1903, pp. 138-9.

[3] Letter of Britannicus, *Cal. Mer.* April 5, 1783.

[4] *Cal. Mer.* April 21, 1783.

[5] Fletcher, *op. cit.* 22-3.

Parliamentary representatives. Owing to the defeat of Pitt's proposals, however, the delegates agreed to lay aside the latter, and confine their attention to the former, a decision which was finally adopted in the convention of October, 1786. Before applying for redress to the legislature the reformers resolved to draw up a report, based on information furnished by the local societies, on the practical evils prevailing in municipal affairs. In this report, published in 1787, the grievances of the burgesses were arranged under the following heads: self-election of town councillors, alienation of public property, illegal contraction of debt, illegal exactions in the name of taxation, misapplication of the town revenues, and partiality in quartering soldiers on the burgesses.[1]

A municipal election was conducted under the "sett" or constitution of the burgh. It was only in 1709, however, that many of the setts had been committed to writing and recorded in the books of the Convention of Royal Burghs.[2] Use and wont, in cases where a written sett did not exist,

[1] Fletcher, *op. cit.* part iii.; *Historical Account of the Government and Grievances of the Royal Burghs of Scotland*, Edin. 1787; *Substance of the Reports*, Edin. 1789. *The General Report of the Commissioners appointed to inquire into the State of Municipal Corporations in Scotland*, Lond. 1835, substantiated the indictment of the early reformers.

[2] The Convention of Royal Burghs must not be confused with the Convention of the Burgh Reformers. The former had its origin in the Court of the Four Burghs, the records of which go back to 1405, though it arose much earlier. "In questions and controversies between different burghs, it has frequently exercised a sort of judicial authority or power of arbitration; and in the administration of particular burghs, besides adjusting the forms and modes of electing their magistrates and councils, it has been not unfrequently appealed to for the purpose either of checking, or of affording its sanction to those Acts which have proved fatal to the original endowments of so many of them. As an executive body, its primary function has been to apportion their respective shares of the general land-tax. . . ." *General Report of the Commissioners*, 1835, p. 19; v. also E. and A. Porritt, *op. cit.* ii. chap. 33. According to the Commissioners' recommendations, the Convention was shorn of its powers, but it still meets to guide public opinion on questions relating to municipal affairs.

had previously regulated the elections, and thus, in the course of time, each burgh came to have its own method of appointing the town councillors. But all the setts, with scarcely any exception, had one principle in common—that of self-election, dating from 1469. Inverness may be taken as a typical example of the manner in which it worked in actual practice. "The town council of this burgh," says the Report, "is composed of twenty-one members, whereof they only change five annually, and these are brought in the succeeding year, if their conduct on former occasions merited the approbation of the party in power; and if that is not the case, any person acting contrary to the ideas of the leading magistrate and his party is turned off the council, never more to be on the list. And thus it happens that the magistrates of Inverness continue to elect their successors, and must do so for ever, if an alteration of the present system is not obtained." Under these conditions, the control of municipal administration often fell into the hands of one family. In Annan, in 1787, the sons, nephews, and brother-in-law of the provost formed the majority of the corporation. In Brechin the chief magistrate and his relatives had maintained themselves in power for forty years. The state of the property and funds of the royal burghs, as revealed by the Report, explains this unusual devotion to public service. In some cases, as in Inverkeithing, the town lands had been "feued" at trifling sums by the municipal authorities to themselves or their friends. In others, such as Dumfries, succeeding generations of provosts seem simply to have annexed them. A former chief magistrate of Rothesay, so the reformers averred, had gifted to a gentleman, "to make him convenient," a piece of ground belonging to the burgh, and when complaint was made to his successor, "he swore that it was in his power to give all the lands away without asking a question of any person." Owing to these alienations many of the burghs were in financial straits. The debt of Perth amounted at this time to £20,000.[1] The creditors of Arbroath, despairing of being repaid, were forced to accept four per cent. interest on their claims. Yet these debts had accumulated in spite of the fact that higher taxes had been levied than could legally be exacted. Little of this money had been spent on public works. In Dunfermline "the want of cleanliness was proverbial," although the inhabitants had offered to bring in an additional supply of water by private subscription. In Banff the rate levied for the upkeep of the streets was devoted to repairing those "contiguous to the dwellings of the leading men of the council." For such works, chiefly of an ornamental kind, as were undertaken, the town was made to pay heavily. When, in 1771, Dunfermline resolved to erect a three-storey tolbooth, the contract was given to a councillor at £700, but eventually, for a one-storey building, £1000 was charged. These details could only be given approximately by the reformers, as they were denied access to the official books and records. In some towns the former consisted only of private memoranda jotted down by the burgh chamberlain.[2]

The evils of self-election were further aggravated by non-residence, although the Scottish Parliament had expressly enacted that the town councillors should be "indwellers." The provost of Inverkeithing, who had held office for the six years preceding 1787, dwelt in Ayrshire. The chief magistrate of Wigtown served in the navy in the West Indies, and other members of the corporation resided at Dumfries, Edinburgh, London, and even in Newfoundland. The presence of these "outdwellers" is explained by the

[1] In 1835 it amounted to £40,000, and by that time Edinburgh had become insolvent. *Commissioners' Report*, 36.

[2] *Ibid.* 37.

fact that the election of the burgh representatives at Westminster was vested in the town councils of royal burghs, as being tenants-in-chief of the Crown. These, with the exception of Edinburgh, were formed into fourteen groups, some consisting of three, and others of four or five burghs. Each town council elected a delegate to a convention held in rotation in one of the burghs of the group, and there the member was chosen. Local magnates therefore exerted themselves to secure by bribes, by intimidation, and by promises of patronage, such a majority in the town councils within their sphere of territorial influence as could be depended upon to vote as they desired; and this interference had been facilitated by an Act passed in 1743, which allowed non-burgesses to be delegates.[1] Whithorn, for example, had been under the direction of the Galloway family for some forty years, when, in 1780, a "breach was made in their interest" by a party of resident councillors. Four years later, however, Lord Galloway, by carrying off some of these independents and corrupting others, succeeded once more in forming a council of his friends.

A Bill to remedy these abuses was finally adopted by the reformers at a meeting of forty-seven delegates in 1785. According to its provisions, the annual municipal elections were to take place on the same day throughout the country. The electors were to be resident burgesses, who were engaged, or had been formerly engaged, in business within the burgh—all honorary burgesses and town or trade servants being disqualified. These electors were also to appoint seven auditors of accounts, whose decisions were to be subject to review by the Court of Session.[2]

Those who defended the existing system maintained that no legislation was required, as the law courts could be called upon to check all maladministration. Two cases tested

[1] Porritt, *op. cit.* ii. 124. [2] Fletcher, *op. cit.* pt. i. 151 *et seq.*

the validity of this contention. In one the burgesses of Nairn complained to the Court of Session that from 1754 to 1784 their municipal affairs had been managed by one family. The Court ordained that all the burgh officials, and six of the other nine councillors, should be "residenters"; but this judgment was reversed by the House of Lords, which held that the Scottish judges had assumed "a discretionary power bordering on the legislative one."[1] The other raised the question of the control of municipal expenditure. In mediaeval times the Lord Chamberlain in his annual "ayre" had supervised the accounts of the burghs in the interest of the king, and in 1535 his powers had been transferred to the Court of Exchequer. In an action brought by the burgesses of Dumbarton against the town authorities, the court disclaimed these powers, and at the same time repudiated the suggestion made by the respondents that the Convention of Royal Burghs could exercise jurisdiction in such matters. As Baron Sir John Dalrymple pertinently asked, "Is a body made up of the defaulters themselves to try these defaulters?"[2]

This judgment was given in February, 1787, and in the same month the standing committee announced their intention of bringing the question before Parliament, thirty-five petitions having been already forwarded to London.[3] The greatest difficulty had been experienced in finding a suitable exponent of their views in the House. George Dempster, "a Scotsman, and a Scots member for burghs," was approached, but he refused because "he thought it would not be becoming in him to assist in destroying Magistracies and Town Councils from whom he derived his situation." Pitt, Wilberforce, and others were then applied to without result, and finally a deputation of the burgesses waited on

[1] *Cal. Mer.* July 12, 1784; May 11, 1785. [2] Fletcher, *op. cit.* 56.
[3] *Cal. Mer.* Feb. 24, 1787.

Fox. He declined, owing to pressure of business. "Go to Sheridan, to whom I shall recommend it," was his advice. "He will bring it forward in all its force, and I shall with infinite satisfaction support him." Sheridan undertook the task, and on May 28, 1787, presented a petition to the Commons from the inhabitants of Glasgow.[1] Meanwhile the Convention of Royal Burghs, far from fulfilling its supposed functions of supervision, had voted £200 to provide a fund for opposing the movement,[2] and its preses, Lord Provost Grieve, had sent a circular letter to all town councils urging them to instruct their Members to vote against the measure. Such a scheme, he pointed out, "would unhinge a constitution which had stood the test of ages," and would be contrary to the fundamental article of the Act of Union.[3] These arguments were to serve Henry Dundas and his supporters on many future occasions, but in the first debate in Parliament on the subject, he confined himself to moving the adjournment of the House in accordance with the decision of the Speaker that the petitions were of a private nature, and could not therefore be accepted so late in the session.[4] Such was the beginning of a series of "shifts and evasions" whereby it was hoped to postpone all fruitful discussion.

Dundas's attitude towards reform, now as always, was based on self-interest. In May, 1782, when Pitt brought forward his first motion on Parliamentary reform, Dundas declared that "the constitution had existed for ages pure, and it was not a proper time now to think of altering it," though he admitted that "if any part of the representation wanted a reform, it was the place from whence he came." [5] Yet by repeating his former eulogy of Chatham, he displayed

[1] Fletcher, *op. cit.* pt. i. 40-60.
[2] *Cal. Mer.* Sept. 8, 1787.
[3] Fletcher, *op. cit.* pt. i. 147-9.
[4] *Parl. Hist.* xxvi. 1215.
[5] *Parl. Hist.* xxii. 1434.

an eagerness to cultivate the goodwill of that statesman's son. On the fall of the Rockingham Administration, Dundas urged Pitt to accept the office of Prime Minister.[1] Pitt refused, and the Coalition came into power. When Pitt introduced his second motion in 1783, Dundas, with that audacious inconsistency which up to this time had marked his public career, voted in its favour. "The granting so much to the wishes of the people," he said, "would be the best means of putting an end to the business entirely, and would certainly, in the popular phrase, give a fresh infusion of fine blood to the constitution of that House." [2] Though the Government itself was divided on the issue—Fox voting for, and North against the proposal—it was thought that Dundas was actuated rather by a desire to embarrass his colleagues than by a sincere wish for reform. This view of his conduct was the result of his growing intimacy with Pitt.[3] Owing to this suspicion, Dundas was dismissed from office,[4] but Lord Chancellor Loughborough indicates what was probably another reason. "I am perfectly convinced," he wrote to Fox, "that the more rigour Administration exerts there [in Scotland], the stronger its influence will be. It

[1] "Certainly the idea did not originate with Henry Dundas, as he afterwards claimed." J. Holland Rose, *William Pitt and National Revival*, 125.

[2] *Parl. Hist.* xxiii. 865.

[3] "Dundas, who had a long and a keen political sight, having already determined on attaching his future political fortune to Pitt, probably thought a speculative tenet to be undeserving of contention. But the recantation pronounced by Thomas Pitt and Dundas rather tended to throw ridicule on the proposition than to recommend it to the House." N. W. Wraxall, *Hist. and Posth. Memoirs*, ed. H. B. Wheatley, 5 vols. Lond. 1884, iii. 67-8.

> "By opposition, he his King shall court,
> And damn the People's cause by his support."

Criticisms on the Rolliad, pt. i. 8th edn. Lond. 1788, p. 44.

[4] G. W. T. Omond, *The Lord Advocates of Scotland*, ii. 114; Lord John Russell, *Memorials and Correspondence of Charles James Fox*, ii. 86.

began to be seriously credited that it was not permitted to them to remove any person protected by Dundas." [1] Henry Erskine was appointed Lord Advocate, but his four months' tenure of office afforded too little time to undermine the Dundas interest.[2] When Pitt became Prime Minister in December, 1783, Dundas was made Treasurer of the Navy, and Ilay Campbell, Lord Advocate.

Pitt's victory at the polls in 1784 was so decisive an expression of the national will that it rendered Parliamentary reform of less practical importance. In 1785 he introduced a Bill dealing with the representation of England, though apparently in a draft of the preamble he proposed to enlarge the electorate of such towns in Scotland as Edinburgh and Glasgow.[3] The measure met with a cold reception, even his henchman Dundas limiting his approval to the principle of compensation.[4] The first reading was rejected by a majority of seventy-four, and for the next few years Parliamentary reform remained in the background. This division was equally fatal to Scottish burgh reform, which was too closely bound up with the general question to allow of its being discussed on its own merits. Powerful though he was, Pitt had not yet an organised following in the House, and he could hardly be expected to inquire into a system which enabled his friend and colleague Dundas to place at

[1] Omond, *ibid.*; Russell, *op. cit.* ii. 203.

[2] Cf. letter of Sir T. Dundas to North, Oct. 1783, recommending him to act on the advice of Mr. Ferguson with regard to patronage as "he and Mr. Robertson are the two persons who have undertaken the Burthen and Management of *Kirk* Politics in this Country, and to whose activity Government is greatly indebted." *Home Office (Scotland) Correspondence*, *Public Record Office*, London, vol. i.—hereafter cited as *Scot. Corr.*

[3] Holland Rose, *op. cit.* 199.

[4] "Mr. Dundas thought it his duty to state some of those reasons to the House which induced him to declare himself a sincere friend to this question. (A hearty laugh.)" *Parl. Hist.* xxv. 469.

his disposal, with unfailing regularity, thirty-nine out of the forty-five votes of the Scottish members.[1]

Dundas's power in his own country, thus practically exemplified, was due, as Professor Hume Brown points out, to family prestige, to his own personal qualities, and to the condition of Scotland at the time.[2] Born in 1742, the son of Lord President Dundas, whose father and grandfather had both been raised to the bench, he was called to the Scottish Bar in 1763.[3] By that time his half-brother was President of the Court of Session. Under such favourable circumstances Henry Dundas soon built up a lucrative practice as an advocate. But it was in the General Assembly of the Church that he, like so many of his contemporaries, developed a talent for public speaking and a natural aptitude for affairs.[4] Such experience stood him in good stead when, in 1774, he entered Parliament as member for Midlothian. His early politics are said to have been of a Whig cast,[5] and later his enemies accused him of having displayed "a passion for democracy."[6] But his political creed was as variable as that of most of his contemporaries. He soon established his reputation as a forcible and fluent speaker,

[1] T. H. B. Oldfield, *The Represent. Hist. of Grt. Brit.* vi. 296.

[2] *Hist. of Scot.* iii. 347.

[3] Omond, *op. cit.* ii. chap. xiv.

[4] T. Somerville, *My Own Life and Times*, 41, 97. Others mentioned by Somerville in the same connection are Sir Gilbert Elliot, Lord Chancellor Loughborough, George Dempster, and Sir Wm. Pulteney.

"'Twas in Kirk Courts he learned his airs,
And thunder'd his oration."

The Melviad, or the Birth, Parentage, Education, and Achievements of a Grete Mon, by I-spy-I, 3rd edn. Lond. 1805, p. 12.

[5] T. Somerville, *op. cit.* 41.

[6] "You wanted to thrust the whole deacons into the ordinary council, nay to rob the guildry of their privileges, and bestow them on the Merchant Company. . . . May not this passion for democracy spread into the counties . . . ?" *A Letter to the Lord Advocate of Scotland* by Eugène, Edin. Nov. 18, 1777.

and a ready and courageous debater,[1] while by a carefully calculated parade of independence he turned every ministerial crisis to his advantage.[2] Lord Advocate under the Tory Ministry of North in 1775, he continued in office under the Whig Administrations of Rockingham and Shelburne. The Treasurership of the Navy, which North seems to have promised him, he received from Shelburne, who added the valuable sinecure of Keeper of the Scottish Signet for life,[3] and "the recommendation to all offices which should fall vacant in Scotland."[4] Even under the Coalition he retained for some time, as we have seen, his post as Lord Advocate.[5] During this period of seven years he laid the foundation of that influence in Scotland which his association with Pitt rendered complete; for the succession of offices he held as Treasurer of the Navy, President of the Board of Control for India, Home Secretary, and Secretary for War, placed

[1] "Far from shunning the post of danger, he always seemed to court it; and was never deterred from stepping forward to the assistance of Ministers by the violence of Opposition, by the unpopularity of the measure to be defended, or by the difficulty of the attempt." Wraxall, *op. cit.* i. 426.

"My friend the Advocate has made a very Brilliant figure; he is really a fine Manly fellow, and I like a Decided Character. He speaks out and is affraid of Nobody." Sir Wm. Gordon to Dr. Carlyle, June 1, 1780. *Edin. Univ. MSS.*, *Letters of Dr. Carlyle*, No. 104.

[2] Mathieson, *op. cit.* 86-91.

[3] *Scot. Entry Book Warrants*, vol. i. July 31, 1782. On March 3, 1777, H. Dundas and Andrew Stuart were appointed Keepers of the Signet, with power "to admit and receive all clerks and writers to the Signet," except sheriffs and their clerks, who were to be appointed by the Secretary of State. On June 23, 1779, H. Dundas was appointed sole Keeper of the Signet during pleasure, "the former grant being revoked." In 1782 the warrant was for life, and empowered him to "admit and receive clerks and writers to the Signet and Sheriff Clerks." *Scot. Corr.* vol. 24, July 29, 1814. According to the second Lord Melville, the right of appointing sheriff-clerks was alone worth more than £1000 a year. *Ibid.*

[4] Lord John Russell, *op. cit.* ii. 29.

[5] According to Lord Campbell, "old Henry Dundas's advice to Ministers of State" was: "Beware of resignation; for when you are out, the Lord Almighty only knows when you may get in again." *Lives of the Lord Chancellors and Keepers of the Great Seal of England*, vii. 599.

in his gift an amount of patronage never possessed by any former "Manager of Scotland."[1]

The political condition of the country enabled this "noted pluralist" to exercise unbounded power in his native land. In the counties the number of voters never reached 3000, and the considerations which weighed with the fortunate possessors of the franchise are fully disclosed in a confidential report drawn up in 1788 to enable Henry Erskine to direct the Whig campaign in the coming election. In it, the "political opinions, family connections and personal circumstances of each of the 2662 voters" on the freeholders' roll of that year are minutely detailed.[2] "Has a family," is a comment, the significance of which is apparent from other entries. John Stewart of Stenton "wants a commission for a younger son." Mr. Cunningham of Lanishaw desires "a second son out as a Writer in India." William Richan of Rapness "got a Lieutenancy through Mr. Dundas, the Treasurer of the Navy." Mr. John Russell is one of a large company who "has received favours from Mr. Dundas." "Married to a niece of Mr. Dundas," or "married to a cousin of Mr. Dundas" appears not infrequently. Places, according to Cockburn, were equally effective in "keeping in order" the town councillors who elected the burgh representatives. The law, the church, the excise, and the public service generally, provided an abundant supply of lucrative posts for them or their relatives.[3]

[1] Referring to the opinion of Pitt's supporters, D. Pulteney writes to the Duke of Portland: "Another jealousy too may break out if Dundas is not a little checked relative to the Scotch, for whom everything is claimed and granted without debate." Aug. 13, 1784. *Hist. MSS. Com. Reports*, xiv. App. i. 1894, *Rutland MSS.* p. 131.

[2] *View of the Political State of Scotland . . . in 1788*, ed. by C. E. Adam, Edin. 1887.

[3] *Life of Jeffrey*, i. 78; Lord Brougham, *Hist. Sketches of Statesmen in the Time of George III.* i. 307-8. "I am not quite certain if, on this occasion, it will be in my power to transmit your lists of names, as was

Dundas's unrivalled knowledge of these relationships made him an ideal electioneering agent. "Here in Edinburgh," wrote Lockhart in 1819, "unless Mr. Wastle exaggerates very much, there was no person of any consideration whose whole connections and circumstances were not perfectly well known to him. And I begin to see enough of the structure of Scottish society to appreciate somewhat of the advantages which this knowledge must have placed in the hands of so accomplished a statesman." [1] A member of a numerous family, he had been brought by intermarriage into close touch with the landed gentry. Of tall and commanding figure, frank and genial in manner, he was a welcome guest at their social gatherings where he could "blend conviviality with business." [2] His broad Doric accent, which, unlike some of his countrymen, he never forsook for the "narrow English," was another trait which "prejudiced in his favour." [3] His inconsistency,

sometimes done formerly; but on this you may confidently rely, that no person whatever shall, with my consent, be admitted into the council, who is not, to the best of my knowledge and belief, not only correct in his political principles, but also firmly attached to your interest." Letter of Lord Provost Stirling to Dundas, Sept. 5, 1799, in *Documents connected with the Question of Reform in the Royal Burghs of Scotland*, 2nd edn. Edin. 1819, p. 71; v. also *The Letter of the Rt. Hon. Henry Dundas unto the Rt. Hon. Thos. Elder, with Notes*, Edin. 1798.

[1] *Peter's Letters to His Kinsfolk*, 2nd edn. 1819, ii. No. 31.

[2] Wraxall, *op. cit.* i. 425-7. "I am this far on my way to the north of Scotland on a visit to Sir James Grant, General Grant, Duke of Gordon, Lord Findlater, and Lord Fife. They are all very hostile to each other; and yet I am told that a visit from me may probably have the effect of uniting their political interests in such a manner as to co-operate for securing five seats in Parliament at the general election in the interest of Government; whereas if I do not interpose, there is a danger of their getting into immediate warfare among themselves.... When I tell you that I was living idly and pleasantly with a few chosen friends in my Highland retreat, you will not suppose that this is a jaunt of pleasure, but I must undertake it." Dundas to Grenville, Sept. 2, 1787, *Hist. MSS. Com.*, *Dropmore MSS.* iii. 421.

[3] "Full weil his ain dear Scotch he'd speak," *The Melviad*, p. 9. "His

which made his name a byword even among English politicians,[1] could not lower him in the esteem of those who were even more intent on the "loaves and fishes."[2] His fidelity to Pitt silenced his detractors. In the "friend and elder brother" of that popular Minister, in one who was the first Scot to gain an eminent place in the ranks of British statesmen, all could take a just pride. "He is a Scotchman," says Cockburn, "of whom his country may be proud."[3] "Tory and Whig agreed in loving him," wrote Lockhart.[4] This admiration was not evoked by the moral grandeur of his character, though in his familiar correspondence he sometimes sounds a note of lofty patriotism.[5] It was based on the unfailing kindliness of his disposition. "Of his private kindnesses," says Somerville, "I have known instances of a nature to exclude all suspicion of their arising from motives of ostentation or selfish policy."[6]

It was therefore with no exaggeration that Dundas could write to Grenville in October, 1789: "A variety of circumstances happen to concur in my person to render me a cement of political strength to the present Administration, which, if once dissolved, would produce very ruinous

oratory was indeed very fine.... Lingua Tuscana in voce Romana." Speech of Lord G. Gordon, *Parl. Hist.* xxi. 337.

[1] Wraxall, *op. cit.* ii. 297; *Criticisms of the Rolliad*, 43.

[2] So Ramsay of Ochtertyre describes their motives. *Scotland and Scotsmen in the eighteenth Century from MSS. of J. Ramsay of Ochtertyre*, ed. A. Allardyce, i. 342.

[3] *Life of Jeffrey*, i. 79.

[4] *Op. cit. ibid.*

[5] "I am here to get sleep, but in truth I am overdone, and unfortunately have got into a habit from anxiety of not sleeping in the night. At the same time I feel perfectly happy. Let happen what will to myself personally, I have the heartfelt satisfaction to know that I have been a main instrument of compleatly rousing the spirit and zeal of the country, and I trust in a little more time to have put it in a state of impregnable security." Letter of H. to R. Dundas, Wimbledon, Ap. 30, 1798. *Edin. Univ. Laing MSS.* No. 500.

[6] *Op. cit.* 317; v. also Stanhope, *Life of Pitt*, i. 311.

effects." The occasion of the letter was the offer of the post of President of the Court of Session. Dundas refused it, not only for the reasons already stated, but because he could not honourably interfere with the Lord Advocate's pretensions.[1] At the time, and long afterwards, he professed to regret his decision, though it may be doubted if such a comparatively insignificant position could now have satisfied his ambition.[2] The office was given to Ilay Campbell, the Lord Advocate, who was succeeded by Robert Dundas, Henry's nephew. Personally popular, the latter proved himself to be a conscientious official, but he had little of his uncle's ability or force of character. At every crisis he had to look to his kinsman for direction.

In 1791, Henry Dundas was appointed Secretary of State for the Home Department. Since the abolition of the Scottish Secretaryship in 1748, its functions had been discharged by the Home Secretary.[3] Though the Lord Advocate remained responsible for local administration, others such as the Lord Justice Clerk, were often consulted on questions relating to Scottish affairs.[4] With the rise of Dundas such communications became rarer, and in 1791, unnecessary; for between uncle and nephew there existed absolute confidence. The concentration of power in the hands of Henry Dundas reduced the government of Scotland to the despotism that bears his name. In the eighteenth century, a succession of managers had exercised a similar, if less complete, control

[1] *Dropmore MSS.* i. 534-5.

[2] J. Sinclair, *Memoirs of the Life and Works of Sir John Sinclair*, 2 vols. Lond. 1837, i. 276.

[3] Hume Brown, *Hist. of Scot.* iii. 210. "I beg leave to address your Lordship as Secretary of State for Scotland," Lord Provost Hunter Blair to North, Sept. 23, 1783. *Scot. Corr.* vol. i.

[4] In applying for the post of Lord President, Lord Justice Clerk Miller calls himself "correspondent of government for this part of the country." *Scot. Corr.* vol. 3, Dec. 13, 1787.

over the destinies of the country, but their authority was almost unquestioned. It was the fate of "Harry the Ninth"[1] that his long and rigorous rule coincided with an awakening of his countrymen which made them realise, for the first time, their political servitude.

By 1787 only a few of the gentry and the middle class had begun to be sensible of their bondage. The people generally remained outside the influence of politics. The county movement was strictly limited in its appeal, and the burgh reformers had expressly condemned such proposals as universal suffrage and the ballot, whereby advanced reformers in England had sought to enlist "the people at large" in their cause.[2] The masses in Scotland had no opportunity to develop an interest in politics, for the only popular element in elections was to be found in those towns which still preserved the mediaeval institutions of Guilds Merchant and Trade Incorporations. In such burghs the trades had originally the right of choosing a deacon who was *ex officio* a member of the town council. This representation was out of harmony with the self-election of the other members, and gradually a compromise arose whereby the trades and the council united to nominate the deacon.[3] The only change suggested in this respect by the burgh reformers was to give the incorporations, where they existed, the right of electing their own deacon. Had they been less anxious to avoid the charge of innovation, they might have added to the number of trade representatives, who were in every case, as may be readily supposed, in a helpless minority. Such as they were, the efforts of the burgesses were supported by the incorporations throughout the country.

Apart from the few members of these incorporations, the

[1] "Mr. Henry Dundas, sometimes called Harry the Ninth." J. Boswell ("Bozzy"), *A Letter to the People of Scotland*, Edin. 1785.

[2] Fletcher, *op. cit.* 203-235.

[3] Porritt, *op. cit.* ii. 63.

common people remained indifferent to the political issues of the day. On one question only had their feelings been aroused—the Roman Catholic Relief Bill of 1778. The eagerness with which they had joined in the crusade against that measure not only testified to the latent power of the lower classes, but revealed the ease with which that power once rendered active might be organised against the Government. Dundas had to bend before the storm of national disapproval, and was forced, amid the taunts of his opponents in the House of Commons, to announce that the proposed legislation was abandoned. These anti-popish riots showed that religious affairs still held the foremost place in the minds of the populace. According to a French observer in 1790, the wild enthusiasm of the seventeenth century was "now chiefly confined to the dregs of the people in manufacturing towns." The clergy did not share their bigotry. "Neither their learning nor example," he says, "has yet been able to banish entirely that enthusiastic spirit which has, for more than two centuries, been the characteristic of the vulgar. Satisfied with discovering truth themselves, they have used no strenuous efforts to reform the multitude, which, they suppose, must always be governed by the grosser systems of mystery and error." [1] It was this lack of sympathy between a large section of the clergy and their parishioners which had led to successive protests against the Patronage Act, and the opposition to that Act had tended to maintain among the latter the sentiment of liberty which had hitherto found no other means of expression. In 1782 the agitation was renewed, and the discussion which it produced showed that it was not unconnected with the reforming spirit of the time.

[1] Mons. B——de, *Reflections on the Causes and Probable Consequences of the Late Revolution in France, with a View of the Eccles. and Civil Constitution of Scotland* (Trans.), Edin. 1790, Letter viii.

Patronage had been restored by the Act of 1712 as a means of political control in the interests of the Jacobites. Patrons, however, did not begin to avail themselves of their rights of presenting to livings till about 1730. The enforcement of the Act led to two secessions from the Kirk, one in 1740, the other in 1761.[1] The second was the more important, for it was the result of the policy of the New Moderates. It was the object of this party to avert a calamity which was threatening the Church.[2] Since the Revolution, and more especially since the Union, it had not possessed that influence which had rendered the General Assembly the real Parliament of the nation. Noblemen and barons no longer sought a place in its courts, and they were being alienated from the services of the Kirk by its conservative theology. The New Moderates hoped by accommodating their creed to the ideas of the "nobility, gentry, heritors, and freeholders" to attract these classes once more. As a means to that end, the law of patronage was firmly upheld and rigidly enforced, although the Assembly, by annually referring the "grievance of patronage" to its standing commission, professed to entertain a hope of effecting a change in the law. This diplomatic method of shelving the question was due to Dr. Robertson, Principal of Edinburgh University, and leader of the Moderates, who, for twenty years, exercised as undisputed a sway over the General Assembly as the political manager of Scotland over the electorate. In 1781 he retired from the leadership of the party, and the question of patronage was at once raised by the High-Flying, Wild, or Popular Party who upheld the right of congregations to a share in the choice of their minister.

[1] W. L. Mathieson, *Scotland and the Union*, chaps. vi. and vii.; *The Awakening of Scotland*, chaps. iv. and v.

[2] Hume Brown, *Hist. of Scot.* iii. 362-70.

Numerous societies and parishes published resolutions denouncing the evils of patronage. Some were drawn up in the language of the seventeenth century,[1] but others showed that the political events of the period were infusing fresh vigour into the old controversy. The Nine Incorporated Trades of Dundee, for example, looked forward to a successful issue to the demand for repeal since they had resolved " to apply to those principles of liberty and regard to the rights of man which actuate the breasts of many of our public representatives in Parliament." [2] In *An Address on Civil and Ecclesiastical Liberty* [3] it was pointed out that the constitution of the Church was republican, that patronage favoured arbitrary government, and breathed a spirit of unlimited monarchy. The law of patronage could serve no purpose but to increase the power of an aristocracy already too powerful, and to add to that system of corruption become already far too prevalent. The Glasgow Society for the Abolition of Patronage especially recommended a pamphlet entitled *An Inquiry into the Principles of Ecclesiastical Patronage and Presentation*.[4] As scriptural expression was liable to misapplication, misconstruction, and cavilling, the author had " drawn his arguments from the soundest arguments of moral and political reasoning, and the great, clear, and open source of natural right." It is interesting to note that the writer was anxious to abolish patronage on the ground that otherwise the people would lose all notion of liberty. " More than once," he says, " we have had occasion to observe and lament that, by the form of the constitution of the country, the great body of the people are, in relation to civil affairs, excluded from the exercise and enjoyment of the rights of freedom. The consequence is what was naturally to have been expected—a total indifference

[1] *E.g.* Collington, *Cal. Mer.* Nov. 27, 1782.

[2] *Cal. Mer.* Feb. 26, 1783. [3] Edin. 1783. [4] Edin. 1783.

approaching to insensibility in relation to the value and advantages of political liberty. . . . It is obvious to all the world that, excepting a mere security for life and a capacity of holding property, they are reduced to the exercise only of the common functions of all animals, the gratification of hunger and thirst and other similar enjoyments." The recognition of the political aspect of the question was no less apparent, though more subtly stated, in the most famous pamphlet of the day, *The Principles of Modern Moderation.*[1] "In the form and appearance of elections," conducted according to the Act of Assembly of 1732, the author, the Rev. Dr. Hardy, found something "highly democratical," and he proposed a plan which "was calculated to secure the confidence of the people without any hazard of awakening their secret ambition." "The political defect of popular elections at large," he wrote, "is that the power is entirely enlarged in one interest, and in that interest in which the genius of legislation does not presume that there is wisdom."

As some three hundred livings in the gift of the Crown formed a ready means of rewarding political supporters, there was little doubt that the genius of legislation would be unwilling to cede to the demands of the Popular Party. In June, 1783, a memorial was placed before the Government, explaining the dangers that might be expected if the Moderates were defeated in the General Assembly.[2] "The

[1] Edin. 1782.

[2] *Scot. Corr.* vol. i. On May 26, 1780, Sir J. M'Pherson had written to Dr. Carlyle: "This will find you in the hurry of Assembly Debates. Pray write me an ostensible Letter, stating to me the pulse of the Kirk, your Labour in keeping it regular, the future Consequence of Inattention in government to the Prejudices and Principles of such a Body as the Kirk influences. Do this and I will make use of it for your good *if possible.* To this Period, government would no more listen to the wishes of the Literati of Edinburgh than to the noise of the waves on Leith Sands." *Edin. Univ. MSS. Letters of Dr. Carlyle,* No. 37.

point on which the Common People of Scotland are maddest," it ran, " is that of patronage (as they call Advowsons). They hold them to be anti-Christian, etc. The ministers who command them always touch this *Key*, and some Liberty-mad people touch it too because they say that it is the only key on which they can be touched." The late motion in the General Assembly to have a report from all the Synods embodying their objections to patronage was preparative to an intended application for an Act of Parliament to abolish patronage, and it was only negatived by a majority of nine. If the greatest attention was not given to the question, the probability was that the motion would be carried next year. The wisdom of Parliament, it was certain, would reject the application. Popular election would involve riots, but rejecting the request of the Kirk would also occasion tumults and new secessions. The Church should therefore be carefully looked after, and it might be easy to keep the Popular preachers in order. The memorialist then proposed a scheme whereby a sum of £20 was to be added to the stipends of two Crown presentees in each county. Thus some sixty clergymen, and those in expectation of succeeding them, would be under government influence. The sixty would be appointed by the Lord Advocate, " who would be careful to name proper persons."

These suggestions were not carried out, but the Moderates spared no effort to secure a majority in the Assembly of 1784. By that time Dundas had entered on his long lease of power, and it was to him that the well-known ecclesiastic, Dr. Carlyle of Inveresk, characteristically announced the triumph of his party.[1] Dundas's nephew, Robert Dundas, following in his uncle's steps, had made a brilliant début in the General Assembly. " In one of the handsomest speeches I ever heard," Carlyle wrote, " delivered with a

[1] *Scot. Corr.* vol. i. May 28, 1784.

manly modesty, he moved the resolution, viz. to reject the overtures as ill-founded, inexpedient, and dangerous to the peace of the Church. Our majority was no less than ninety that day, but that was owing to a division among our opponents. . . . Next day . . . we followed up our victory close . . . and without a vote resolved to expunge the Grievance of Patronage from our instructions to the commission. So that the Wild Brethren are compleatly routed, and Fanaticism has received a greater blow than ever it did in our time. To say the truth, such was the spirit of the clergy that even the prudence and political timidity of our friend the Principal could not have restrained them had he been their leader. He has, however, marked the most sincere joy upon this occasion, and I say that he, like King William, trained the army which was afterwards victorious."

During the following year, the conflict raged outside the Assembly, in synods, presbyteries, and kirk sessions. So acute did the crisis appear, that Robertson felt himself obliged to issue from his learned seclusion to denounce, in the General Sessions of Edinburgh, the idea of applying to Parliament for relief. Neither the Ministry nor the Opposition, he said, would give such petitions the least countenance. Some had argued that no harm would ensue if they were rebuffed. It was an easy matter to alarm the populace, but who could appease them? All remembered what had happened in the metropolis and her sister city during the anti-popish riots. "Sir," he concluded, "the same causes will ever produce the same effects, and once open the gate of novelty, bold is the man who will pretend to foretell when it will be shut." [1]

In 1785, the Popular Party raised the question once more in the Assembly, by a motion to consult the landed interest and the royal burghs as to the repeal or the alteration of

[1] *Cal. Mer.* Aug. 21, 1784.

the law. It was rejected by a majority of thirty-six, and from that date the agitation gradually subsided, although as late as 1789 the Glasgow Society for the Abolition of Patronage was still engaged in circulating petitions.[1] The opponents of patronage were themselves divided as to the remedies to be applied to the evil. Some supported the election of the minister by the whole congregation. The majority, on the other hand, wished to revive the practice of 1690 whereby the right was exercised conjointly by the elders and heritors. This division in the ranks of the "Wild Brethren" gave strength to the Moderates. Moreover, there existed in Scotland the churches of the Seceders, with a membership of some one hundred thousand, ready to welcome those who were discontented with the principles of the Established Church.

Unsuccessful as the movement was, it throws no little light on the relations between the governing classes and the general mass of the people at this time. The language of the patronage controversy of 1782 is more distinctly political than that of 1761.[2] Under the guise of ecclesiastical liberty, political ideas were gradually insinuating themselves into the minds of the common people. It was the distrust and even dread of democracy which gave added force to the pen of Hardy and the voice of Robertson long before events in France appeared to justify them; and when the shock of the French Revolution roused the industrial classes to political life, the very phraseology of the defenders of patronage became the commonplaces of the opponents of reform.

[1] *Cal. Mer.* Aug. 6, 1789.

[2] Andrew Crosbie in his *Thoughts of a Layman concerning Patronage and Presentation* (1769) had indicated the political consequences of patronage. Mathieson, *op. cit.* 174.

CHAPTER III.

THE FRENCH REVOLUTION.

As yet none of the issues raised indirectly by the American War had appealed to the Scottish people as a whole. Each class of society regarded with indifference the grievances of the other. By 1788 burgh reform had indeed made some progress. The number of towns adhering to the movement had risen from forty-seven in 1785 to fifty-three, and the Commons had ordered the charters of the royal burghs to be laid before the House. But the cause of the reformers had aroused no such general enthusiasm as the demand for a national militia or the opposition to the Roman Catholic Relief Bill. A lively interest in purely political affairs was still lacking, and the nation was still in a state of complacent acquiescence in what Galt calls "the taciturn regularity of ancient affairs." [1] In November, 1788, when the centenary of the Revolution was commemorated in all the churches on the recommendation of the General Assembly, Scottish pulpits resounded with praises of "Our Happy and Glorious Constitution." [2] Had not foreigners,

[1] Galt, *Annals of the Parish*, chap. xxix.

[2] Henry Brougham, then a boy of ten, was taken to hear his kinsman, Principal Robertson, preach on this occasion. "One sermon I can never forget. . . . I well remember his referring to the events then passing on the Continent as the forerunners of far greater ones which he saw casting their shadows before. He certainly had no apprehensions of mischief, but he was full of hope for the future, and his exultation was boundless in

Montesquieu among others, regarded it as a model? Had not Scotland peculiar reasons for remembering what Wodrow had called "the glorious and never-to-be forgotten" event? The Jacobite risings had brought home to the great majority of Scots the true benefits of the Revolution Settlement; and what was the political apathy of which Scotland had been accused but the silent testimony to the perfection of that system of government under which it had made extraordinary progress in industry and trade? Even the reformers had never ventured to call in question the principles of 1688, and it was their constant endeavour to meet the charge of innovation by asserting, in the conventional language of the day, that they were merely attempting to repair a few loose joints in the timbers of the ship of state which a hundred years' service had revealed.

Little more than two years passed, and the claim of the British constitution to be "the wonder and envy of the world"[1] was seriously challenged by the new constitution of France; and the challenge was rendered all the more dramatic by the series of momentous events that preceded it—the meeting of the States General, the taking of the

contemplating the deliverance of 'so many millions of so great a nation from the fetters of arbitrary government.'" *Life and Times of Henry, Lord Brougham*, written by himself, i. 26. Robertson's son refused later to publish the sermon "because, in the violence of the times, the author would be set down for a Jacobin, how innocent soever he was at the date of its being preached"; *ibid.* 27. Another Lord Chancellor, John Campbell, records that his "earliest recollection of eloquence" arose from a sermon delivered by his father on the same occasion. Mrs. Hardcastle, *Life of John, Lord Campbell*, i. 12.

[1] "We feel ourselves called upon to commemorate that glorious event, the Revolution of 1688, which delivered us from Popery and arbitrary power, and fixed that constitution of government which is the wonder and envy of the world. . . ." Address of the General Assembly to the King. *Scots Mag.* June, 1788, p. 307. Cf. Mons. B——de: "Many of them imagine it to be the most perfect plan of human policy." *Reflections on the Causes and Probable Consequences of the late Revolution in France*, Edin. 1790, p. 174.

Bastille, and the Declaration of the Rights of Man—and all the more impressive by the fact that it was made by a nation whose government had hitherto been regarded as the most despotic in Europe.[1] Like the American War this crisis created a keen desire for news.[2] The press published full accounts taken chiefly from the *London Gazette*. Scottish newspaper enterprise was limited, and the public curiosity was to be gauged by an increased importation of English journals,[3] well known in the larger towns where they could be obtained at the booksellers', or consulted in the coffee-houses and tap-rooms.[4] An absence of systematic comment, a notorious defect of Scottish periodicals of the time, renders

[1] "The Revolution that has taken place in France astonishes every politician in Europe to whom the news has reached. That a nation whose characteristic for several centuries has been unconditional submission to slavery should have on a sudden, in the twinkling of an eye, been animated with the boldest spirit of liberty and patriotism, is an event to be contemplated with wonder." *Edin. Evening Courant*, July 25, 1789.

[2] "We have narrated, as copiously as the limits of our paper would permit, the Revolution and the politics of a neighbouring nation, in which we have the satisfaction of having received the approbation of our readers. Yet while we presented them with the correct reasoning and elegant harangues of a Mirabeau and a Necker, we in no case omitted any local occurrences worth noting." *Cal. Mer.* Jan. 23, 1790.

[3] "To the Public. . . . The article in question, the publication of Journals and Newspapers has for some time increased astonishingly in this country ; but that increase has been chiefly promoted by the importation of English Newspapers." *Edinburgh Herald*, No. 1, March 15, 1790. Cf. the advertisement of the *Courier de Londres* in the *Caledonian Mercury*, Sept. 17, 1789 : "By means of this paper the higher orders of English readers have been provided with a variety of incidental and important intelligence, arising from the momentous occurrences of the times."

[4] "The great subscription coffee-room is supported by certain annual contributions of more than six hundred of the principal citizens of Glasgow and members of the university. Half the newspapers of London, the Gazettes from Ireland, Holland, and France, and a number of provincial journals and chronicles of Scotland and England, besides reviews, magazines, and other periodicals, are objects of the subscription." I. Lettice, *Letters on a Tour through various Parts of Scotland in the year 1792*, Lond. 1794, pp. 59 and 60.

it difficult to give a precise account of the general opinion regarding the Revolution. The tone of the press was, however, sympathetic, and it is significant that as early as March, 1790, the *Edinburgh Herald* was established to supply the want of a " truly constitutional paper." [1]

The only public expression of opinion came, as was to be expected, from the Whigs. As early as June 4, 1789, the Reform Burgesses of Aberdeen at their annual dinner, had pledged the Estates General.[2] A year later, the Whig Club of Dundee, following the example of the Revolution Society of London, voted this address to the National Assembly : [3]

> " The triumph of liberty and reason over despotism, ignorance, and superstition, is an interesting event to the most distant spectators. But the regeneration of your kingdom is rendered doubly interesting to us inhabitants of Great Britain : for the example of your former abusive government proved in the last century extremely prejudicial to ours. It excited in our princes and their ministers an inordinate desire for power which was often hurtful and sometimes fatal to themselves, but always injurious to the state.
>
> " Accept, Sir, our sincere congratulations on the recovery of your ancient and free constitution and our warmest wishes that liberty may be permanently established in France. We observe for the honour of the age and nation that your renovation has been effected without a civil war, and that neither the superfluous domains of the Prince nor the possessions of the Church have been divided among rapacious subjects but converted to the use of the State to which they

[1] Letter to the Lord Advocate, Feb. 27, 1798. *Edin. Univ. Laing MSS.* No. 500.

[2] *Cal. Mer.* June 11.

[3] *Cal. Mer.* Sept. 2, 1790.

belong. That some disturbances and even acts of violence should have attended this great Revolution is in no way surprising: that these have not been more numerous is the wonder of every politician. Our hopes are that your example will be universally followed, and that the flame you have kindled will consume the remains of despotism and bigotry in Europe.

"We not only hope, but are confident, that the National Assembly of France and the Parliament of Great Britain will from henceforth be inseparably united in promoting the peace and prosperity of the two kingdoms, and in diffusing those blessings through the whole extent of the globe.

"We congratulate you on having an army of citizens and a wise monarch, who, by lending himself graciously to the views of his people, has added lustre to the House of Bourbon, and rivetted the crown of France on the heads of his posterity. . . .

"Our climate is cold and our country mountainous. Yet since public liberty has been restored to us by the Revolution, our cities become daily more populated, our inhabitants more industrious, our mountains less barren, and our whole country more healthy and happy. Our Sovereign, the guardian of our constitution and the father of his people, is almost an object of our adoration, and our nobility and clergy form useful and illustrious members of a state where all are subject to the laws."

The reply of the National Assembly was communicated to the members of the club at their annual dinner in July of the same year. "Il est donc vrai," it ran, "qu'il existera bientôt plus de barrières entre l'Angleterre et la France; et ce grand exemple doit préparer le jour où tous les hommes vont se regarder comme frères. . . . Nous pourrions dire aussi, pour nous servir de vos propres expressions, que le Roi des Français est *presque l'objet de notre adoration.*"

Such were the only addresses that passed between Scotland and France during the Revolutionary Era. The President's reply was the only answer the Dundee Whigs received, and the patriotic societies of France did not render their action conspicuous by opening up a correspondence. Unlike the later addresses of the English political clubs, that of the Dundee society made no invidious reflections on the British constitution, but the various aspects of the new *régime* in France which were selected for commendation afford indirect testimony that a division of opinion regarding these was beginning to manifest itself in Scotland. That division of opinion had existed in England since the discussion on the Army Estimates in the House of Commons on February 6, 1790,[1] and the Dundee address was but an echo of that debate. Burke had stated the fatal influence of French despotism on the neighbouring countries, had animadverted on the recent disorder and confiscations, and had warned the House that "the present distemper might be as contagious as the old one." Fox, on the other hand, had seen in the new order of government the augury of happier relations between Great Britain and its ancient enemy, and had eulogised its citizen army. These speeches had "an immense and immediate effect"[2] in England, and the address of the Dundee Whig Club shows that they excited some attention in Scotland; but it was not until the publication of Burke's *Reflections on the Revolution in France* in November of the same year that these opinions in Scotland, as in Europe generally, became a subject of engrossing interest.

Three months before the appearance of that work, a pamphlet bearing on the same subject was published in

[1] *Parl. Hist.* xxviii. 352 *et seq.* [2] Lecky, *Hist. of England*, v. 461.

Edinburgh.[1] Badly arranged, and written with no distinction of style, it made little impression at the time; but it is worthy of note as a contemporary account by a Frenchman resident in Scotland of the political condition of the country, and of the current opinion of the French Revolution and its probable effects. In dedicating to the members of the National Assembly his short delineation of "the ecclesiastical and civil government of the freest nation upon earth except that which they had framed," the author did not do so "with a view to information of which they did not stand in need, but to afford his countrymen the most incontestible proof of the superior excellence of their own constitution." [2] The effects of their labours would not be confined within the limits of France. The world was their theatre, and generations yet to come would taste the fruits derived from the seeds of liberty they had sown. A great and respectable part of the British race was prepared to second their views, and aided by it they must become the arbiters of Europe and enabled to diffuse the blessings of freedom, happiness and peace through all the nations.[3] Englishmen, however, would not adopt a revolution. There was little to change in the constitution. They appreciated their liberty, and the privileges still to be acquired were not worth the risk of a convulsion in the state. "Among the Scots," he continues, "where I have already remarked that sentiments of freedom are neither so lively nor so universally felt, these maxims are still more generally adopted." A majority of voices in Britain would favour only a few alterations in the equality and adequacy of the representation in Parliament, in the mode of choosing its

[1] Mons. B——de, *Reflections on the Causes and Probable Consequences of the Late Revolution in France with a View of the Ecclesiastical and Civil Constitution of Scotland*, (Translated), Edin. 1790.

[2] *Ibid.* vii. and viii.

[3] *Ibid.* vi.

members, and in its duration. The Majesty of the People, Liberty, and Reform had long been familiar to British ears, and it was significant that the word "Patriot" was beginning to convey an idea of contempt and irony rather than of approbation. There was no distinction of ranks. In Scotland the clerical system was good, though not well paid, and hence low bred and fanatical.[1] Some remains of feudal institutions had still to be removed. There was an agitation in progress for burgh reform. In the counties the evil effects of superiority in creating fictitious votes were especially apparent. Every sentiment of liberty was thereby extinguished in Scotland; the commonalty were ignorant of every measure of Government, and frequently did not know even the names of those entrusted with its administration.[2] The want of juries in civil cases rendered the Scottish press ludicrously careful of expressing opinion, and hindered the diffusion of political knowledge.[3]

With regard to the current opinion of the Revolution, he found that the more enlightened part of the community viewed the transactions of the National Assembly "with great approbation." "The stability of the infant constitution was that alone concerning which they entertained a doubt."[4] These statements are confirmed by the few memoirs of the period which have come down to us.[5] In

[1] *Op. cit.* Letter xxi. [2] *Ibid.* Letter xii. [3] *Ibid.* Letter xv.

[4] *Ibid.* 6. "You say true that the French will have a hard struggle to go through before they fix on a proper form of government. They have certainly been more adventurous than wise." Rev. R. Small to Dr. A. Carlyle, Dec. 9, 1791. *Edin. Univ. MSS. Letters of Dr. Carlyle*, No. 130.

[5] "Every man of upright principles and sound sense must wish well to the cause of freedom; but every man acquainted with the human heart and the principles of government is aware of the difficulties that must ever stand in the way in an attempt radically to alter the constitution of any country. . . . From this mode of reasoning, without entering into any particular examination of the circumstances, the true friends of freedom will be moderate in their congratulations of the happiness of the people in France." *Bee*, Edin. 1791, vol. i. Jan. 26.

Edinburgh, not only Whigs like Erskine and Fletcher welcomed the Revolution, but even Principal Robertson "was dazzled by its splendour."[1] Dugald Stewart, who had visited Paris in the summers of 1788 and 1789 to study French politics on the spot, was another enthusiast.[2] In Professor Millar of Glasgow it excited the fondest hopes,[3] though he reprobated the confiscation of property and the extinction of ranks.[4] Somerville, minister of Jedburgh, whose autobiographical memoirs present a vivid picture of his times, "hailed it as the dawn of a glorious day of universal liberty."[5] Among those who were more concerned with the stability of the new Government was Beattie, the poet, the author of the *Essay on Truth,* and his opinions as revealed in his correspondence closely parallel those of Burke.[6] "One knows not what to say of this wonderful revolution that is likely to take

[1] Grey Graham, *Scottish Men of Letters*, 93, fn.

[2] *Collected Works of Dugald Stewart*, vol. x. cxxii-cxxxv, where extracts from his letters from Paris are given. Writing from Edinburgh in Jan. 1793 to his friend the Rev. Archd. Alison, he says, "I rejoice at the birth of your son . . . and I engage, as soon as he begins to snuff (which, I suppose, he will do in a dozen years hence) to make him the present of a very handsome box which I received lately, with the *Rights of Man* inscribed on the lid." *Ibid.* cxxxv. By the irony of fate this son was afterwards to be known as the Tory historian of the French Revolution.

[3] Craig, *Life of Millar*, prefixed to the *Origin of Ranks*, Edin. and Lond. 4th edn. 1806, p. cxii *et seq.* One of Millar's pupils, Lord Maitland, afterwards Earl of Lauderdale, accompanied Dugald Stewart on one of his visits to Paris, and "harangued the mob in the streets 'pour la liberté.'" J. Rae, *Life of Adam Smith*, 390.

[4] As became the author of the *Origin of the Distinction in Ranks.* This work is said to have been translated into French by Garat, the Minister of Justice after Danton, and was much esteemed on the Continent. Craig, *op. cit.* lxxvi.

[5] *Own Life*, 264.

[6] V. quotations from Burke's correspondence in Lecky, *Hist. of England*, v. chap. xxi.

place in France," he writes to Mrs. Montagu on July 31, 1789. "As I wish all mankind to be free and happy, I should rejoice in the downfall of French despotism, if I thought it would give happiness to the people; but the French seem to me better fitted for that sort of government which they want to throw off than for any other that they could adopt in its stead."[1] By September of the same year he finds "Confusion worse confounded." "The generality are actuated by a levelling principle of the worst kind which one is sorry to see likely to extend its influence beyond the limits of France."[2] In April, 1790, in a letter to Sir William Forbes, he notes with pleasure "how averse the Parliament is to civil and ecclesiastical innovation." "I hope," he adds, "our people will take warning from France."[3] In the course of the same month he wrote to his friend Arbuthnot: "No despotism is so dreadful as that of the rabble: the *Bastille* was never so bad a thing as the *Lanterne* is. . . . The old government was not rigorous; it was the mildest despotism on earth. . . . I wish Mr. Burke would publish what he intended on the present state of France. He is a man of principle, and a friend to religion, to law, and to monarchy, as well as to liberty."[4] When the *Reflections* eventually appeared, Beattie, who had himself contemplated a similar publication, felt that any attempt on his part "would be not only useless but impertinent."[5]

Burke's work, which, as Beattie shows, had been awaited with lively feelings of expectation, is an even greater landmark in the political history of Scotland than of England. In the latter country, as is well known, the *Reflections* at once put an end to that mingled astonishment and sympathy with which the French Revolution had hitherto

[1] Sir W. Forbes, *Life of Beattie*, ii. 246. [2] *Ibid.* ii. 250.
[3] *Ibid.* 254. [4] *Ibid.* 256. [5] *Ibid.* 278.

been regarded.[1] As Mackintosh said: "That performance divided the nation into marked parties." Political ferment, however, had long existed in England. In Scotland where it was as yet unknown, the discussion evoked by Burke's pamphlet, and more especially by the replies which it drew forth, was the means of awakening to political life every class of society, hitherto only somewhat feebly stirred by the narrower questions of burgh, county, or ecclesiastical reform. From the first Burke's publication awakened keen interest. All the newspapers printed long extracts, including not only as a matter of local interest the denunciation of the Dundee Whig Club,[2] but also those passages which, since the day of publication, have been regarded as among the finest examples of English rhetoric. Burke himself, writing to his Scottish friend, Sir Gilbert Elliot, expressed his astonishment that "about a book published only the 1st November, there should be an attack and so able a defence on the 11th in Edinburgh."[3] The attack referred to was probably that of the *Edinburgh Evening Courant*,[4] and its criticism represented a common opinion of the *Reflections*. "In his statement of what was done at the Revolution of 1688 we think him unanswerable. In

[1] J. Morley, *Burke*, 152.

[2] "These [issue of assignats] are the grand calculations on which a philosophical public credit is founded in France. They cannot raise supplies; but they can raise mobs. Let them rejoice in the applauses of the club at Dundee, for their wisdom and patriotism in having thus applied the plunder of the citizens to the service of the state. I hear of no address upon this subject from the directors of the Bank of England, though their approbation would be of a *little* more weight in the scale of credit than that of the club at Dundee. But, to do justice to the club, I believe the gentlemen who compose it to be wiser than they appear; that they will be less liberal of their money than of their addresses; and that they would not give a dog's-ear of their most rumpled and ragged Scotch paper for twenty of your fairest assignats."

[3] Countess of Minto, *Life and Letters of Sir Gilbert Elliot*, i. 366, 367.

[4] Nov. 11, 1790.

many of his remarks on the former and present constitution of France he is just and sensible, but the general complexion of the book presents us with what we consider as a total dereliction of those principles which Mr. Burke has been for many years known to hold. . . . In a word, such a work as the present, from any man but Mr. Burke, would deserve a place among the most valuable dissertations of the constitution of Great Britain, but coming from *him* it leaves us altogether at a loss to know what political principle or integrity means, not to speak of what is intimately connected therewith, *consistency*!"[1] In the next issue "A Rockingham Whig"[2] combated this charge, and proved by citations from Burke's other writings and speeches that he had always been opposed to speculative principles in government and metaphysical considerations of the rights of man.

Burke does not seem to have influenced the opinion of those who had already expressed their enthusiasm for the Revolution. Principal Robertson talked of the "ravings of Burke"[3] and Somerville could find in the "eloquent publication," nothing but "the ranting declamations of aristocratic pride and exuberant genius."[4] There is no doubt that in official circles the book was heartily welcomed. As early as December, 1790, traces of its influence may be seen in the loyal address voted by the Town Council of Edinburgh on the successful issue of the negotiations with

[1] Cf. *Glasgow Mercury*, Nov. 9—Nov. 16, 1790. "Last Monday morning, died at an advanced age, the Whiggism of the Rt. Hon. Edmund Burke, once an eminent Patriot and Whig under the Rockingham Ministry, much and deeply regretted by his numerous friends and acquaintances."

[2] "With a signature so soothing to my ears," Burke to Elliot, *op. cit. ibid.* The writer was John Wilde, Professor of Civil Law in the University of Edinburgh. V. his *Address to the . . . Friends of the People*, Edin. 1793, pp. x-xv.

[3] Grey Graham, *op. cit.* 93, fn.

[4] *Own Life*, 264.

Spain, which for some time had withdrawn public attention from French affairs.[1] Even the Edinburgh Revolution Society in November of the same year was content with pledging the cause of liberty throughout the world without making specific reference to France, and the chairman of the annual gathering dwelt impressively on the glories of that constitution " upon which other nations wished to model their governments but which they had not yet been able to effectuate." [2] That the Edinburgh Society should adopt language in such striking contrast to that of the London Revolution Society was a sign that as yet the contagion from France so dreaded by Burke and his admirers had not spread to Scotland. Commendation of the Revolution was " speculative and platonic " ; was confined to a few members of the upper and middle classes ; and had produced no apparent effect on the people at large. The style and the language of Burke made no popular appeal, and the price of the book was prohibitive.[3]

Of the many replies to the *Reflections* still addressed to this limited audience, two are noteworthy as the work of Scotsmen—the *Letters on the French Revolution* [4] by Thomas Christie, and the more famous *Vindiciae Gallicae* of James Mackintosh. Thomas Christie was the member of a Montrose family well known for its liberal opinions.[5] His father, Alexander, was for many years provost of the burgh. His uncle, William, who founded in the same town the first

[1] *Scot. Corr.* vol. iv. Nov. 24, 1790.

[2] *Cal. Mer.* Nov. 18, 1790.

[3] An abridged edition, price 8d., was published. *Cal. Mer.* June 18, 1791. From the number of more popular pamphlets against the French Revolution issued in Scotland towards the end of 1792, it does not seem to have appealed any more than the original to the ordinary reader. Adolphus states that the price was never reduced. *Hist. of England*, Lond. 1841, iv. 555.

[4] Part i. Lond. 1791. Part ii. never appeared.

[5] For an account of the Christies v. *Dict. Nat. Biog.*

Unitarian church in Scotland, published in 1791 *An Essay on Ecclesiastical Liberty*[1] in which he made an admirable plea for religious toleration. Like his co-religionists in England with whom he was closely allied, William Christie was an ardent admirer of the French Revolution, and did not refrain from bearing testimony in its favour.[2] His brother, Alexander, as a member of the Church of Scotland, was censured by the Kirk Session for having "occasionally frequented the Unitarian Society." *The Holy Scriptures, the Only Rule of Faith and Religious Liberty*[3] was the outcome of this controversy in which he defended his cause by citing such authorities as Dr. Price and Necker, the French Minister; and, "as a work eminently calculated to promote civil and religious liberty," he printed as an appendix the former's famous sermon of November 5, 1789. Thomas Christie, son of the provost, after spending some time at Edinburgh University, settled in London where he established the *Analytical Review*.[4] In 1789 he visited Paris where his literary reputation and the introductions he bore from influential friends soon procured him intimate relations with Mirabeau, Sieyès, Necker and other leaders of the constitutional party.[5] In 1791 appeared his *Letters on the French Revolution*.

[1] Montrose, 1791.

[2] "The mention of the Bastille recalls to my memory the late glorious revolution in France in favour and approbation of which I am happy to bear a public and sincere testimony." *Essay on Eccles. Liberty*, 26, fn.

[3] Montrose, 1790.

[4] Miss Seward, the "Swan of Lichfield," characterised him as "a young prodigy in science and literature." *Letters of Anna Seward*, i. Letter lxxi.

[5] At the request of the National Assembly, Christie, in 1792, translated the constitution into English. Alger, *Englishmen in the French Revolution*, p. 78. *The French Constitutional Code as Revised, Amended, and Finally corrected by the National Assembly*, was published by W. Creech, Edin. 1791.

To his antagonist's ability and the charm of his style Christie was by no means indifferent. Feeling what was due to Mr. Burke, he apologised for not entering into an elaborate review of that work in which " with majestic grace worthy of a nobler office he conducts us to the Temple of Superstition," and by the " magic of his language soothes our hearts into holy reverence and sacred awe." [1] But the question at issue was one of "*facts* not of *declamation* and *oratory*," [2] and Christie, who had already published a sketch of the new constitution in two folio sheets, proceeded to refute the arguments of Burke and of his authority, Calonne, by a more detailed description of that pledge of settled government. He candidly confessed that Burke's method of reforming by engrafting new principles on the stock of old ones was in general a good one. But it was not the only one nor would it suit in all cases. " When the whole mass of juices are corrupted, as M. Mirabeau well observed, it will not do to cut off some of the members." [3] The evils that had attended this more drastic process—the riots, burnings, and murders—had been exaggerated by Burke in the highest degree. " I went over to Paris immediately after the king's arrival there, and I lived in that city six months in the middle of the great events then accomplishing in the most perfect harmony and security. I walked about everywhere, mixed with all classes of society, spoke my opinion publicly of every public measure, and was abroad at all hours, and never met with injury, nor even experienced alarm." [4] The conduct of the French mob, as eye-witnesses had assured him, had been exemplary, and if a few rich proprietors in some provinces had suffered, it was not till they had excited the vengeance of the people. Equally misinformed was Mr. Burke regard-

[1] *Op. cit.* 6.
[2] *Ibid.* 7.
[3] *Ibid.* 20.
[4] *Ibid.* 121.

ing the labours of the legislators, and his account of the mode of election to the Assembly "teemed with errors." The method in reality "resembles the constitutions of the towns in Scotland where magistrates or municipal assembly choose an *Assembly of Delegates,* and these delegates appoint the Member of Parliament. It is far superior to it in another respect, for the Electoral Assemblies of France are chosen by the *Primary Assemblies* which consist of *all* the citizens except paupers, servants and bankrupts; while the delegates of Scotland are appointed by municipal officers who elect one another *ad infinitum,* without the concurrence of, and frequently contrary to, the general service of the citizens."[1] Among the benefits he enumerated as resulting from such a constitution was the simplification of the laws; and the history of his own country appeared to justify the change. "The old Scotch Acts rarely contain so many lines as the modern British ones do pages. Yet they occasioned fewer controversies than arise from the present method of multiplying words without wisdom."[2] Interesting as the work is, and still valuable for its account of the state of Paris during the earlier stages of the Revolution, it was soon to be discounted as a contribution to the controversy by the later tragic developments. But indirectly the author had much influence in Scotland. His native Montrose and the district around were soon to become notorious as one of the centres of democratic propaganda, and the Government was led to believe that this was largely due to Thomas Christie, the friend of Condorcet.

Like Christie, James Mackintosh, the author of the *Vindiciae Gallicae*[3] had been subject to liberal impressions from his youth. Even as a schoolboy he had evinced a decided interest in politics, and had conducted in the class-

[1] *Op. cit.* 155-6. [2] *Ibid.* 271, fn.

[3] The references are to the 4th edition, Lond. 1792.

room a series of debates on the American War, based on the reports of the *Aberdeen Journal*, the only newspaper then circulating in the north of Scotland.[1] At Aberdeen University he came under the tuition of Professor Dunbar, a man of strong Whig principles;[2] and when later he proceeded to Edinburgh University, the "Speculative" and other societies, testifying to what he himself calls a general "fermentation of mind," provided scope for the maturing of his powers. In 1788 he went up to London where he attracted the attention of Horne Tooke and other advanced reformers, and displayed his early interest in the cause of freedom by contributing articles to the *Oracle* on the affairs of Belgium and France. In April, 1791, he published his brilliant *Vindiciae Gallicae*, which was at once received as an adequate answer to the *Reflections*. An important section of the book dealt with the new constitution of France, for a more complete account of which he referred his readers to Christie. More important for our purpose are the fifth and sixth chapters where, in vindicating English admirers of the Revolution and in speculating on its probable consequences, he eulogised the early spirit of freedom that had distinguished his countrymen in the past, and called upon his fellow Scots to emulate the fame of their ancestors. When "the science which teaches the rights of man and the eloquence which kindles the spirit of freedom had for ages been buried with the other monuments of the wisdom and relics of the genius of antiquity," Buchanan

[1] R. J. Mackintosh, *Life of Sir James Mackintosh*, i. 8, fn.

[2] "In spring, 1782, when the news arrived of the dismissal of Lord North, he met me in the street and told me, in his pompous way, 'Well, Mr. M., I congratulate you, the Augean stable is cleansed.'" *Ibid.* 12. Mr. Ogilvie, another of his professors, published *An Essay on the Right of Property in Land*, which "by its bold agrarianism attracted some attention during the ferment of speculation occasioned by the French Revolution." *Ibid.* 17.

was the first scholar of the Revival of Letters "to catch the noble flame of republican enthusiasm."[1] The Revolution Whigs did not escape the Toryism of an age which saw the University of Oxford offer its congratulations to Sir George Mackenzie for his confutation of the abominable doctrines of Buchanan and Milton. Hence the absurd debates in the Convention in England about such palliative phrases as "abdicate," "desert," etc. It was the Scottish Parliament which cut the matter short by using "the correct and manly expression that James II. had forfeited the throne."[2]

It was the desire of the English admirers of the Revolution of 1688 to remedy grievances according to its *principles.*[3] What was the source of these grievances—the remains of feudal tyranny still suffered to exist in Scotland, the press fettered, the right of trial by jury abridged, manufacturers proscribed and hunted down by excise? "No branch of the Legislature represented the people."[4] All therefore should unite to procure a reform in the representation of the people. The grievances did not justify a change by violence; but they were making rapid progress to that fatal state in which they would both justify and produce it. There was only one opinion about the French Revolution on which its friends and enemies were agreed. Its influence would not be confined to France. It would produce important changes in the general state of Europe. These effects would depend on the stability of the new settlement, and that very moment (August 25, 1791) was peculiarly critical.[5] A confederacy of despots against the new *régime* was announced. But even if war did break out, there could

[1] *Op. cit.* 313. "It is also worthy of note that in the year of the French Revolution, 1789, an English translation [of the *De Jure Regni*] was published in London." Hume Brown, *George Buchanan*, 292.

[2] *Vind. Gall.* 319. [3] *Ibid.* 344. [4] *Ibid.* 349. [5] *Ibid.* 360.

be no doubt as to the result. History recorded no example where foreign force had subjugated a powerful and gallant people governed by the most imperious passion that can sway the human breast. The ancestors of a nation now stigmatised for servility felt that powerful sentiment. The Scottish nobles contending for their liberty under Robert the Bruce spoke thus to the Pope: "Non pugnamus propter divitias, honores, aut dignitates, sed propter *Libertatem* tantummodo quam nemo bonus nisi simul cum vita amittit!" Reflecting on the various fortunes of his countrymen, he could not exclude from his mind the comparison between their present reputation and their ancient character—"terrarum et libertatis extremos"—nor could he forget the honourable reproach against the Scottish name in the character of Buchanan by Thuanus, "Libertate genti innata in regium fastigium accibior." This melancholy prospect was, however, relieved by the hope that a gallant and enlightened people would not be slow in renewing the era of such reproaches.[1] Thus did Mackintosh trust that even in Scotland the Revolution would serve, not as a model, but "to invigorate the spirit of freedom."

Among the author's friends in Edinburgh, the *Vindiciae* was highly appreciated.[2] Professor Wilde, writing in June, 1791, though severely critical of some passages, declared that he was "inter ignes luna minores."[3] None of the Literati had bought the book save Tytler, who said that there was a good deal of thought in it. Malcolm Laing

[1] *Op. cit.* 362, fn. [2] *Life*, i. 76.

[3] Wilde published a voluminous *Address to the Lately formed Society of the Friends of the People.* Edin. 1793. It was partly a vindication of Burke's consistency (v. *ante*, p. 52) and partly a reply to Mackintosh and other defenders of the French Revolution. According to Brougham (*Memoirs*, i. 231), Burke "conceived the greatest admiration" for Wilde in consequence, but the book does not merit particular notice. V. also J. Wilde's *Sequel to An Address to the lately formed Society of the Friends of the People.* Edin. 1797.

affirmed that it was the best he had ever read. Grant of Corrimonie thought it "admirable." Thomas Reid of Glasgow, the founder of the Scottish school of philosophy, characterised the *Vindiciae* as "one of the most ingenious essays in political philosophy he had ever met with."[1] Nor is it likely that the case of Robert Haldane of Airthrey, a typical country gentleman, was exceptional. Before the French Revolution, having nothing to rouse his attention, he lived in the country almost wholly occupied in the usual pursuits. Like most of his class he had read Delolme's *Treatise* and Blackstone's *Commentaries*, and was a sincere admirer of the British constitution. The first books he read on the subject of government after the change that had taken place in France were Burke's *Reflections*, Mackintosh's *Vindiciae Gallicae*, and afterwards some of the pamphlets of Christie, Paine, Priestley, and others. "Although I did not exactly agree with these writers," he says in his *Address on Politics*,[2] "a scene of amelioration and improvement in the affairs of mankind seemed to open itself to my mind which I trusted would speedily take place in the world, such as the universal abolition of slavery, of war, and of many other miseries that mankind were exposed to. . . . I rejoiced in the experiment that was making in France of the construction of a government at once from its foundation upon a regular plan, which Hume in his *Essays* speaks of as an event so much to be desired." Mackintosh exerted considerable influence on the better educated type of reformer in Scotland. His list of the defects in the constitution was often the theme of the abler democratic pamphlets of the day; and, as we shall see, his references to Scottish history were not forgotten.

[1] A. Campbell Fraser, *Thomas Reid* (Famous Scots Series), 116.

[2] *Address to the Public concerning Political Opinions*. . . . Edin. 1800, p. 4.

Meanwhile the works of another writer, Thomas Paine, were being disseminated among a large section of the community indifferent to the charms of rhetoric or to the niceties of political controversy. The first part of his *Rights of Man* appeared in February, 1791, and was followed by the second in February, 1792.[1] Paine did not make direct references to Scotland as his friend Christie had done, nor could he like Mackintosh appeal to Scotsmen as a fellow-countryman. But with dogmatic assurance, and a homeliness of illustration that gave vigour to his style, Paine exposed the grievances of the nation more definitely than either of these opponents of Burke, by an elaborate comparison between the English and the French Constitutions. He showed that every man in France paying sixty sous a year in taxes had a vote.[2] The Members of Parliament were distributed according to the number of taxable inhabitants.[3] Parliament was elected for two years. There were neither oppressive game laws nor chartered towns enjoying monopolies in trade and election. Corruption was unknown since placemen and pensioners were excluded from the Assembly.[4] Taxes were thus directed to their legitimate end, and were neither dissipated in maintaining a corrupt set of courtiers nor increased by war. The powers of peace and war resided in the nation in France.[5] Nobility had been done away with, and the peer was exalted into the man.[6] Primogeniture no longer perpetuated such a class in society. Tithes were abolished, and a universal right of conscience was established. All these principles were derived from the Declaration of the Rights of Man which Paine printed in full.[7] How were such rights to prevail in England? Not under the existing system of Parliament. There was a paradox in the idea of vitiated

[1] *Works*, ed. M. D. Conway, vol. ii. [2] *Ibid.* 312. [3] *Ibid.* 313.
[4] *Ibid.* 315. [5] *Ibid.* 316. [6] *Ibid.* 319. [7] *Ibid.* 351 *et seq.*

bodies reforming themselves. "The true constitutional method would be by a general convention elected for the purpose." [1] Burke had affirmed that a hereditary crown was necessary to preserve the liberties of England. Paine's answer was Lafayette's phrase, "For a Nation to be free, it is sufficient that she wills it." [2]

As events were to prove, Paine's ideas on the grievances of the nation, and even on the manner of removing them, found ready acceptance in Scotland. Not only were the defects of the constitution glaringly exhibited in its political state. The progress of industry and trade since the 'Forty-Five was creating new social conditions making for independence of thought and action among the middle and lower classes, and towards the close of the century a new spirit of energy accelerated these effects. The Government itself showed some signs of activity. In 1784 a contemporary newspaper could point to the large sums of money voted for the construction of public works and to the Parliamentary committee on the fisheries as likely to stimulate Scottish enterprise.[3] It was by a grant from the funds of the Forfeited Estates that the Forth and Clyde canal was completed in 1790. The prosperity of the Carron Iron Works since 1760 had rendered the canal an economic necessity.[4] In the twenty-eight years succeeding their establishment the annual output of iron was 1500 tons, but before the beginning of the nineteenth century foundries had been set up in various parts of the kingdom, so that by 1796 the production of iron had risen to 18,600 tons per annum.[5] The manufacture of linen, still the staple industry of Scotland, flourished from Glasgow in the west to Dun-

[1] *Op. cit.* ii. 312. [2] *Ibid.* 363.

[3] *Cal. Mer.* Sept. 6, 1784.

[4] W. L. Mathieson, *The Awakening of Scotland*, 250.

[5] Mackintosh, *Hist. of Civilisation in Scotland*, iv. 347.

fermline in the east. In the counties of Forfar, Perth and Fife, however, was to be found the greatest number of looms. In Dunfermline alone they had increased from 900 in 1788 to 1200 in 1792.[1] Nearly twelve million yards were manufactured in 1768, thirteen million in 1778, and twenty and a half million in 1788.[2] Paisley, whose trade in silk outrivalled for a time that of Spitalfields, had 1767 looms at work in various textile industries in 1766. In 1773 the number was computed to be 2233, and in 1792, 3602.[3] In 1782 Dale in partnership with Arkwright set up three cotton mills at New Lanark; and the new industry spread with such rapidity over the whole district of the Clyde that by 1790 it had almost superseded that of linen in Glasgow and of silk in Paisley.[4] As in England, such prosperity was accompanied by an increase of population and the rise of large towns which further emphasised the anomalies of burgh government and representation. In 1755 the population of Edinburgh was 47,815, of Glasgow 30,000, of Paisley 6799, of Perth 9019, and of Dundee 12,477. By the year 1795 Edinburgh had 71,645 inhabitants, Glasgow 56,028, Paisley 24,592, and Dundee 23,500. Perth in 1790 had a population of 19,871.[5]

During the same period wages steadily advanced. "The mason, the weaver, the carpenter who could in 1750 only earn his 6d. a day, in 1790 made his 1s. or 1s. 2d." [6] Many Paisley firms in 1785 had a weekly wage bill of £500.[7] Under such conditions, these classes began to assert themselves.

[1] E. Henderson, *Annals of Dunfermline.*

[2] Bremner, *Industries of Scotland*, 220.

[3] Metcalfe, *History of Paisley*, 460. [4] Mathieson, *op. cit.* 372.

[5] *Parochial Statistics of Scotland 1755-1795. Brit. Mus. Add. MSS.* 15746. These were compiled by George Chalmers from Dr. Webster's and Sir John Sinclair's *Statistical Accounts of Scotland.*

[6] H. G. Graham, *Social Life of Scotland*, 261.

[7] *Social England*, ed. H. D. Traill, v. 691.

" A spirit of independence in the progress of opulence has arisen especially among the more substantial part of the people," wrote the parish minister of Wigtown in the *Statistical Account of Scotland*.[1] Less friendly observers noted the same effects in the larger towns. One of Beattie's correspondents, referring to the meal riots in Peterhead in 1793, declared that they were " the evil fruits of our manufactories." " Numbers of scoundrels are brought from all parts," he wrote, " knaves who hardly ever possessed a whole shilling at once before ; they are introduced to high daily pay ; they think themselves equal to any persons they can see ; they are rude, insolent and riotous." [2] Even in the laws of the Leadhill miners Ramsay of Ochtertyre detected " somewhat of a republican spirit." " They anxiously stipulated that on no pretext shall the Earl of Hopetoun and his factors, or the company's manager or deputy, attempt to influence the proceedings or resolves of the society." [3] Strikes, then known as " combinations," were another new phenomenon of industrial life which provoked the adverse comment of conservative minds. The first of any importance seems to have occurred in July, 1787, when the weavers of Glasgow refused to work at the usual rates of pay. Having assembled on Glasgow Green, they proceeded to appoint committees " to meet with the masters, receive their ultimatums, and report." Negotiations having proved fruitless, the strikers took the webs out of the looms of those willing to work and carried them in procession through the town. A riot followed ; the military were called out ; and as a result of the firing that ensued three of the weavers were killed and three mortally wounded. In

[1] Vol. xiv. 483.
[2] M. Forbes, *Beattie and His Friends*, 281.

[3] *Scotland and Scotsmen in the Eighteenth Century*, ed. A. Allardyce, ii. 324-5. "Yet in their *proper* business," Ramsay characteristically adds, "they were obliged to give up their *natural* rights and obey the commands of their superiors without calling them in question."

the following July, Lord Eskgrove sentenced one of the strikers to be whipped and banished for seven years.[1]

In the country the general improvement in agriculture was effecting similar changes. "I travelled," says a writer in 1790, "through some places where not many years ago the people were wretchedly poor, want sat upon every brow, hunger was painted on every face; neither their tattered clothes nor their miserable cottages were a sufficient shelter from the cold; now the labourers have put off the long clothing, the tardy pace, the lethargic look of their fathers, for the short doublet, the linen trousers, the quick pace of men who are labouring for their own behoof, and work up to the spirit of their cattle, and the rapid revolution of the threshing-machine." [2]

To this independence of thought was now joined an interest in politics, occasioned by the upheaval in France,[3] and conditioned by the spread of education. Although the standard of teaching degenerated during the latter half of the century, a school was yet to be found in nearly every parish, and such schools were supplemented in many cases by those of the Society for the Propagation of Christian Knowledge.[4] Ability to read and write was thus comparatively widespread, and was remarked by foreign visitors.[5]

[1] *Scots. Mag.* July and Sept. 1787, July 1788. Burnett gives the generally accepted view of "combinations" at this time. "There is hardly any offence more dangerous in its consequences to the public at large." *Criminal Law*, chap. xii.

[2] Quoted by Graham, *op. cit.* 214.

[3] "The French Revolution first raised a general curiosity, and newspapers were generally sought after, procured, and read." Jas. Mitchell, Kirriemuir (to Henry Dundas?). *Scot. Corr.* vol. vi. Nov. 29, 1792.

[4] T. Pettigrew Young, *Histoire de l'Enseignement en Écosse*, chap. vi. In only four parishes was there no school. *Ibid.* 150.

[5] Cf. Mons. B——de, *op. cit.* pp. 160 and 161. "This is perhaps the only country in the world where all are taught to read and write. . . . With respect to education, the peasantry of Scotland as far excel those of England, as the latter are superior to the same order of men in those nations which adhere to the Catholic religion."

Towards the close of the century there arose a demand for libraries,[1] and reading clubs were formed. Even in country districts debating societies were not unknown. In manufacturing towns and the larger villages the mill was beginning to provide a natural means of social union for discussion,[2] and quicker methods left the home working weaver free to devote some time to public affairs. The desire for newspapers testified to this new interest. " Although the parish consists wholly of the poorer ranks of society," wrote the minister of Auchterderran in 1790, " newspapers are very generally read and attended to, and the desire for them increases." [3] " An attention to public affairs," wrote another, " a thing formerly unknown among the lower ranks, pretty generally prevails now. Not only the farmers, but many of the tradesmen, read the newspapers and take an interest in the measures of Government." [4] The secular spirit, always associated with material prosperity, was beginning to affect the lower, as it had already affected the higher ranks of society ; and the same acuteness which the former had displayed in religious controversy was now to be transferred to political discussion.[5] The year 1792 was to show how far the writings of Paine had replaced Boston's *Crook in the Lot*, the *Fourfold State*, and Bunyan's *Pilgrim's Progress* [6] as the favourite reading of a large section of the Scottish people.

[1] J. Colville, *By-ways of Scottish History*, 274.

[2] Cf. Galt, *Annals of the Parish*, chap. xxix.

[3] *Stat. Acc. of Scot.* vol. i. 457.

[4] *Ibid.* vol. xiv. 483, Wigtown.

[5] Referring to the growth of political discussion among his parishioners, the minister of Urr (Kirkcudbrightshire) wrote : " In a quarter where (till of late) religious controversies used to be agitated with great freedom and warmth, it is not to be supposed that the minds of men should be deprived of that acuteness which results from such disquisitions." *Stat. Acc. of Scot.* vol. xi. 79.

[6] These, according to Somerville, were to be found "in almost every cottage." *Own Life*, 350.

CHAPTER IV.

POLITICAL AND SOCIAL UNREST.

THE Tory riot at Birmingham in 1791, and the rise of the democratic societies during the same year, showed that in England the writings of Burke and of Paine were beginning to influence popular action. It was not until the middle of the following year that riots in Perth, Aberdeen, and Edinburgh, revealed similar tendencies at work in Scotland. By that time the vague sense of grievance created by the existing political conditions in Scotland, and fostered by such publications as the *Rights of Man,* had been rendered more definite by the action of the Government, represented by Henry Dundas, now "*de facto*" King of Scotland. The rejection of the petition in favour of the repeal of the Test Act in so far as it applied to Scotland, the Corn Bill of 1791, the opposition to burgh reform and to the abolition of the slave trade, and the issue of the proclamation against seditious writings, had added fuel to the flame of popular discontent.

As has already been noted, Burke had avowed his dread of the contagious example of France as early as February, 1790, and he had stated his views with greater precision in the debates in the House regarding the repeal of the Test and Corporation Acts. In their catechisms the dissenters evinced a decided hostility to the Established Church, and from the praise of the French Revolution by two of their leading divines,[1] he inferred that the Church of England was " in a much more serious danger than the Church of France a year or two ago." In rejecting by 294 votes to 105 a motion which in the previous year had only been defeated by 20, the House showed that it shared Burke's apprehensions.[2]

This debate had been followed by Dr. Somerville, minister of Jedburgh, with " vigilant anxiety." [3] Certain statements made by Pitt and Fox induced him to believe that Parliament might be willing to relieve members of the Kirk of Scotland from the operation of the Test Act. Accordingly, through his instrumentality, there came before the General Assembly of May, 1790, an overture to the effect " that the extension to Scotland of the Test Act of Charles II. was a violation of the privileges stipulated to them by the Treaty of Union, and injurious to the interests of religion and morality." In the discussion which ensued, the motion was strenuously opposed by all the lay members of the Assembly, including the Lord Advocate and the President of the Court of Session, whose speeches reflected the spirit of the debates in Parliament earlier in the year.[4] It was urged that the times were inauspicious, and that by such an innovation the public peace might be endangered. An able speech by Sir Henry Moncreiff, one of the leaders of the Popular Party, enabled Somerville to carry the day, and he was empowered to proceed to London in charge of a petition to Parliament. Accompanied by his friend, Sir Gilbert Elliot, who had promised his assistance, he interviewed the most prominent Parliamentary leaders with the view of soliciting their support. Dundas " frankly owned " that he was in favour of the proposal, but, as the Archbishop of Canterbury was adverse, he wished it to be with-

[1] Dr. Priestley and Dr. Price. [2] *Parl. Hist.* xxviii. 431 *et seq.*

[3] *Own Life*, chap. vi. *passim.* [4] *Cal. Mer.* May 31, June 3, 5, 7, 1790.

drawn.[1] Such a reception was ominous, and when Sir Gilbert Elliot presented the petition in the House on May 10, 1791, it only secured 62 votes. The Lord Advocate,[2] Robert Dundas, urged that the tenor of the petition was against the Treaty of Union, and his uncle in the same strain declared that any attempt to repeal the Test Act " would be playing a shameful game at fast and loose with England, and retreating from our contract after we had got possession of great and invaluable benefits which she could not retake from us." [3] Such was the beginning of the adverse influence of the French Revolution on Scottish reforms, and on this

[1] The Moderate Party in Scotland had warned the Archbishop. "Being at a distance from Town and ignorant of the Progress of Dr. Somerville's Petition, I thought your letter, and the Protest deserved the Archbishop of Canterbury's Attention, and I therefore took the Liberty of sending them to His Grace, who has expressed himself obliged to me for the Communication. It was natural that our Dissenters, who wish to have the Corporation and Test Acts repealed, should endeavour to call upon your Assembly to their Assistance. But their Alliance with the Protesting Catholics is rather an extraordinary Step. It is fortunate for our Establishment in the Church that its Enemies have loudly declared their Enmity to our Establishment in the State, and while we have such strong Proofs of their eager Desire to convert our Parliament into a National Assembly, and to introduce all the levelling Projects of the French Patriots into this Country, there seems to be little Probability of their being successful in any Application to the Legislature at this Juncture." Dr. Douglas, Bp. of Carlisle, to Dr. Carlyle, April 4, 1791. *Edin. Univ. MSS. Letters of Dr. Carlyle*, No. 29.

[2] Dr. Hill, the leader of the Moderates, seems to have supplied him with arguments against the motion. *Edin. Univ. Laing MSS.* No. 500, Mar. 14, 1791.

[3] *Parl. Hist.* xxix. 500. Burke, "from prudential reasons," took no part in the debate. "He said . . . he had never heard the Test Act complained of, and never expected that an application for the repeal of it would have come from the clergy of the Church of Scotland, who, on former occasions, appeared culpably obsequious to all the measures of government. . . . A predominating dread of innovation seemed to engross all Mr. Burke's thoughts and feelings at this time. When he spoke of the French Revolution he grew warm and animated. He showed me a few letters which he had lately received from France giving an account of the multiplied atrocities arising from the dissolution of the Government." Somerville, *op. cit.* p. 251.

occasion there was nothing in the petition itself, nor in the political state of the country, to justify the attitude of the Government.[1]

Two months later, the Birmingham riot proved that Burke's fears and prejudices were spreading beyond the confines of Parliament.[2] But neither at this time nor later did the rank and file of the Scottish people make any turbulent demonstrations in favour of Church and Crown. The dramatic incident of Varennes had renewed public interest in French affairs,[3] and in Edinburgh, Glasgow, Dundee, and other towns, the fall of the Bastille was duly

[1] "The rejection of the petition from the General Assembly of the Church of Scotland we do not class among the symptoms of amendment in our constitution. What was requested was moderate and just. Could any evil have arisen from granting that request, it might have been rejected, but that was neither proved nor even asserted, and indeed cannot possibly exist." *Cal. Mer.* May 21, 1791.

[2] Full accounts are to be found in the Scottish press. V. *Cal. Mer.* July 21-25.

[3] On this event there appeared in the *Cal. Mer.* "An Heroic Tale, Translated from the French of M. la Fontaine the Younger." He tells

. . . .

How they were stopt *in all their glory*.
A fly old soldier twigged the Queen
    Whom he had seen,
    Like Mr. Burke, *some years ago*,
And took it in his head to know.
He then went on, with reason, to suppose,
And soaking till he look'd as wise
As ever he was known to look,
    When from a nook,
    Out popt *La Reine*,
    That is the Queen,
Like a *delightful vision* from above,
    Or Queen of Love
    Descending in her car,
And glittering like the morning star.
    In justice be it known
This latter line is not my own,
But written by one Master Burke.

. . . .

Cal. Mer. July 7, 1791

commemorated. Yet these celebrations passed off as quietly as those of the London Revolution Society to which prominent Scottish officials had been expressly invited.[1] At the Glasgow dinner where Lieut.-Colonel Dalrymple of Fordell and Professor Millar presided, the toasts included the standing army of France, the natural rights of man, and the abolition of the slave trade.[2] At Dundee the Revolution Society pledged the rights of men, an equal representation of the people, a speedy abolition of the slave trade, and the abolition of all religious tests for civil offices.[3] Two groups of admirers of the French Revolution joined to commemorate in Edinburgh " an event so interesting to mankind as the redemption of twenty-six millions from servitude, an event that promised unexampled happiness to the human race." [4] On this occasion, Mackintosh, Paine, and Priestley " were all toasted with distinguished applause." [5] Even as far north as Portsoy, Alexander Leith, a distiller, " by distributing a considerable quantity of spirits, procured a mob to assemble to celebrate the anniversary of the French Revolution, which was accordingly done in the most tumultuous manner by firing cannon, etc." [6]

[1] On June 27, 1791, R. Dundas forwarded to London an invitation which he had received to dinner at the Crown and Anchor Tavern, the Strand, to celebrate the second anniversary of the French Revolution, "to show how industrious the Revolutionists are in propagating their intended anniversary. . . . I presume every man in Scotland whose name appears in a Scots Almanac is honoured with a similar invitation." *Scot. Corr.* vol. iv.

[2] *Edinburgh Herald*, July 18. [3] *Ibid.* July 20.

[4] The second advertisement added: "Though the lateness of this call to the friends of Liberty and of Mankind must operate in rendering the Meeting more thinly attended than might otherwise be expected from the ancient independent character of the Scots nation, yet the proposers are satisfied their numbers will be so considerable as to accomplish the end they have in view, which is nothing more than a public avowal that the principles of liberty are cherished in Edinburgh, as well as in London and in Dublin." *Edinburgh Herald*, July 6.

[5] *Cal. Mer.* July 16. [6] *Scot. Corr.* vol. v. June 13, 1792.

Though the Lord Provost of Edinburgh sent Henry Dundas the names of those who were present at Fortune's Tavern, none of these proceedings seem to have given rise to any anxiety on the part of the authorities. The provost's list included such advocates as John Clerk, Jr., of Eldin, Malcolm Laing, afterwards known as an historian of Scotland, John Millar, the Glasgow professor's son, Archibald Fletcher, the leader of the burgh reform movement, Fergusson of Craigdarroch, various merchants and "writers," and some fifteen university students, one of whom was John Allen, later of Holland House fame.[1] "If any judgment is to be formed from the present sample," commented the provost, "they do not seem qualified to do much mischief in this or any other country. The meeting I can assure you, Sir, incurred the universal censure of the community, in which, with I believe as few exceptions as in any other place whatever, the greatest harmony, peace, and respect for the present government prevail." [2]

An Act which came into force in November of the same year had ultimately more effect in undermining this prevailing respect for the Government than any annoyance at the failure to repeal the Test Act, or even enthusiasm for what were beginning to be known as "French Principles." In the recess of 1790, a report of the Privy Council on the question of the regulation of corn was widely circulated to prepare the nation for the new Corn Bill which was discussed during the ensuing session. Hitherto the corn laws

[1] Allen and James Craig, afterwards Sir James Gibson Craig, took a leading part in the preparations. John Allen, *Inquiry into the Rise and Growth of the Royal Prerogative in England, a new edn. with . . . biographical notices.* Lond. 1849.

[2] *Scot. Corr.* vol. iv. July 15, 1791. In all seventy-three were present. Another dinner was held in the house of Stewart, Royal Exchange, where the low price of the ticket, half-a-crown, attracted "Joseph Lauchlan, J. Fairbairn and other violent reformers." *Ibid.*

had been of a more or less temporary nature, but it was hoped that the Bill, following the lines of the report, would permanently solve the difficulty of providing the British Isles with food supplies.[1] The main feature of the new Bill (which was highly approved of by the landed interest) was the giving of bounties to encourage exportation and the imposing of duties to restrain importation. Against such a principle the growing manufacturing centres in the west made vigorous protests. The Town Council of Glasgow, among others, declared that the state of the manufactures of Scotland rendered a free importation of corn and meal at all times necessary.[2] More significant of the opposition was a meeting of thirty-two delegates from the Incorporated Trades and Friendly Societies of Paisley, who passed a resolution that the new regulations adversely affected "the peace and welfare of the labouring poor who are the radical instruments of British opulence and prosperity."[3] Apart from the principles of the Bill, there were definite grievances in its actual provisions. Oatmeal, for example, could be imported into England when the price of oats was 16s. a quarter, but not into Scotland until it exceeded 16s. per boll, that is, 19s. a quarter. It was also urged that, as there were no regular corn markets in Scotland, the price of meal should be regulated by the price of the meal itself, and not by that of oats, as was proposed. Further, for the purposes of the Act, Scotland was divided into four districts. The average price of grain obtained by the sheriff in each district determined the importation of cereals for three months, and their exportation for one month, throughout that district. When the price of wheat was under 44s. a quarter, a bounty

[1] *Bee*, Edin. 1791, i. 304. An abstract of the Corn Act as it affected Scotland is to be found in vol. vi. p. 17 *et seq.*

[2] *Edin. Herald*, Jan. 31, 1791.

[3] *Ibid.* Feb. 2, 1791.

of 5s. a quarter was allowed; when it was at or above 46s., exportation was forbidden; and at or above 50s., import duty was imposed according to a sliding scale. Little care was taken to group districts according to their fertility. Grain-producing counties were joined to others which were not. Thus prices were kept up, and the ports of a district closed, which otherwise would have been open. Before the Bill finally became law, the more clamant objections to it had been removed; but when to its vexatious regulations, carried out with all the notorious harshness of Scottish excise officials, was added the scarcity of the year 1792, it became a fruitful source of local disturbance and of democratic invective.

Dundas appears to have taken no active share in the Corn Bill debates, though he incurred all the odium excited by the administration of the law; but the part he bore in opposing burgh reform, and the abolition of the slave trade, and in issuing the proclamation against seditious writings still further embittered his relations with the lower classes whose interest in political affairs was steadily increasing. In May, 1791, Sheridan moved in the House of Commons "that the several petitions, and other accounts and papers presented in the last Parliament be referred to a committee."[1] When Dundas opposed the motion on the ground that the session was too far advanced for the magistrates to attend in person, the House agreed, on the suggestion of Fox, to take the matter into consideration early next session. In the interval signs were not wanting that the subject was exciting keener attention than before. In April, 1790, the London committee of the burgesses had warned the burgh reformers that their cause was being compromised by the alarm of the French Revolution to which some of them had referred in their printed proceedings. This induced Henry Erskine to bring forward a motion in their annual convention of the same year that their proposals "had not the remotest tendency to alter or infringe in any respect the political institutions of their country."[1] Outside the Whig ranks in Scotland, however, the movement was definitely associated with the momentous changes abroad. The *Historical Register*, a new organ of advanced opinion, complained that the agitation was "carried on more by the spirit of individuals than the united endeavours of the people"; but it asserted that "the example of some other states of Europe who had so nobly and so successfully asserted the rights of man could not fail to awaken the attention of Scotsmen to their true interest, after which it was impossible that they could long continue in a state of wretched slavery."[2] At a meeting of the Glasgow Society for Burgh Reform in March, 1792, it was reported[3] that, "along with several letters from

[1] Fletcher, *op. cit.* 109.

[2] October, 1791.

[3] *Cal. Mer.* March 24, 1792. In January, 1792, a subscription had been opened in Glasgow "to aid the French in carrying on the war against the emigrant princes, or any foreign power by whom they were attacked." "It is said that £1200 have already been subscribed." Contemporary newspaper quoted in Chambers's *Life and Works of Burns*, ed. W. Wallace, vol. iii. 319. Thomas Reid seems to have been among those who remitted money to the National Assembly. M. Forbes, *Beattie and His Friends*, 273. One of Reid's university colleagues, John Anderson, was in Paris when Louis XVI. was brought back from Varennes. He presented to the French people the model of a gun of his own design which was hung up in the hall of the Convention with the inscription, "The gift of Science to Liberty." Guns of this pattern are said to have been used with great effect at the battle of Maubeuge in June, 1792. By means of another of his inventions—small paper balloons varnished with boiled tar—revolutionary manifestos were sent across the hostile frontiers of Germany and Spain. *Glasgow Courier*, April 3 and 5, 1792; Alger, *Englishmen in the French Revolution*, 52; Chambers's *Biog. Dict. of Eminent Scotsmen; Glasgow and the French Revolution*, a paper by the present writer in the *Transactions of the Franco-Scottish Society*, Edin. 1912. In Feb. 1792, Burns sent four carronades as a present to the French Assembly. Chambers, *op. cit. ibid.*

societies in that city testifying their concurrence with the plan of reform and offering very liberal subscriptions for its support, the Society was presented with a box containing an elegant silver medal." On one side was engraved the following inscription: "Men are by nature free and equal in respect of their rights; hence all civil or political distinctions are derived from the people, and can be founded only on public utility. . . . The deprivation of rights, or the abuse of power, justifies resistance and demands redress. . . . Public justice, liberty of conscience, trial by jury, the freedom of the press, the freedom of election, and an equal representation, ought ever to be held sacred and inviolable." On the other side were the words, "Glasgow Society for Borough Reform. Friends of reform, be unanimous, active, and steady, asserting and constitutionally establishing the rights of man, and be 'not weary of well-doing' for by wisdom, prudence and courage, 'in due time ye shall reap if ye faint not.'"

When, therefore, Sheridan again brought forward his motion on April 18, 1792,[1] he had some justification for warning Dundas that "he was vigilantly watched in England, and would be faithfully reported in Scotland. . . . If he thought that his petty shifts would pass upon the people of North Britain he was deceived in them, and did not know them so well as he thought he did. . . . He ought to know them better than to think that they would for ever bear such insults." From the first Sheridan's conduct in forwarding the cause of the reformers had revealed his lack of business capacity, and on this occasion he displayed a singular want of tact. He did not content himself with rehearsing all the "flimsy evasions" whereby Dundas had hitherto postponed discussion. In direct opposition to the methods of the burgesses, he needlessly introduced a long panegyric

[1] *Parl. Hist.* xxix. 1183 *et seq.*

on the French Revolution, and indirectly on the new association of the Friends of the People which was in process of formation. The lesson of the recent events in France, he declared, was to introduce a timely reform. Otherwise the increasing desire for redress of grievances might lead to "anarchy and confusion." If they suffered that, it would be too late to talk about the probable mischief of reform.[1] As the House was doubtless of the opinion of the honourable Member who declared that Sheridan had delivered "one of the most inflammatory, wicked, and dangerous speeches ever heard," Dundas and his nephew, the Lord Advocate, hardly required to invent any new arguments against the motion. Nothing came of the discussion save the admission by Robert Dundas that there was no legal authority in Scotland to control the accounts of the Town Councils.

Five days later, Dundas was at issue with an even greater number of his fellow-countrymen by introducing his motion in favour of the gradual, as opposed to the immediate, abolition of the slave trade. On no question since the Catholic Relief Bill had Scotland appeared so unanimous as in the cause of Wilberforce and his fellow-labourers. From January to May, 1792, the advertisement columns of the newspapers teemed with resolutions in favour of the anti-slavery crusade. Town Councils, Trade Incorporations, Presbyteries and Sessions of the Kirk and of the Seceders, private societies of every kind, united in denouncing the slave trade as immoral and unchristian. Under the auspices of the parent Abolition Society in London, branches were

[1] "Écoutons M. Sheridan, le second orateur de l'opposition, parlant dans la séance du 18 avril, et proposant de réformer la représentation parlementaire dans les burgs d'Écosse. . . . On nous proposoit, comme fait M. Sheridan, une réforme modérée, et l'on nous a donné une révolution atroce. . . . Burke ! O sage Burke. . . . C'est la première tête de l'hydre qui se montre." A. Dillon, *Progrès de la Révolution Française en Angleterre, ce 27 avril, 1792.*

instituted in such centres as Edinburgh and Perth. A meeting held in the Circus of the former city, presided over by Henry Erskine, was attended by 3000 people, and led to a petition containing 10,885 signatures.[1] It was noted at the time that few if any of the landed interest passed resolutions against the traffic,[2] and Dr. Somerville of Jedburgh, by publishing a sermon against it, gave great offence to some gentlemen in the country who imputed it to seditious principles.[3] In the higher circles of Edinburgh, where the influence of Dundas was more immediate, the agitation was said to be taken up only by those unfriendly to the Government. As Pitt had delivered one of his most eloquent orations in favour of abolition, such assertions might have been hard to justify, had not some of the petitioning societies in their resolutions made specific references to the rights of man.[4]

"Seditious principles," however, were as yet confined in Scotland to individuals. In England not a few societies had been established to propagate Paine's teaching. Foremost among them was that at Manchester, whose ostentatious vote of thanks to the author of the *Rights of Man* was duly published in the Scottish press. The spirit of the French Revolution had also infused new life into older associations such as the Society for Constitutional Information, which had been moribund since Pitt's abortive motions in favour of reform.[5] In 1791, Thomas Hardy, a native of Falkirk,

[1] *Cal. Mer.* Mar. 29, 1792. [2] *Ibid.* Feb. 27, 1792. [3] *Own Life*, 263.

[4] The Medical Society of Edinburgh, for example, adopted the following resolution: "All men are born free and equal in rights. The first object of government is to secure to *all* the right which *all* derive from nature to *civil* liberty. The object of *political* liberty is to prevent the abuse of power in government. Slavery, therefore, if political, must be contrary to the *cause*, if civil, to the *end of* good government: and in both cases it is a violation of the first and most sacred rights of man." *Cal. Mer.* Mar. 10, 1792; Neil Douglas, *American Slave Trade*, 193.

[5] E. Smith, *Story of the English Jacobins*, 14.

founded the London Corresponding Society, and it came definitely before the public on April 2, 1792, with a series of resolutions advocating drastic measures of reform.[1] Its low subscription of one penny a week was designed to attract a more popular class than adhered to the Constitutional Information Society, whose annual subscription was five guineas. In the same month Grey, Sheridan, the Earl of Lauderdale, and other Whigs of the younger school, founded the Society of the Friends of the People, whose members paid two and a half guineas a year.[2] It was the professed aim of this body to counteract the more radical tendencies of the others,[3] and a week after its formal institution, Grey gave notice in Parliament of his intention to submit early next session a motion, the object of which was a reform in the representation of the people. The irregular debate which Pitt initiated revealed a schism in the Whig ranks. Fox, though he abstained from joining the association, supported Grey; but Windham, speaking for the older Whigs, "avowed his intention to oppose the motion whenever it appeared."[4]

A variety of motives, therefore, induced the Government to issue the proclamation against seditious writings on May 21. There is little doubt that Pitt was really alarmed at the progress of Paine's principles among "mechanics and cottars." On the other hand, it afforded him an opportunity of strengthening his party by still further widening the breach in the Whig ranks.[5] Such at least

[1] *Place Coll. Brit. Mus. Add. MSS.* 27808, f. 4.

[2] *Proceedings of the Society of the Friends of the People*, Lond. 1793, April 11, 1792.

[3] *Ibid.* Correspondence with Society for Constitutional Information, May 12, 1792.

[4] *Parl. Hist.* xxix. 1327.

[5] This motive is unduly emphasised in W. T. Laprade's *England and the French Revolution*, chap. iii.

was the result of the debate on the loyal addresses voted by both Houses when the proclamation was published.[1] In Scotland it provoked a storm of disapproval in all but official circles. The *Historical Register,* quoting the *Morning Chronicle,* affirmed that the proclamation introduced the spy system by rendering the magistrates accusers instead of judges. If complaining of abuses was sedition, then Members of Parliament were guilty of the most horrible kind that ever existed.[2] Even the learned and genial editor of the *Bee* admitted into its columns a scathing criticism of the Government's action. Paine's book had received an excellent advertisement. "I know," added the editor in a footnote, "that in a small town in the north of Scotland before the proclamation, there was just *one* copy of Paine's pamphlet; and the bookseller of the place declared three weeks ago that he had since then sold seven hundred and fifty copies of it. And a bookseller in Edinburgh told me that he had before the proclamation a good many copies of it that lay so long on his hand that he would gladly have sold them all at two shillings a copy. He has since then sold the whole of these and many more at three shillings and sixpence each." [3]

While the people were anxiously inquiring for "the book that was forbidden to be sold," corporations were zealously following the example of the Houses of Parliament in voting loyal addresses. In county meetings also the freeholders and the commissioners of supply were equally eager to manifest their principles. Each country gentleman made it his duty to see that his presence was duly noted in the public prints. Absence, on such an occasion, might be construed as a sign of revolutionary sympathies. The

[1] The proclamation had been submitted to the Duke of Portland, *Life and Letters of Sir Gilbert Elliot*, ii. 26.

[2] May, 1792.

[3] *Bee*, vol. x. 85.

loyalty of the addressers was doubtless stimulated by a succession of popular demonstrations against Dundas and the governing classes. In May "a very disagreeable state of tumult and disorder" in the town of Lanark lasted for eight days.[1] In Aberdeen, Perth, and Dundee, "and almost every village in the North of Scotland," the mob burned Dundas in effigy,[2] and as June 4, the King's birthday, drew near, inflammatory placards warned the magistrates that Edinburgh intended to do the same. The premature introduction of troops into the city led to a three days' riot.[3] On the first night a "prodigious" crowd made a bonfire of a sentry box of the city guard, and stoned the soldiers as they returned to the castle. On the following evening a knot of workmen attempted to burn an "image" of Dundas in George Square, and when they were dispersed, they came back in greater numbers to storm the Lord Advocate's town house. The reading of the Riot Act and the firing of the troops brought the disturbance to an end. "With extraordinary persistency" the mob reappeared next night, and shivered to pieces the Lord Provost's windows in St. Andrew's Square before the military arrived. "An evil spirit seems to have reached us which I was in hopes John Bull would have kept to himself"[4] was Lord Provost Stirling's comment to Dundas. To the workings of the same evil spirit were assigned in the month of July the destruction of the newly erected toll bars in the neighbourhood of Duns, and the sheep riots in the county of Ross. Three troops of dragoons were required to quell the former

[1] *Scot. Corr.* vol. v. May 8, 1792.

[2] *Hist. Register*, June, 1792. "At Peebles, the Right Hon. Secretary has twice undergone the fire ordeal, and passed through the flames unhurt."

[3] A full account of the riot by the present writer will be found in the *Scot. Hist. Rev.* Oct. 1909; v. *Scot. Corr.* vol. v. June.

[4] *Scot. Corr.* vol. v. June 12, 1792.

disorder,[1] and it was not till the 42nd regiment had been requisitioned that the latter subsided.[2]

Officially all these signs of popular unrest were attributed to the writings of Tom Paine. The sheriff of Lanarkshire informed Henry Dundas that the real cause of the outrages was "an almost universal spirit of reform and opposition to the established government and legal administrators which has wonderfully diffused through the manufacturing towns of this county, and is openly patronised by many county gentlemen of fortune." [3] At a meeting held in St. Giles' after the Edinburgh riot, the Lord Advocate insinuated that there had been a premeditated design of the people to rise in revolt,[4] and the Town Council passed a motion denouncing the propagators of sedition. The resolutions adopted by the county gentlemen of Ross were to the same effect.[5] Yet real grievances were known to exist, and were admitted in private. The magistrates of Lanark by proposing to enclose a small part of the burgh moor had exasperated the long-suffering townsfolk.[6] In Berwickshire, it was alleged, not improbably, that the money raised by the toll dues had been expended in repairing the roads in the neighbourhood of the gentry.[7] The half-humorous, half-satirical placards posted up in the streets of Edinburgh had stigmatised Dundas's opposition to burgh reform and other progressive measures.[8] Lord Adam Gordon, Commander-in-Chief in Scotland, while giving an official version of the

[1] *Scot. Corr.* Suppl. vol. lx. July 8, 1792.

[2] *Ibid.* vol. v. Aug. 6, 1792.

[3] *Ibid.* May 8, 1792.

[4] *Hist. Register* (*Universal Monthly Intelligencer*).

[5] *Scot. Corr.* vol. v. July 31, 1792.

[6] "The ostensible cause of these outrages." Sheriff's letter, *Scot. Corr.* vol. v. May 8, 1792.

[7] *Hist. Register* (*Universal Monthly Intelligencer*), July, 1792.

[8] *Scot. Hist. Rev.* Oct. 1909, p. 23.

sheep riots, sent in another marked "private."[1] "If I were to hazard an opinion upon the matter," he wrote, "it is a decided one—that no *disloyalty* or spirit of *rebellion* or dislike to His Majesty's *Person* or *Government* is in the least concerned in these tumults. They solely originated in a (too well founded) apprehension that the landed proprietors in Ross-shire and some of the adjacent Highland counties were about to let their estates to sheep farmers, which meant all the former tenants would be ousted and turned adrift, and of course obliged to emigrate, unless they were elsewhere received, any probability of which they could not discover. And it is an undoubted fact that, in several instances within these last two or three years, such speculations have been realised, and the proprietors have by those means greatly increased their rent rolls, and diminished the number of the people on their respective estates. Of this last but too many proofs might be adduced, and if the strength of a nation depends on the number of its people, measures which tend directly and unavoidably to dispeople it ought not in reason and sound policy to be encouraged." Dundas had long been of Gordon's opinion. In 1775 the question of emigration had seriously occupied the attention of the Government, and the newly appointed Lord Advocate, in a long letter to Auckland, explained, partly in the same terms as Lord Adam Gordon did now, the root of the evil.[2] The destruction of clanship, and the consequent decrease in the value of men, appeared to him to be deeper reasons of the distress, and he mooted the idea of restoring the "old proprietors" to their forfeited estates whereby the kind and beneficent sway of the landlord-chieftain might in some degree be brought back. This patriotic policy Dundas had carried out in 1784, and in the

[1] *Scot. Corr.* vol. v. Aug. 19, 1792.

[2] *Auckland Papers*, *Brit. Mus. Add. MSS.* 34412, f. 352.

same year the Highland Society was founded to interest the public in the development of the Highlands and Islands.[1] But the evils which still continued were too great for its labours. When in August, 1792, a boatload of emigrants was visited by a Custom-House official, they gave as reasons for leaving for North Carolina three long-standing causes of emigration—poverty, oppression of landlords, and encouraging letters from friends already settled in America.[2]

Such a state of affairs was frequently denounced both in pamphlets and in the press. But for the present there was no appearance of a desire on the part of the Government to consider these and other grievances on their merits. Parliamentary reform of one kind or another was beginning to be put forward as the panacea for all the ills of the body politic,[3] and Parliamentary reform would involve the end of the rule of Dundas and his supporters. The dread of mobs was genuine,[4] and it was not difficult for the " friends of administration," with exaggerated reports of French excesses fresh in their minds, to persuade themselves and others that reform and revolution were identical. As Lord Provost Stirling, referring to the riot, put the matter to Dundas: " The favourers of reform and innovation . . . have, by their late intemperance and zeal, overshot the mark, and given an alarm to the sober and well-minded part of the community which they did not

[1] A Royal Charter setting forth the objects of the society was granted in 1787. *Home Office* (*Scotland*) *Entry Book Warrants*, vol. ii. May 21, 1787.

[2] *Scot. Corr.* vol. v. Aug. 17, 1792.

[3] *Historical Register* (*Universal Monthly Intelligencer*), Aug. 1792, attributed the riots in Ross-shire to the fact that the people had "no one to represent them."

[4] Justice Clerk Millar's letter, July 19, 1784, *Scot. Hist. Rev.* Oct. 1909; *Scot. Corr.* vol. ii.

intend. . . ."[1] When, therefore, associations of the Friends of the People were founded in Scotland, their constitutional agitation was studiously confounded with rioting, sedition, and revolution, and the cause of reform compromised ere it had well begun.

[1] *Scot. Corr.* vol. v. June 16, 1792.

CHAPTER V.

"THE FRIENDS OF THE PEOPLE."

THE first society of the Friends of the People in Scotland met in Edinburgh on July 26, 1792,[1] but it was not until two months later that the increasing number of such associations began to alarm the Government. In the interval the principles of reform were being actively propagated by the distribution of Paine's *Rights of Man,* and by discussion in the press. As in France itself, the Revolution produced in Scotland a mushroom growth of journals and periodicals. In 1782, there were only eight Scottish newspapers; but by 1790 there were twenty-seven,[2] and during the years 1791 and 1792 additions were made to their number. The first to be established avowedly in consequence of the stir in the political world was the *Edinburgh Herald,* which appeared in March, 1790.[3] In August of the same year the *Glasgow*

[1] *Cal. Mer.* July 28, 1792. The Glasgow Society of the Friends of the People, usually reckoned the first in Scotland, was not founded until October, but there was a society for effecting Constitutional and Parliamentary Reform already in existence, for on July 23, it expressed its "warmest sentiments of veneration and regard" for the Friends of the People in London. Wyvill, *Polit. Papers*, iii. No. xviii. 45.

[2] Statement by Lord John Russell in his motion for Parl. Reform, April 22, 1822. *Annual Register*, 1822, p. 69, quoted by Alison, *Hist. of Europe*, 1815-1832, ii. chap. x. par. 126, fn.

[3] "The politics of France, and of other parts of the Continent by which the example has been followed, give an importance to the public affairs of the present period beyond those of almost any other æra that can be remembered." *Edin. Herald*, No. 1, March 15, 1790.

Courier was founded, " the apology for this offering " to the public being, besides domestic occurrences, " the politics of France and of the other Continental Powers, whether considered abstractedly or as affecting the politics of this country." [1] The *Courier* was not in favour of reform, but to such an extent had the older newspapers been affected by French ideas that in April, 1792, the *Edinburgh Herald* was described to the Lord Advocate as " the only newspaper in Scotland *truly* and *sincerely* affected to Government." [2] By the beginning of June the periodicals in Edinburgh alone numbered ten,[3] and on June 20, 1792, the *Political Review of Edinburgh Periodical Publications* was started to give an account of these, from the anti-Ministerial point of view, beginning with June 4, " as a remarkable æra." [4] According to its trenchant criticism, the *Edinburgh Advertiser* was the " least political." The *Caledonian Mercury* was the " most free-spirited "—though the proclamation against seditious writings was evidently beginning to affect its impartial discussion of affairs. The *Courant* was " more attached to Ministers " than the *Mercury*. The *Herald*, however, was " the vehicle of Ministerial dirt . . . the subjects of its vengeance being the French Constitution, the National Assembly, and the Reform Society." An equally ardent supporter of the Government was to be found

[1] Advert. in *Edin. Herald*, Aug. 8, 1791.

[2] Henry Mackenzie to Ld. Advocate, April 14, 1792, *Edin. Univ. Laing MSS.* No. 501.

[3] An excellent account of the Edinburgh press will be found in W. J. Couper's the *Edin. Period. Press*, 2 vols. Stirling, 1908. The present writer is also indebted to Mr. Couper for information regarding the Glasgow newspapers.

[4] Copy in Brit. Mus. Few of the Scottish democratic newspapers of this period have been preserved. Owing to later political developments they became dangerous possessions. June 4 was the date of the King's Birthday Riot in Edinburgh.

in *Constitutional Letters*. The career of the *Historical Register*[1] was even more symptomatic of the times. Originally intended to advocate reform, this review, on the issue of its tenth number, was published in two parts, the one having for sub-title the *Edinburgh Monthly Intelligencer*, the other the *Universal Monthly Intelligencer*. While the former represented the views of the original paper, the latter was much more extreme. Thus it denounced war—the Commanders in the East Indies being designated "murderers"—the slave trade, the extravagance at court, the notorious immorality of the Duke of Clarence,[2] the evils of solitary confinement, and the rapacity of landlords who were driving thousands of Highlanders abroad. For success in the cause of reform, it showed the necessity of unanimity among the reformers, and such an accession of numbers as would enable them to form something like a National Convention.[3] Even more significant of the political atmosphere of the capital were the essays in the *Bee*, which was first published in 1791 under the editorship of Dr. Anderson, a well-known authority on the agriculture and fisheries of Scotland.[4] This magazine confined its attention, after the manner of Adam Smith, to the exposure of glaring defects in administration without committing itself to party politics. The oppression of the tacksmen in the Highlands, the harshness of the excise duties and of customs officials, the injustice of the corn laws, and the necessity of a jury in civil cases were among the subjects of its shrewd and temperate criticism. In 1792, a series of articles appeared in its columns which aroused no little comment. The "Political Progress of

[1] There is a copy in the Signet Library, Edinburgh.

[2] Cf. Sir Gilbert Elliot: "If anything can make a democracy in England it will be the Royal Family." *Life and Letters*, ii. 13.

[3] Sept. 1792. Cf. Paine, *ante*, ch. iii. p. 62.

[4] V. James Anderson in *Dict. Nat. Biog.*

Britain," which condemned the whole system of government since the Revolution of 1688, was considered by some of the subscribers as an attack on Dundas.[1] An essay entitled "Hints respecting the Constitution," by one of the Friends of the People in London, was probably inserted as an antidote.[2] The writer, after showing the illogical position of those who based their faith on the inalienable rights of man, pointed out the strictly constitutional aims of his party. In August, even this series came to a close. The alarming incidents in France had raised doubts in the author's mind as to the propriety of adopting certain modes of conduct that did not appear liable to objection before. The writings of Paine and his associates had too rapid a circulation, and the essayist was now prepared for an inundation of writings of an opposite tendency. Under the influence of this apprehended frenzy much mischief might be done, and he therefore suspended his remarks.

Yet at this very time the Friends of the People were making rapid progress in Edinburgh. On the last day of August, a certain Robert Watt wrote to Henry Dundas[3] that he had been present at some of the committee meetings and had been astonished at the language used by the reformers, such as "government expenses must be retrenched"; "Ministry must be displaced"; "none belonging to the Treasury should have a seat in Parliament." "In short," he added, "France must be imitated." One of their number in a committee in a tavern had said: "It is

[1] *Bee*, viii. 171.

[2] *Polit. Rev. of Edin. Per. Publications*, No. 3; *Bee*, ix. June, 1792.

[3] *Scot. Corr.* vol. 5. *State Trials*, xxiii. 1323. Watt was not a member of the Friends of the People. "As I could not be prevailed on to subscribe their book of admission, notwithstanding their using several arguments to persuade me to it on three different occasions, they sent me for my information and conviction Paine's *Rights of Man*, Mackintosh's answer to Paine, and Flower's publication."

a maxim of mine that a king should be sacrificed to the nation once in every hundred years." "They propose to accomplish their h—— designs," he concluded, "by pretending moderation at first in their demands and proceedings, and by degrees artfully to insinuate their dangerous ideas into the minds of their adherents, and when they suppose themselves sufficiently powerful, then to attack perforce the throne and the friends of the constitution. This they think they can do with more ease and safety than even the French." Two hundred had attended the general meeting and discussed a plan of organisation. As they expected their numbers to increase, the society was to be divided into smaller ones for the more convenient dispatch of business. Three weeks later [1] he informed Dundas that the society numbered three hundred. They were in communication with the London Corresponding Society, whose seditious papers they were circulating, and they were even thinking of joining in a congratulatory address to the Jacobin Club of Paris.[2] He enclosed one of the papers, *An Address to the Nation at Large,*[3] which contained as an argument for reform the fact that the single county of Cornwall sent forty-four members to Parliament, one less than the total representation of Scotland. About the same time [4] Lord Provost Stirling forwarded to Dundas a broadsheet, large

[1] *Scot. Corr.* vol. v. Sept. 21, 1792.

[2] This was not carried out. "A letter was read from the Association of the Friends of the People in Edinburgh, cautiously declining joining in the address, but giving a very favourable account of the spirit of liberty in these parts." *Journal of the London Corresp. Socy.* Nov. 1792. *Place Coll. Brit. Mus. Add. MSS.* 27812, f. 24. Cf. entry dated Jan. 1793: "A letter was read from the Friends of the People [in London] signifying their acceptance of our proffered correspondence, their regard and veneration of the original principles of our constitution, and a friendly admonition to abstain from intermixture of foreign correspondence and domestic reform."

[3] *Scot. Corr.* vol. v.

[4] *Ibid.* Sept. 22, 1792.

impressions of which were being thrown off. The first part contained a reprint of the *Declaration of the Rights of Man.* The second consisted of an outline of the origin of government, condemned impress warrants and Dundas's conduct in opposing burgh reform, and advocated equal representation, just taxation, and liberty of conscience.[1] This was the most direct application of the Rights of Man to the political condition of Scotland that had yet been made. The authorities were still further alarmed by the appearance of another organ of advanced opinion, the *Edinburgh Gazetteer*,[2] and by the circulation of medals inscribed with revolutionary mottoes.[3]

Such "political madness," according to the *Caledonian Mercury* of September 30, 1792, was not limited to Edinburgh. "That keenness of political enquiry," it said, "which for a long time seemed to be confined to England, has now reached this northern clime and extended its influence with rapid strides, so that it now pervades the whole of Caledonia. Societies are everywhere formed and clubs instituted for the sole purpose of political debate."[4] Thus the Dundee Friends of the Constitution, founded on September 17, 1792,[5]

[1] Printed in *State Trials*, xxiii. 27.

[2] Prospectus in Couper, *op. cit.* ii. 191-9. There are numerous references to its influence in the *Scot. Corr.* As early as Nov. 29, 1792, Mrs. S. B——, Montrose, one of Dundas's regular correspondents, wrote: "That newspaper, the *Gazetteer*, puts them [the reformers] in a flame. I believe it has done more hurt than anything else."

[3] *State Trials*, xxiii. 30.

[4] Cf. *Whitehall Evening Post*, Nov. 22-4, the editor of which was a Scotsman, Dr. W. Thompson, formerly minister of Auchterarder. *Scot. Corr.* Dec. 4, 1792. "The spirit of association and remonstrance is stronger in Scotland, as vegetation is powerful in soil fresh and newly reduced from the forest."

[5] *Cal. Mer.* Oct. 4, 1792. The word "Constitution" was included in the designation of some of the societies as an answer to the insinuations of their opponents.

was said to consist of fifty members.[1] By September 23, Perth was reported to have four societies with a total membership of a hundred, and during the same month, the newspapers published the resolutions of numerous societies in the eastern district.[2] The activity of the reformers was as keen in the west. In the Star Inn on October 3, the Glasgow Associated Friends of the Constitution and of the People was formed, with Lieut.-Colonel Dalrymple of Fordell as President, Thomas Muir, younger, of Huntershill, Advocate, as Vice-President, and George Crawford, "Writer," as Secretary.[3] Under the stimulus of these leaders, similar associations sprang up in Paisley, Kilmarnock, Kirkintilloch, and other towns and villages in the neighbourhood.[4]

The organisation of the Glasgow Society may be taken as typical of the others.[5] Each member, besides paying a quarterly subscription of threepence, had to sign two resolutions to the effect that the society would co-operate with the Friends of the People in London in all proper measures to accomplish an equal representation of the people in Parliament, and to obtain a shorter duration of Parliamentary delegation. As a safeguard against admitting avowed republicans, and as an answer to their enemies, members were further required to declare that they would be faithful to the British Constitution as consisting of a King, House of Lords, and House of Commons, and would discountenance

[1] Watt to H. Dundas, Sept. 21, 1792, *Scot. Corr.* vol. v.

[2] Adverts. in *Cal. Mer.* Oct. to Dec.

[3] *Cal. Mer.* Oct. 13, 1792. The *Glasgow Courier* of Oct. 20 contains an account of the third meeting of the association. 400 were present, of whom 121 were new members. Several other societies were affiliated. Muir's speech recommending moderation and order is given in outline. Macleod, M.P. for Inverness, joined the society on October 27.

[4] Muir's propagandist tour may be traced in the evidence of the witnesses at his trial.

[5] *Plan of the Internal Government of the Society of the Friends of the Constitution and of the People* [*Glasgow*]. *Scot. Corr.* vol. v.

and suppress all sedition, riots and disorder.[1] A Committee of Direction met weekly to manage the affairs of the society and enrol new members. As the numbers increased, branches were set up in each district which sent monthly reports to the central society and delegates to a convention of the local associations. Thus there was an essential difference between the Friends of the People in London and in Scotland. The high subscription of two guineas kept the former a select body of Members of Parliament, country gentlemen, and the professional classes. No branches were formed in England, though country members were admitted. The low subscription and the organisation of the Scottish associations were based on those of the London Corresponding Society, and the Scottish Friends of the People were drawn from a similar grade of society—weavers and shoemakers in the country districts, tradesmen and shopkeepers in the towns.[2]

Amid this growing excitement, Dundas, the Home Secretary, arrived in Edinburgh about the middle of October. The appearance of a new class of politicians was sufficient in itself to disturb his peace of mind, and his apprehensions

[1] Some of the societies, in imitation of the English associations, published longer declarations, *e.g.* Paisley, *State Trials*, xxiii. 122-3. The Montrose Friends of the People issued *An Address to the People of Great Britain*, which enumerated six advantages which would result from their activity. These included the spread of political information and the preservation of order—"such societies cannot be concealed." *Cal. Mer.* Nov. 3, 1792.

[2] Cf. *The Reformers*, Edin. 1793:

> "The worthy members of these worthy meetings
> Are cobblers some, some brewers to their trade,
> Weavers are some, some finely thrive by beatings,
> And some by their smart feet do make their bread.
>
> Old toothless schoolmasters, and furious tanners,
> Tailors, hair-dressers, deep-read butchers too,
> All list with zeal under fair Reform's banners,
> And that they will be great men vow."

were increased by the flood of confidential letters that was pouring in from all quarters of Scotland warning him of the dangerous spirit abroad in the land.[1] Some of these Dundas forwarded to Nepean, an official of the Home Office, for the inspection of Pitt and Grenville. Writing on October 14, he says, " I am more and more satisfied that unless something effectual can be done to check the indiscriminate practice of associations, they will spread the fermentation of the country to such a height it will be impossible to restrain the effects of them." [2] The letter from Glasgow which he enclosed gave point to his remarks. " The success of the French Democrats," it ran, " has had a most mischievous effect here. Did it go no further than give occasion for triumph to those who entertain the same sentiments here, there would be little harm, for they are very few in number, and but two or three of them possessed of any considerable influence or respectability. But it has led them to think of forming societies for reformation in which the lower classes of people are invited to enter, and however insignificant these leaders may be in themselves, when backed with the mob they become formidable." An anonymous correspondent confirmed these statements.[3] " Within these few months," he wrote, " I have visited several places in Scotland and corresponded with others, and find from every intelligence that all the lower ranks, particularly the operative manufacturers, with a considerable number of their employers, are poisoned with an enthusiastic rage for ideal liberty that will not be crushed without coercive measures."

[1] As a rule the government of Scotland was carried on without much trouble. Thus one volume suffices for the Scottish correspondence preserved in the Record Office for the years 1789-91. Owing to the crisis in 1792, the correspondence of the months of November and December alone occupy one volume, and three are required for that of 1793.

[2] *Scot. Corr.* vol. v.

[3] *Ibid.* vol. vi. Nov. 1792.

With another communication to Nepean, dated from Melville Castle, November 24, 1792,[1] Dundas sent several papers for further inspection and preservation. The first from Sir William Maxwell in Dumfriesshire struck him as a proof of the rapidity with which these " mad ideas " had made progress. He had met this baronet at the Duke of Buccleuch's, at Langholm, on his way north, and Sir William had then assured him that there was not a symptom of unrest in all that countryside. Now he wrote that unknown emissaries of sedition were at work in his neighbourhood, and by infinite address, artifice, and falsehood, were operating on the credulity of the people, affirming that the King and his family were useless and burdensome and ought to be sent adrift, and that taxes only served to support them. Paine's pamphlet, or " the cream and substance of it," was in the hands of almost every countryman, and could be had for twopence. Medals with inscriptions expressive of liberty and equality had been forwarded in anonymous letters to several of the clergy, and were even in circulation among the commonalty. Dundas's third enclosure related to the disposition of the troops under Lord Adam Gordon. " Mr Pitt," he remarked, " will see the necessity of immediate consideration being given to what I wrote to him on the subject of military force requisite for this country. . . . I am persuaded it will very soon become necessary to aid the military force, by arming, under proper authority, bodies of men of respect and who can be trusted." According to Watt, even the regular troops were being tampered with, four members of the Edinburgh Friends of the People having so inflamed the minds of the guard at the Register House that they exclaimed, " D—— the King ! " There were more reports from another spy regarding the progress of the Friends of the People in Edinburgh.

[1] *Ibid.*

They were being visited by Colonel Dalrymple and Muir from Glasgow, who, while emphasising the necessity of moderation, were urging the members to persevere until they succeeded. At a meeting of delegates of the societies in and around Edinburgh, three hundred had been present. They had been addressed by Dalrymple, Muir, Macleod,—Member of Parliament for Inverness,—Major Maitland, and Messrs. Millar and Morthland, advocates. Macleod had declared that his purse, his sword, and his influence were at their service, and that he would stand by them to the last drop of his blood. A general convention of all the societies in Scotland was to be held early in December.

A more legitimate cause for apprehension was the continued unrest throughout the country which found vent in riots. Perth was justifying Lord Adam Gordon's description of it as a "very dangerous place." On November 6, "several hundreds of the lower class" burnt Dundas in effigy,[1] and the sheriff reported that it was not uncommon for even boys at the west end to shout "liberty, equality, and no king!"[2] Little more than a fortnight later, the entry of Dumouriez into Brussels was celebrated by the erection of a Tree of Liberty at the Cross. The bells were rung from eight in the morning till six at night, and the inhabitants were compelled to illuminate their windows.[3] Some days before, Dundee had given an example of similar manifestations. On Friday, November 16, a few people assembled in the High Street, where they attempted to plant a fir tree as a Tree of Liberty,

[1] *Cal. Mer.* Nov. 12, 1792: "The magistrates of Perth much to their honour did not take any violent measures. The Duke of Athole went among the mob, and being desired by some of them, his Grace, in a very prudent manner, honoured them and cried out, 'Liberty and Equality.'" *The Execution of Dundas at Perth* was hawked in the streets of Glasgow. *Scot. Corr.* vol. vi. Nov. 1792.

[2] David Smyth to H. Dundas, Nov. 24, 1792, *ibid.*

[3] *Cal. Mer.* Nov. 29.

but some young gentlemen pulled it down. On the Monday following, a mob threatened to unload a cargo of meal which could not be landed because of the corn laws. Next day the rioters, having assembled to the number of some hundreds, paraded the streets shouting "Liberty and Equality," and carrying the effigies of the gentlemen who had pulled down their tree. A man with a flaming barrel on his head led the way. Proceeding to the Town Hall, the mob rang the bells. The provost, however, successfully intervened, and the crowd, after breaking a few windows, made their way back to the High Street, where a huge bonfire was lit. A Tree of Liberty, bearing the scroll "Liberty, Equality and no Sinecures," was decorated with apples and lit up with a lantern and candles.[1] The tree remained till Wednesday night. On Friday another was set up in the market place and stood till Sunday, when the provost ordered its removal. On Monday the troops arrived and the disorders subsided.[2] In Aberdeen, the sailors, following the example of Leith and other British seaports, went on strike, and although "the tree of liberty business ended in nothing," they unrigged the vessels going to sea.[3] The dispute was settled by arbitration, the provost apologising for such weakness by pleading that nothing else could be done.[4]

During the eighteenth century rioting had been almost the only method of popular protest, but such tumults had never been associated as they now were with universal principles of reform and even of revolution. The same cries of "Liberty and Equality" were at that very moment

[1] Dr. John Moore thus describes the Tree of Liberty he found at Aire in France on Oct. 8, 1792: "It was hung round with garlands of flowers, with emblems of freedom and various inscriptions." *A Journal of a Residence in France*, Lond. 1793, ii. 7.

[2] Provost Riddoch to Ld. Adv. Dec. 8, 1792, *Scot. Corr.* vol. vi.

[3] Ld. Adam Gordon to H. Dundas, Dec. 7, 1792, *ibid.*

[4] *Ibid.* Dec. 9, 1792.

resounding all over France. There the Tree of Liberty had become the symbol of democracy. Clubs had spread republican ideas to its remotest corners, and in every town, riots had signalised the rise of the people. To all lovers of order, the lower classes in Scotland seemed to be rushing headlong down that path of innovation which in France had led to revolution and finally to the massacres of September. It was in vain, therefore, that the Friends of the People strove to distinguish themselves from those wilder spirits who inevitably accompany all popular movements. In Edinburgh, Glasgow, Dundee, and Perth, the societies published resolutions in which they declared that all who took part in such disorders would be expelled from their membership. It was currently believed that privately the leaders were republicans, only biding their time to reveal their true sentiments.[1] Thus "one Palmer, a disciple of Priestley's," was held responsible for "the promotion of levelling doctrines" in Dundee,[2] and ultimately for the riot itself.[3] In other quarters it was supposed to be due to revolutionaries from the surrounding districts of Forfarshire, whose correspondent was Thomas Christie, "an associate of Condorcet, Horne Tooke, and Thomas Payne." Even when the reformers gave unmistakable proofs of their repudiation of such proceedings, they were still held responsible for them.[4] It was at their meetings that "those with

[1] "Notwithstanding their public professions respecting the Constitution, I am well informed that it is easy to discover from the conversation of the leading men in the Society that they think a republic a much preferable form of Government." Sheriff of Perth to H. Dundas, Nov. 24, 1792, *Scot. Corr.* vol. vi.

[2] Letter of R. Graham, Nov. 22, 1792, *ibid.* [3] *Ibid.* Nov. 25, 1792.

[4] Sheriff Smyth reported to Dundas that during the riots in Perth "even the most violent reformers had concurred as readily as the other inhabitants" in watching the prison, etc., day and night. *Scot. Corr.* vol. vi. Dec. 3, 1792. At the beginning of December the Edin. Friends of the People offered their assistance to preserve order, but the Provost

nothing at stake" had picked up their loose notions of equality and liberty, for among the lowest classes it was commonly understood that these involved an equal distribution of property and exemption from all taxation.[1] Further, many who had not joined the societies were known to be in sympathy with their aims, and to be unwilling to repress the activity of the reformers or "the violence of their friends the mob."[2] The Government, by its resistance to all reform, was now reaping the fruit of such a policy in the loss of the moral support of the growing class of shopkeepers and well-to-do artisans.

The lower stratum of society, incapable of appreciating the issues at stake, could not fail to realise the harshness of many of the prevailing customs and laws. The lack of a jury in civil cases, economic changes in the Highlands, the stern repression of combinations or strikes, and above all

replied that he did not know any "legally constituted society under that designation." *Cal. Mer.* Dec. 8, 1792.

[1] "An opinion got amongst the lowest class that a division of property should also take place, and that they would be equally free and equally rich." Jas. Mitchell, Kirriemuir, Nov. 29, 1792, *Scot. Corr.* vol. vi. "Scots peasants understand nothing of parliamentary reform, equal representation, and other grievances of which the discontented in a higher rank of life complain, while they may be tempted to unite to try their strength and risk their necks in the hopes of bringing about a division of the landed property, and of getting ten acres each, which, they have been told, will fall to the share of each individual." Sir W. Maxwell to Duke of Buccleuch, Nov. 19, 1792, *ibid.* The Convention of the Friends of the People, as well as the individual societies, repudiated such misrepresentations of their views; yet in 1794 it was believed that the Friends of the People in Dunfermline "had the whole of Pittencrieff estate mapped off and allotted amongst its members." E. Henderson, *Annals of Dunfermline*, Glasgow, 1879, p. 351.

[2] "Many of the inhabitants [of Perth] though they censure the Friends of the People, and think it an improper season, do yet think a reform bill both in Parliament and the Burghs necessary; and I apprehend that neither they, nor the other inhabitants who wish for no alteration or change, would be very active in their endeavours to suppress the violence of the society, or their friends the mob, though that should become necessary." Sheriff Smyth to H. Dundas, Nov. 24, 1792, *Scot. Corr.* vol. vi.

the evils of excise administration, more especially in connection with the recent corn laws, created a spirit of antagonism to all constituted authorities. Thus in Dundee the real cause of the riot was to be found in the practical working of the corn laws. George Dempster, Member of Parliament for Forfar, though hostile to the reformers, thought that every real grievance should be inquired into. "There is a very absurd law, passed last session," he wrote, referring to the disturbances in Dundee, "restraining the free commerce in corn between the different parts of this island when prices are at a certain height in London. . . . One of the causes of discontent at Dundee was the impossibility of landing for sale a cargo of oatmeal from Berwick. It was at last landed by a *Dispensation* from the Board of Customs at Edinburgh. There never was so odd a law."[1] Balfour of Pilrig, writing in the same strain, described the corn laws as "the only measure of which the common people justly complain of their interests being sacrificed to the wealthy landholder."[2] This seems to have been recognised even in Government circles. The official comment on a précis of this letter, drawn up probably for Dundas or Pitt, was to this effect: "It is to be observed on this subject that more than one Jacobin publication has already taken notice of the Corn Laws. The Bounty has been called 'a premium for starving the poor, etc., etc.' This, it must be expected, will be urged with more violence the more strongly the landed interest attach themselves to Government. The suppression of the Bounty deserves consideration as an object of Revenue. Would country gentlemen dare to oppose it?"[3] There could only be one answer to this question. Dundas knew full well the basis of his power. Yet always, within certain limits, attentive to the interests

[1] *Scot. Corr.* vol. vi. Dec. 1, 1792.
[2] *Ibid.* Nov. 28, 1792.
[3] *Ibid.* Supp. vol. lxi.

of his country, he sent a circular to all the sheriffs of Scotland asking particulars as to the threatened scarcity of corn and the high price of fuel. Though the corn laws remained unchanged, it was ultimately considered safe to repeal the coal duty, and effusive votes of thanks from corporate bodies throughout the land welcomed this popular action.

Meanwhile the crisis in foreign affairs had compelled Dundas to return to London. Since August 10, the French, under the growing influence of the Jacobins, had been assuming a menacing attitude. On November 16, the Convention issued a decree throwing open the navigation of the Scheldt to all nations, and on the 19th, a decree of fraternity, offering assistance to all peoples who were striving for liberty. Both of these acts were a direct challenge to the British Government. By the treaty of 1788 Britain had guaranteed the independence of the Dutch Netherlands now threatened by the first decree, and the Convention by its enthusiastic reception of deputations and addresses from democratic societies in England, emphasised the significance of the second.[1] Under these circumstances the Government determined to call out a portion of the English militia.[2] "I believe myself that the chief danger at home is over for the present," wrote Pitt to Dundas, "but I am sure that there is still mischief enough afloat not to relax any of our

[1] No Scottish society sent greetings to the Convention, though a group of English, Scottish and Irish, resident in Paris, appeared at the bar with a congratulatory address on Nov. 28, 1792. *Adresse des Anglois, des Écossois, et des Irlandois résidans à Paris à la Convention Nationale. Imprimé par ordre de la Convention Nationale*; v. also *Collection of Addresses transmitted by certain English Clubs to the National Convention of France*, Lond. 2nd edn. 1793.

[2] Owing to the small number of troops in Scotland, Dundas was strongly in favour of this step. Lord Adam Gordon wrote to him on Nov. 29, "You must give us more troops and embody the English militia."

preparations, and things abroad still wear such an aspect that nothing but our being ready for war can preserve peace." [1] In view of the anticipated criticism on the part of the Opposition, he advised the Home Secretary to be ready with a full account of the Dundee riot, which was to be the specific ground for alleging the existence of "insurrection or rebellion" required by the Militia Act. Dundas was therefore prepared when it fell to him, in the absence of Pitt, to defend in Parliament the action of the Cabinet. After referring to the disorders in Dundee and elsewhere, and the alarm among manufacturers, country gentry, and magistrates, which he had witnessed during his six weeks' stay in Scotland, he justified the calling out of the militia as being necessary to restore confidence in the country.[2] A majority of two hundred and forty for the address corroborated Pitt's forecast that there would be little difficulty in securing public approval for the measure.

In Scotland, as in England, such approval was endorsed by the loyal addresses voted by corporate bodies of every kind, and judging from their tenor, Dundas had not exaggerated the dread of the classes with whom he had come in contact. These addresses, indeed, formed but one of the many schemes Dundas had set on foot during his recent sojourn in Scotland for concentrating public opinion on the side of the Government; and such was the confidence he inspired in his less capable officials, that it was with difficulty

[1] Stanhope, *Life of Pitt*, ii. 177.

[2] Gilbert Elliot, who had joined the Duke of Portland's party in supporting Pitt, wrote: "The Scotch insurrections consist of the planting of the Tree of Liberty at Perth, and the Dundee mob, and some others of less note. This is certainly ridiculous to those who live in Scotland and know the truth. The conduct of ministry imposes on those who wish to stand by Government the heavy task of defending, or at least approving of, an *unconstitutional* Act relating to the military, the subject on which it is easier to raise jealousy than any other." *Life and Letters of Sir G. Elliot*, ii. 80.

he had been allowed to return.[1] He left behind him as an adviser of the Lord Advocate, William Pulteney, Member of Parliament for Bath, and he proved of invaluable assistance.[2] On behalf of Dundas he wrote to influential persons suspected of revolutionary sympathies, urging them to declare themselves for law and order. Thus to George Dempster of Dunnichen he sent Adams's *Answer to Payne* and Dr. Hill's *Sermon,* and received Dempster's assurances of support.[3] Dundas was especially anxious lest the dissenters in Scotland should take the opportunity of manifesting their dislike of the established order of Church government, but Pulteney was soon able to assure him that they were steadfast upholders of authority.[4] His chief work was to assist in the organisation of an anti-reform society on the lines of the Association against Levellers and Republicans founded in London on November 28 by John Reeves. On December 7, a meeting of the "gentry of the city and county of Edinburgh" was held to consider the state of the country. A series of resolutions was passed declaring that "the subscribers would stand by the constitution with their lives and fortunes,"[5] and would use "their utmost endeavours to counteract all seditious attempts, and in particular, all

[1] "If I was to give way to the importunity and anxiety of those who wish to retain my assistance here, I would never get away. So many recent things have occurred, I may perhaps stay a day or two more than I mentioned in my last to Mr. Pitt, but beyond Monday the 3rd or Tuesday the 4th December, I have told them all, no consideration shall detain me here, and they must make up their minds to act upon their own judgment and discretion. It is one great point that with respect to spirit they are all up to anything." H. Dundas to Nepean, Nov. 24, 1792, *Scot. Corr.* vol. vi.

[2] "Let us keep Pulteney *here* as long as possible." R. to H. Dundas, Dec. 15, 1792, *ibid.*

[3] Pulteney to H. Dundas, Dec. 4, 1792, *ibid.*

[4] Rev. J. Peddie to Pulteney, Dec. 26, 1792, *ibid.*

[5] Hence they were popularly known as "Lives-and-Fortune Men."

associations for the publication or dispersion of seditious and inflammatory writings, or tending to excite disorders and tumults within this part of the kingdom." It was further determined to circulate pamphlets in defence of the Constitution. The resolutions were left for signature at the Goldsmiths' Hall, and a committee was appointed to carry out the objects of the association.[1] Soon two hundred names were secured, and the Lord Advocate reported that the work was proceeding with vigour.[2] Pulteney wrote that there was much general zeal, though shyness, about standing forth. He had attended the committee, but at his own request he had "not been named a member." It would be necessary to moderate their zeal and prevail with them to act coolly, but soon things would get into a regular system.[3]

Two parties were now competing for support in the capital—the Friends of the People, and the Goldsmiths' Hall Association as it was beginning to be called. Outside both was the small band of Whigs with whom the burgh reformers were identified. Strenuous efforts were made by the Friends of the People to win over their acknowledged leaders, Henry Erskine and Archibald Fletcher. But the former refused to imitate the example of his two brothers, the Earl of Buchan and Thomas Erskine, by joining the London branch so that there might be "*tria juncta in uno*" in a good cause. In a long letter to Sir Gilbert Elliot he explained the reasons for his conduct. Though he rejoiced in the downfall of despotism in France, yet he thought it had excited in the minds of many "ideas on the subject of government highly hostile to the constitution." Two evils,

[1] Cockburn, *Exam. of Trials for Sedition in Scot.* i. 152.

[2] R. to H. Dundas, Dec. 12, *Scot. Corr.* vol. vi. The number of names exceeded 1000, *Cal. Mer.* Dec. 13.

[3] Pulteney to H. Dundas, Dec. 12, 1792, *Scot. Corr.* vol. vi.

he predicted, would result from the propaganda of the societies. A flame of reform would arise which the associations would be unable to extinguish. The lower classes would be alienated by frustrated hopes, and so the real leaders would lose authority at a later date when reform was practicable. He was determined, therefore, to use such influence as he possessed in moderating the violent spirit of innovation which was stirring even Scotland, and in preventing his friends, who favoured reform, from taking part in the existing agitation.[1] In this endeavour Erskine was successful, and even Fletcher, who at considerable risk continued for many years to celebrate the anniversary of the French Revolution, refused to listen to Muir's solicitations. "I remember," his wife records in her *Autobiography*, "Mr. Muir's calling on my husband one evening in Hill Street, and I heard them at high words in an adjoining room. When his visitor went away, Mr. Fletcher told me that Muir quitted him much dissatisfied because he could not persuade him to join the Society. Mr. Fletcher added: 'I believe him to be an honest enthusiast, but he is an ill-judging man. These violent reformers will create such an alarm in the country as must strengthen the Government. The country is not prepared to second their views of annual parliaments and universal suffrage.' "[2]

In the midst of such political tension the first General Convention of the Delegates from the Societies of the Friends of the People throughout Scotland met in Lawrie's Rooms, James's Court, Edinburgh, on December 11 and the two following days.[3] The delegates, some hundred and sixty in number, represented eighty societies of thirty-five towns and villages situated for the most part in the manufacturing

[1] Fergusson, *The Hon. Henry Erskine*, 341-4.

[2] *Autobiography of Mrs. Fletcher*, 65.

[3] For the minutes, v. Appendix A.

district bounded on the north by Dundee, on the west by Glasgow, and on the east by Edinburgh. Some of the associations lying both within and outside this area did not send delegates, probably owing to the distance from the capital and lack of funds,[1] so that the Edinburgh societies accounted for more than half the assembly. The principal leaders were Lieut.-Colonel Dalrymple of Fordell, Lord Daer, Thomas Muir, and a few of his fellow advocates, such as Millar, Morthland, and Forsyth. Dalrymple was well known as the President of the Glasgow Society.[2] Lord Daer, the eldest son of the Earl of Selkirk, had been in Paris at the commencement of the French Revolution, and was an ardent reformer: he was a member of the London Friends of the People, the London Corresponding Society,[3] and a delegate to another convention then assembled in Edinburgh to discuss measures for abolishing the anomalies of county representation.[4] Muir was the son of a Glasgow merchant, who had a small property at Huntershill near Glasgow.[5]

[1] *E.g.* Wigtown. *Cal. Mer.* Dec. 8; Kincardine Friends of Liberty and of the People, *Edin. Gazetteer*, Dec. 25, 1792.

[2] On Dec. 8, the *Glasgow Courier* reported that Dalrymple and Macleod had received intimation that His Majesty had no further occasion for their services. Lord Sempill, a Scottish peer, was also cashiered about this time. He had signed the address of the Constitutional Information Society to the French Convention, and had also taken some part in the Scottish burgh reform movement. V. *A Short Address to the Public on the Practice of Cashiering Military Officers* . . . by Hugh, Lord Sempill, Lond. 1793. Macleod did not attend the Convention, Parliament being in session. Cf. his speech in the House of Commons on Dec. 17, where he defended his action in joining the Glasgow Society.

[3] Thos. Hardy, the secretary, in forwarding "his new ticket at 1d. a week," July 14, 1792, hopes that he will inform him of the progress of liberty in Scotland. *Place Coll. Brit. Mus. Add. MSS.* 27811 f. 15.

[4] *Cal. Mer.* Dec. 6, 1792. "Several of his contemporaries speak of his abilities in very high terms, and he might not improbably have played a considerable part in the politics of the period." Stanhope, *Life of Pitt*, ii. 215. He died at the age of 26. *Account of the Proceedings of the British Convention*, Lond. n.d. 2, fn.

[5] P. Mackenzie, *Life of Thomas Muir*, Glasgow, 1831, *passim.*

He had been a student of Professor Millar's, but had been forced to retire from Glasgow University for writing political squibs against some of the professors. After spending two years at Edinburgh University, he became an advocate in 1787. Although of no great ability, he was distinguished by his enthusiastic temperament and a talent for public speaking. He was popular among his colleagues at the Bar, who nicknamed him the "Chancellor," owing to a story that his mother had dreamt that he would some day become Lord High Chancellor of England.[1] In July, 1792, he had defended some of the King's Birthday rioters.[2] By that time he was probably engaged in his work of establishing the first society of the Friends of the People, for although his name does not appear among the officials of the Edinburgh Association in July, he himself claimed that the first proposal came from him.[3] After helping to organise the movement in the west, he returned to Edinburgh, and was elected Vice-President of the Associated Societies in and around Edinburgh.

The first day of the Convention was devoted to formal business. The election of a chairman called forth some curious remarks from Lord Daer. Addressing the members by the "familiar epithet of 'Fellow-citizens,'" he argued that, according to the principles of liberty and equality, there was no necessity for such permanent officials as President, Vice-President, etc. As the Ministry "had its eye on them," the responsibility should be divided. After some discussion, Colonel Dalrymple was elected chairman for

[1] G. W. T. Omond, *The Lord Advocates of Scotland*, ii. 187.

[2] "Mr. Muir stated and admitted the dangerous tendency of mobs, and observed that when mobs were set on foot in order to obtain redress of grievances, or from any other cause, they defeated the cause they meant to serve." *Cal. Mer.* July 19, 1792. One of the accused was sentenced to fourteen years' transportation to Botany Bay.

[3] Appendix A, p. 239.

the day, though he objected that, being a military man, he might be accused of raising a rebellion. William Skirving, the secretary of the Edinburgh societies, was appointed to the same office for the Convention. Next day revealed a contentious spirit among the delegates. Lord Daer's motion regarding procedure, though based on the methods of the French Assembly, was stoutly opposed by Muir, but was ultimately adopted by the Convention. Muir, however, caused a more serious division of opinion when he insisted on reading an address from the Society of United Irishmen at Dublin. Daer, Dalrymple, and the more moderate section were opposed to this, on the ground that it "contained treason or at least misprision of treason." Muir, however, having been allowed to read it, moved that an answer should be sent. This provoked a lively debate, one delegate selecting as objectionable a phrase in which Scotland was described as "rising to distinction not by a calm, contented, secret wish for a reform in Parliament, but by openly, actively, and urgently willing it, with the unity and energy of an embodied nation."[1] In spite of Muir's defence of the address, it was decided by a majority that it should not lie on the table. At the evening sitting the matter was brought up again, when Muir agreed to withdraw the document and return it to the chairman of the United Irishmen, pointing out the passages objected to that they might be "smoothed." The subject was again raised on the following day, but finally dropped. The chief work of the Convention was the drawing up of a series of resolutions on Parliamentary reform. Despite the efforts of a few extremists, these were all passed in such a moderate form as to win the approval, according to one delegate, of Henry Erskine himself. The Convention declared that the Friends of the People would defend the Constitution, that they would assist the civil magistrates in suppressing riots,

[1] This passage appeared in Muir's indictment, *State Trials*, xxiii. 124.

and that their true object was to agitate for an equal representation of the people and a frequent exercise of their right of election, by the proper and legal method of petitioning Parliament. Thus, though Muir and others wished to "restore" the Constitution to its supposed purity in King Alfred's days, when every freeman had a vote and Parliaments were annual,[1] the Convention decided to keep to general terms, and to be guided by the petition which Grey was known to be preparing on behalf of the parent society in London. Two other subjects claimed the attention of the delegates that day. One was their attitude to the burgh reformers, whom they decided to welcome as individuals to their societies. The other had a more important bearing on the fate of the reform movement generally. Mr. Millar drew the attention of the Convention to the Goldsmiths' Hall resolutions, evidently intended to throw discredit on their societies, and proposed that they should go in small parties and sign the resolution, "which contained nothing that any friends of reform could disapprove of." This being agreed to, one group signed the declaration; but each member added after his name, "delegate of the Society of the Friends of the People," lest it should be understood that he had abandoned his principles. A subsequent deputation was refused the privilege, and ultimately the Goldsmiths' Hall Committee ordered all such names to be deleted, Muir's among the rest.[2]

After providing for its general expenses by appointing a Committee of Finance to receive the contributions from

[1] This had been a tenet of advanced reformers since the Duke of Richmond's Reform Scheme in 1780. "To the zealous advocates for annual parliaments, and the perfect equality of representation, they are most ready to concede that those propositions may be supported by the ancient practice of the constitution and the genuine theory of civil liberty." Wyvill, *Polit. Papers*, i. 316.

[2] Cockburn, *Exam. of Trials for Sedition*, i. 152-3.

all the societies in Scotland, the Convention was adjourned till April. A dramatic incident marked its close. On the motion of a Mr. Fowler that "all should take the French oath to live free or die," the members rose as one man, and holding up their right hands, took the oath "amid reiterated plaudits." Thereupon Dalrymple pointed out that their indiscretion might be magnified into sedition, and Fowler, acknowledging the justice of the Colonel's remarks, explained "that he meant no more by the motion than simply to impress upon the minds of all present, uniformity and steadiness in the cause of freedom and virtue." On Dalrymple's suggestion, the motion was not recorded in the official minutes, though it duly appeared in the spy's account forwarded to Dundas. Taken in conjunction with another proposal made on the same day, that the Friends of the People should be armed with a "Brown Janet" to aid the magistrates in suppressing disorder, it was considered by the Administration sufficient evidence of the more revolutionary schemes which the delegates hid under the mask of reform.[1]

Thus ended one of the most noteworthy assemblies in the history of modern Scotland. Insignificant in point of numbers, and even in its personnel, it gave voice for the first time to the newly awakened aspirations of democracy. Though its deliberations had no immediate effect, they were justified at the time by at least one sympathiser on Montesquieu's principle: "Il est très souvent indifférent que les particuliers raisonnent bien ou mal; il suffit qu'ils

[1] The following comment was made by some Government official on the publication of the official minutes: "The minutes of the Convention are published. No notice is taken of the oath to live free or die, or of the proposition for arming themselves. These circumstances should surely be made public." *Scot. Corr.* Supp. vol. lxi. It was also noted that the petition circulated by the Friends of the People was "enormously insolent." "Relying on the virtue of some and the prudence of many individuals, we request . . . ."

raisonnent."[1] That shopkeepers and artisans should have begun to reason at all on political matters, was sufficient to alarm those at the head of affairs, and taking advantage of the strength which accrued to them through the growing panic among the middle and upper classes, they were now prepared to strike a crushing blow at the reformers.

[1] R. Fergusson, jr., of Craigdarroch, in *The Proposed Reform of the Counties in Scotland*, Edin. 1792. The author was not a member of the societies.

CHAPTER VI.

THE STATE TRIALS.

In January, 1793, the law officers of the Crown in Scotland began a series of trials for sedition which were to continue, more or less intermittently, until the cause of reform triumphed.[1] James Tytler was the first to be cited. He was charged with having published two seditious libels, one of which concluded, "If the King hear you not, keep your money in your pockets, and frame your laws, and the minority must submit to the majority."[2] Tytler failed to appear and was outlawed. On the following day, three printers were accused of having entered a canteen in the Castle of Edinburgh, and having drunk to "George III. and last and damnation to all crowned heads," while holding out to the soldiers that they would get increased pay by joining the Friends of the People.[3] Though they called witnesses to prove that their visit was a casual one, and that they did not belong to any of the reforming societies, they were condemned to nine months' imprisonment, and

[1] Cockburn, in his *Exam. of the Trials for Sedition in Scotland*, discusses twenty-five cases between 1793 and 1849. Twenty-two occurred before 1820.

[2] *State Trials*, xxiii. 1-6; Cockburn, *op. cit.* i. 95.

[3] *State Trials*, xxiii. 7-26; Cockburn, i. 95-108. A common toast in certain circles. Cf. Burns: "Here's the last verse of the last chapter of the last Book of Kings." *Life* by Chambers, ed. W. Wallace, iii. 379; v. also *Glasgow Courier*, Jan. 22, 1793.

ordered to find security for good behaviour for three years. Considering the temper of the times, this was a lenient sentence, though one of the judges, without dissent from the others on the bench, pronounced transportation to Botany Bay to be a possible, though hitherto unknown, punishment for sedition.[1] Since the day on which Fox had praised the French for proving that a man by becoming a soldier did not cease to be a citizen,[2] the authorities had been peculiarly apprehensive regarding the loyalty of the troops. At one time it would be reported that Paine's works were being freely circulated among them;[3] at another, that some of Colonel Macleod's regiment had set out for Scotland to propagate his opinions among their comrades.[4] Military officers pointed out the dangerous principles their men might pick up while billeted in private houses,[5] and, as a precaution, barracks were eventually erected for the first time in Glasgow and some other Scottish towns, whereby another grievance was added to the popular list.[6] Among the next to be prosecuted were the publishers of the *Declaration of the Rights of Man.* They had also issued the medals which had excited the alarm of the Lord Provost of Edinburgh in September.[7] The case, however, was not proceeded with. The *Political Progress of Britain* which had originally appeared

[1] Cockburn, *op. cit.* i. 106-7.

[2] Lecky, *Hist. of England*, v. 455.

[3] "A Mr. Thomson, a bookseller near Edinburgh, gave to one of our men in passing his shop to-day, six pamphlets saying that they were for the amusement of his comrades." They turned out to be abridgments of Paine's works. Letter of Sir Chas. Ross, Edinburgh Castle, Nov. 23, 1792, *Scot. Corr.* vol. vi.

[4] Information transmitted to the Ld. Adv. Dec. 16, 1792, *ibid.*

[5] Ld. Dundonald to Ld. Adv. Dec. 16, 1792, *ibid.*

[6] *A word in Season to the Bakers, Brewers, Butchers, Spirit Dealers, etc., in Glasgow respecting a Dangerous and Deep-laid Scheme of Garrisoning this City by Barracks.* Handbill, Nov. 26, 1792, *ibid.*

[7] *State Trials*, xxiii. 25-34; Cockburn, *op. cit.* i. 109-114.

in serial form in the *Bee* led to another trial.[1] Great difficulty was experienced in tracing the author. A man Callender was suspected, but, on being examined by the sheriff, he denied all connection with it, and tried to incriminate his benefactor, Lord Gardenstone, unique among the judges of the Court of Session as a reformer. It was not until Lord Gardenstone himself had made an official declaration, and Dr. Anderson, the editor of the *Bee,* had been threatened with imprisonment, that Callender's treachery was revealed.[2] Callender thereupon fled,[3] and the bookseller and printer were sentenced to three and six months' imprisonment respectively.

The mildness of these proceedings was doubtless due to the comparative insignificance of the offenders, but one had been arrested who was not to escape so easily. This was Thomas Muir, regarded by the Ministerialist party as the organiser of the whole agitation. By his conduct in defending the Address of the United Irishmen, he had played into the hands of the Lord Advocate. On December 15, the latter, in forwarding the minutes of the Convention to Henry Dundas, wrote that he was endeavouring to get hold of the paper characterised therein as treasonable.[4] " In that event, the Solicitor and I are resolved to lay him by the heels on a charge of High Treason." [5] An accident provided further

[1] *State Trials*, xxiii. 79-114 ; Cockburn, *op. cit.* i. 128-143.

[2] Precognitions, Dec. 29, 1792—Jan. 3, 1793, *Scot. Cor.* vol. vii.

[3] He reached America, where he published an enlarged edition of his pamphlet. (Phila. 1795, Brit. Mus.) When Jefferson was shown a copy of the original, he is said to have declared that "it contained the most astonishing concentration of abuses that he had ever heard of in any government." Cobbett, then a loyalist pamphleteer, in his *Bone to gnaw for Democrats*, affirmed that Jefferson must have said 'abuse'! Callender has been regarded as the founder of Yellow Journalism in America. For his career v. *Cyclopædia of American Biography*.

[4] The minutes were taken in shorthand by the Government spy. Letter of Sheriff Pringle, Dec. 17, 1792, *Scot. Corr.* vol. vi.

[5] *Ibid.* Dec. 15, 1792.

materials for the public prosecutor. A certain Mr. Muir received a letter intended for Thomas Muir. Having heard something of its contents, the sheriff interviewed the former, and was told that the letter, which had been returned to its rightful owner, was from a correspondent in Kirkintilloch, acknowledging the receipt of a number of pamphlets which he had distributed with "most beneficial effects." [1] This clue was followed up, and Muir was arrested on January 2, 1793, and examined before the sheriff as to his movements in the west of Scotland, and his alleged circulation of certain works, including Paine's. On principle, Muir refused to answer these questions, and he was liberated on bail. A week later, Robert Dundas reported to his uncle that Muir had set out for London to attend a reform meeting there, but that there was sufficient evidence against him, and his indictment was being prepared.[2]

There is no doubt that such vigorous action commended itself to the vast majority of the middle and upper classes. There was not a corporation, municipal or ecclesiastical, not a society however humble, but felt itself called upon to denounce the reformers and testify its loyalty. The declaration of the Burgh of Culross, for example, fills nearly a column of the *Caledonian Mercury*.[3] The Highland Society, on the initiative of Henry Erskine, ordered to be translated into Gaelic a series of resolutions expressing "their greatest

[1] *Ibid.* Dec. 18, 1792. On Dec. 26, Dundas consulted the legal advisers of the Home Office as to the advisability of preferring against Muir the charge of having circulated various papers which he enclosed. He was informed that "the papers, if prosecuted at all, must be prosecuted in Scotland where they were published." Messrs. Chamberlayne and White, 6 Lincoln's Inn, to H. Dundas, Dec. 26, 1792, *Scot. Corr.* vol. vi.

[2] *Scot. Corr.* vol. vii. Jan. 9, 1793. Referring to Muir and Tytler he writes to Nepean on Jan. 21: "The great object is to satisfy the country that within the British dominions none of these fellows are safe, and that every exertion will be made by government to bring them to justice."

[3] *Cal. Mer.* Dec. 15, 1792.

abhorrence of the exertions of evil-designing persons."[1] In like strain are those of the United Grocers of Edinburgh, the Bakers of Stirling, the Burgess Golf Club of Edinburgh, the Free Masons of Newton Douglas, and a hundred others. Some went further. St. Andrews resolved "not to employ any tradesman or other person whatever who discovers principles adverse to the spirit of the resolutions."[2] In other cases the reformers mustered in such force as to alter materially the significance of the motions proposed at public meetings, by carrying amendments that defects did indeed exist in the Constitution, though they were such as would be corrected by the wisdom of Parliament.[3] Such unsatisfactory proceedings were carefully noted at the Home Office. Associations against Levellers and Republicans, on the model of the Goldsmiths' Hall Association, were established throughout the country, and soon every village was divided into rival camps of Government Men and Democrats.[4]

As an additional means of counteracting the reformers, the secret service fund was drawn upon to meet the expenses of defending the Constitution in the press.[5] On December 12, 1792, the Lord Advocate applied to the Home Secretary for £400 for the *Edinburgh Herald* "to be repaid immediately,"[6] and it was eventually allowed £50 every half year. Payments to various writers in the *Caledonian*

[1] *Cal. Mer.* Jan. 12 and 19, 1793. [2] *Scot. Corr.* vol. vi. Dec. 28, 1792.

[3] *Glasgow Advertiser*, Dec. 17, 1792; Jan. 11, 1793.

[4] *E.g.* Selkirk, Craig Brown, *Hist. of Selkirkshire*, ii. 126; Dumfries, Chambers, *Life of Burns*, ed. Wallace, iv. 132. The Dalkeith Farmers' Society, consisting of representatives of twenty parishes, had the following toasts: "May we have no *Fox* in our folds nor *Greys* [wild oats] among our corn; may we never have reason to reflect with *Pain* on our constitution; may our patriotism never depend on *Price* or *Priestly* influence." *Scot. Corr.* vol. vii. Jan. 4, 1793.

[5] Statement of Secret Service Fund, Feb.-June, 1793; Sept. 1793—Jan. 1794; April, 1794; *Edin. Univ. Laing MSS.* No. 500.

[6] *Scot. Corr.* vol. vi. Dec. 12.

Mercury during the winter of 1792 seem to have amounted to the substantial sum of £134. Similarly the Lord Provost of Glasgow spent £40 in providing loyalist literature for the masses.[1] The same work was performed by the Goldsmiths' Hall Association, which not only undertook to distribute any pamphlets sent down from London by Dundas, but itself published anti-democratic leaflets.[2] Its most ambitious effort in this line was the *Patriot,* written to order by the Rev. Dr. Hardy, who had earned his laurels as a pamphleteer by his *Principles of Moderation* in the patronage controversy.[3] With like success he now addressed himself to the "politicians of the clubs." Thinking men, he owned, admitted that there was room for improvement in burgh elections, qualification of voters, the Test and Corporation Acts, etc., but the Legislature was competent to effect this, and was solely and exclusively competent to judge of the times and the seasons. If the clubs wanted a republic, let them consider the hypocrisy and oppression of Cromwell's.[4] After defending the Pension List, and denouncing "Paine's system of pillage," the author concluded with the usual eulogium on the felicity of the British nation.[5] Hardy was only the best of the clerical champions of the

[1] "In consequence of the conversation that passed at Arniston amongst you, Mr. Secy. Dundas, the Lord Provost, and myself last winter." Sheriff Orr to Ld. Adv. July 29, 1793, *Scot. Corr.* vol. vii.

[2] Ld. Adv. to H. Dundas, Dec. 9, 1792, *Scot. Corr.* vol. vi.; *Cal. Mer.* Dec. 27.

[3] Edin. 1793. "I hope Hardy's *Patriot* meets with the same approbation in London that it universally does here. Moodie's *Political Preaching* in answer to Dunn at Kirkintilloch has had the most beneficial effects.' Ld. Adv. to H. Dundas, Jan. 13, 1793. A copy of the *Patriot* was forwarded for Pitt's inspection on Jan. 4; v. also Kay, *Orig. Portraits* ii. 50, "The Reverend Patriot."

[4] This, of course, was the accepted opinion of Cromwell at the time.

[5] The Pension List had been published with adverse comments in the Opposition press. *Scots Mag.* Dec. 4, 1792.

established order of things. It would be difficult to estimate the number of sermons based on such texts as : " Fear God and honour the King," " My son, meddle not with those that are given to change," or, " Who is like unto thee, O people, saved by the Lord ? "[1] In these the reader was reminded, or rather informed, that God's government of the whole world was a monarchy, and that the language of the reformers was, " No King, no nobility, no Parliament, no clergy."[2] Not a few laymen, " Lovers of their Country," warned the Friends of the People that political affairs were " above the comprehension of tradesmen," that they were responsible for encouraging the unprincipled poor and stirring up workmen to demand an increase of wages, and that arrayed against them were " the Genius, the Virtue, the Industry, the Property, and the Religion of their country."[3] Innumerable pamphlets dwelt with circumstantial detail on the massacres in France, and gave reasons to prove that the Scottish reformers were but Dantons in disguise.

With fewer resources, and with the threat of prosecution hanging over their heads, the Friends of the People were content with denying in their published resolutions the designs with which they were charged. One of their number, however, Colonel Macleod, safeguarded by his privileges as a Member of Parliament,[4] undertook their

[1] V. book lists in the *Scots Mag.* Oct. 1792 *et seq.*

[2] Rev. W. Dalgleish, D.D., *The Excellence of the British Constitution and the Evil of changing It*, Edin. 1793.

[3] *An Address to the Association of the Friends of the People*, by A Lover of His Country, Edin. 1792 ; *Facts, Reflections and Queries submitted to the Consideration of the Associated Friends of the People*, Edin. 1792.

[4] Referring to Col. Macleod's "most wonderful production in last [*Edinburgh*] *Gazetteer*," the Ld. Adv. wonders if it is "actionable or contrary to the privileges of the House of Commons, which I doubt." Letter to H. Dundas, Jan. 14, 1793, *Scot. Corr.* vol. vii.

defence in his *Letters to the Friends of the People*.[1] Having the honour to be the first member of the present legislature who had the virtue openly to join the associations of the people of Scotland, instituted for the purpose of obtaining a reform of Parliament, he felt the strongest impulse to address them at this interesting and alarming period. What were the calumnies against the Friends of the People? "The destruction of a despotic throne has been represented as a probable precedent for the demolition of a limited monarchy; the extinction of the most degenerate set of nobles that ever existed in any kingdom has been stated as a forerunner of the ruin of our respectable peerage; the cruelties which have been committed at Paris by a few execrable ruffians have been imputed to the whole French nation; and we are now insulted with affected apprehensions that similar atrocities may be expected in the capitals of London and Edinburgh." Convulsions in the past had never been tainted with the crimes of popular executions and assassinations, and there was no reason to believe that the national character had changed. No one denied that a reform was desirable, but the cry was that the people could not be trusted. In England, every class of society had some voice in the election of their representatives. In Scotland, the manufacturer, the farmer, and the artisan had none, though it was a well-known fact that these classes were much better educated than the corresponding classes in England. "Such a people," he declared, "is marked by the finger of God to possess, sooner or later, the fullest share of liberty which is compatible with that order and

[1] *Two Letters from Norman Macleod, M.P., to the Chairman of the Friends of the People at Edinburgh*, Edin. printed for A. Scott, Gazetteer Office, 1793. The same pamphlet, with the title *Letters to the People of North Britain*, was published in London. Macleod was also the author of *Considerations on False and Real Alarms*, Lond. 1794.

those institutions which form the basis of well-regulated communities. . . . By violence you can do nothing; by constitutional patience and endeavours you will accomplish all your objects." Unfortunately the author, in referring to English troops sent against "imaginary Scotch insurrections," made most mischievous allusions to the valour of his countrymen in the days of the "Edwards and Henrys." "March your standing army," he wrote, apostrophising the Ministry, "march your militia into the heart of Scotland; my countrymen will greet them with peace and welcome, with hospitality and fraternity; they will receive them into their houses, and will communicate to them the knowledge of those rights which are essential to the happiness of mankind." Such language tended to discount the concluding exhortation of the first letter: "Be not rash; be not impetuous; imitate the Great Pattern of long-suffering; venerate the Constitution as it is; and search only for loyal and gentle corrections."

These pamphlets were intended for the trader and the artisan, but there were others for still more popular consumption. One Brown of Dundee, by a leaflet entitled *Look before Ye Loup*, brought himself under the notice of Henry Dundas, who established him in Edinburgh as the editor of a new Government organ, the *Patriot's Weekly Chronicle*.[1] As in the days of the Reformation, ballads and songs spread the new doctrines among the common people. Those of Burns and of Wilson, the Paisley weaver poet, are the best known. Wilson, indeed, in his *Address to the*

[1] Correspondence of Brown with the Ld. Adv. and others. *Edin. Univ. Laing MSS.* No. 500. The Solicitor General declared that his compositions rivalled those of Principal Robertson. As late as March, 1798, the Goldsmiths' Hall Association recommended to the favourable notice of the Home Secretary a Mr. White, who, in 1793, had written four pamphlets. One was entitled, *The Cat let out of the Pock.*

Synod of Glasgow and Ayr struck a clearer, if less poetic note than Burns himself:

The *Rights of Man* is now well kenned,
And red by mony a hunder;
For Tammy Paine the buik has penned,
And lent the court a lounder.
It's like a keeking-glass to see
The craft of kirk and statesmen,
And wi' a bauld and easy glee,
Guid faith, the birky beats them
Aff hand this day.

Though G——dy be deluded now,
And kens na what's a-doing,
Yet aiblins he may find it true
There is a blast a-brewing.
For British boys are in a fiz,
Their heads like bees are humming,
And for their rights and liberties,
They're mad upon reforming
The court this day.[1]

Burns, in his "Tree of Liberty" and other poems, some of which, for obvious reasons, have not survived, did not conceal his sympathy for the French Revolution.[2] But sooner than Wordsworth and Coleridge he lost his enthusiasm; for, in the beginning of 1795, he came forward with public proof of his loyalty to the King in his song, "Does haughty Gaul invasion threat?" More familiar productions of his genius due to the influence of the French Revolution are "Scots wha hae" and "A man's a man for a' that." In the former he gave expression to those memories of the past which were now subtly blended with the political struggles

[1] *Works*, Belfast, 1844. Life of Wilson by Sir W. Jardine in *American Ornithology*. Ed. C. L. Bonaparte. Lond. 1832.

[2] R. Chambers, *Life and Works of Robert Burns*, ed. W. Wallace, iv. 133. Burns and the French Revolution is fully discussed in A. Angellier's *Robert Burns, Sa Vie et Ses Œuvres*, i. chap. vi. sect. 2, ii. chap. ii.; v. also Hume Brown, *Hist. of Scot.* iii. 394.

of the hour;[1] while in the latter—"The Marseillaise of Equality" as Angellier calls it—he embodied not only the philosophy, but even the very words of Paine.[2]

Amid the strife of pamphleteers, the exhortation of friends, and the denunciation of foes, the reforming societies continued to meet, though the prosecutions were beginning to tell on their numbers. On January 3, 1793, the spy reported that further investigation of "this kind" would be unnecessary. The most influential members were absenting themselves from the weekly meetings, and even when they did attend the monthly local conventions, they were endeavouring to persuade the enthusiasts to "lie by" until the atmosphere should clear, and to refrain from further action until the result of their petition to Parliament should be known. Through the exertions of Millar and Morthland, the Edinburgh Associated Societies rejected a resolution against the threatened war with France, It was proposed by T. F. Palmer, the Unitarian minister of Dundee, who, having established himself in Edinburgh, was now President of the Lawnmarket Association.[3] Morthland argued that the Convention had only to do with Parliamentary reform, and though one or two of the individual societies published declarations against the war, the moderates carried their point.[4] A visit from Lord Daer and Colonel Macleod

[1] "The accidental recollection of that glorious struggle for Freedom, associated with the glowing ideas of some other struggles of the same nature, *not quite so ancient*, roused my rhyming mania." Burns to Thomson, Chambers, iv. 37-8. Chambers suggested that he had in mind the message of the Scottish barons to the Pope. If so, he may have got the idea from Mackintosh, v. *ante*, chap. iii. p. 59.

[2] So Professor MacCunn pointed out. Chambers, iv. 186.

[3] Palmer was an M.A., B.D. of Queen's College, Cambridge. After adopting Unitarian views, he left Cambridge for Montrose, where W. Christie had opened a Unitarian chapel. *State Trials*, xxiii. 377-382, where his biography is given.

[4] *Scot. Corr.* vol. vii. Jan. 3, 1793.

towards the end of January infused new energy into the Friends of the People,[1] and the work of circulating the reform petition was actively carried on in spite of strenuous opposition. The Lord Justice Clerk's sister, for example, threatened to withdraw the patronage of herself and her friends from the shopkeeper bold enough to have it lying on his counter for subscription; a zealous doctor in Edinburgh carried off one of the advertising placards, while the soldiers at Dalkeith stole the petition itself.[2] Under these circumstances, some of the societies began to lose heart. At the beginning of March, the Abbeyhill Association burnt its books, and the Lawnmarket Society suspended its meetings;[3] while the better to hide the fact of its diminishing numbers, Canongate No. 2 branch amalgamated with No. 1.[4] Yet this did not discourage the enthusiasts; for at the convention of the same month Fowler failed to carry a motion to the effect that, since the majority of the nation seemed content with their political state, the Friends of the People should take leave of their country with a final declaration of their true aims.[5] Palmer appears even to have secured the adoption of a revised form of his peace resolutions, though the *Gazetteer* "rejected them in toto."[6] The more ardent members were doubtless encouraged by the reports from the country received by the indefatigable Skirving.[7] While the monthly fourpences were with difficulty collected in Edinburgh, the country subscriptions soon cleared all expenses. According to Watt, the spy, there was even more

[1] *Scot. Corr.* vol. vii. Jan. 24.

[2] *Ibid.* Mar. 6.

[3] *Ibid.* Mar. 1.

[4] *Ibid.* Mar. 20.

[5] *Ibid.* vol. viii. Mar. 6.

[6] *Ibid.* Mar. 13. Johnston, the editor, had just been ordered by the Court of Justiciary to find security for his good behaviour. He had inserted in the *Edinburgh Gazetteer* a too accurate report of Braxfield's language in one of the trials. *State Trials*, xxiii. 43; Cockburn, *Exam. of Trials for Sedn.* i. 119.

[7] *Scot. Corr.* Mar. 15.

enthusiasm for the petition in the provinces than in the capital; for he found that in Perth and Pathhead, it was being largely signed by many who had never joined the Friends of the People.[1]

A more popular topic among these societies was the war. Some handbills had been distributed as early as December, 1792,[2] and in the following January the delegates of the associations in Perth and the neighbourhood printed a broadsheet giving their views on the cause of strife. "By universal right and general sanction," it declared, "all rivers are free in those nations through whose countries they flow; and as no good reason can be given why the Scheldt only should be an exception to the laws of nature and nations, the opening of that river can never justify a war with the French."[3] On February 16, Sheriff Orr of Glasgow wrote to the Home Secretary that the Friends of the People in his county had of late been publishing violent resolutions in the newspapers about reform, and expressing a strong aversion to war. He enclosed the manifesto of the Paisley United Societies, which, after referring to the dispute over the Scheldt, concluded: "It is of the utmost importance to your commercial interests as well as to the great cause of humanity." The manufacturers of Stirling and the neighbourhood joined in a similar protest,[4] and the Friends of the People in Glasgow who had been very quiet since January began to hold their meetings again.[5]

[1] *Scot. Corr.* vol. viii. Feb. 9, 1793; Dundas's agent in Montrose gave a similar report. Mrs. S. B—— to H. Dundas, Feb. 24, 1793.

[2] *Ibid.* vol. vi. Dundee, Dec. 30, 1792.

[3] *Scot. Corr.* vol. vii. The following societies in the west published resolutions against the war: Bridgetown (near Glasgow), Renton, Irvine, Kilmarnock, Loch Mill, Lennox Town, Torrence, Campsie, Cambuslang, Darvel. *Glasgow Advertiser*, Jan. to Mar. 1793.

[4] *Scot. Corr.* vol. vii. Feb. 15; *Cal. Mer.* Feb. 18.

[5] *Ibid.* Sheriff Orr to W. Scot, Mar. 15.

This activity, especially in the west, accounted for the success of the second General Convention which met in Edinburgh on the last day of April. One hundred and sixteen delegates from the societies of some twenty-eight towns and villages were present.[1] While some of the associations, such as Stirling, were no longer represented, others, like Selkirk, appeared on the list for the first time. A greater change was evident in the character of the delegates. Not more than a dozen had been present at the first Convention, and none of the Edinburgh advocates, who had formerly figured so conspicuously, attended the second. Only two of the prominent members were present, Aitchison and Skirving, and there is evidence that the delegates as a whole were of a lower type than their predecessors. The dominating personality in the assembly was one Sinclair from Glasgow, and it was with difficulty that Aitchison and "James Sommerville, Esquire, of Holmes," succeeded in counteracting his influence. One of Sinclair's motions, "that they should make a declaration of their rights as men and as Britons," occasioned a long and warm discussion, "some being excited by the cheerful glass." Their rights as men, Aitchison argued, took in a much wider range of political ideas, and would, if entered on, involve them in a labyrinth from which they might find it impossible to extricate themselves. These words comprehended the essence of the French Constitution, and of Paine's *Rights of Man,* a book already condemned by a British jury. All that they could wish for was a renovation of the constitution. Let them therefore stick to their rights as Britons but delete the words "rights as men." Ultimately the motion was withdrawn, though another, to

[1] The minutes, as extended from the Spy's shorthand notes, are in vol. viii. Unfortunately they only give the proceedings of the first day and part of the second. The list of delegates will be found in Appendix B.

the effect that the societies should dissolve after the decision of Parliament regarding their petition, was defeated by a large majority. It was decided "to recommend the different societies to persevere in the cause of Parliamentary reform until such time as they should obtain the end for which they had associated." The moderates, however, prevailed on the others to postpone the consideration of resolutions against the war till the evening sitting of the second day. Further information regarding the proceedings is lacking, but the Convention was so far successful in its main object, that Grey's famous petition, when presented to Parliament in May, was supported by thirteen from Scotland, Colonel Macleod's from Edinburgh extending the whole length of the House.[1]

Grey's motion was rejected, and the conservative reaction, due to dread of the French Revolution, drove the English Whig reformers into the political wilderness for nearly forty years. The Scottish burgh and county reformers shared the same fate. After the defeat of Sheridan's motion in May, 1792, Dundas had brought in a Bill to control municipal expenditure, the one defect officially admitted in burgh administration. This concession was refused by the burgesses, as the auditors were to be appointed by the self-elected magistrates. In March, 1793, Sheridan succeeded in obtaining the appointment of a committee of the Commons, which, in June, gave in a report establishing most of the grievances complained of. But the London committee of the burgesses warned their friends in Scotland that there was no prospect of further success—the very sound of liberty having become odious to British ears. The

[1] *Cal. Mer.* May 11, 1793. "The petitions from the Convention of the Friends of the People at Edinburgh would arrive this morning as you will see by the enclosed. I doubt not Macleod will present it. So consider if such a *body* of petitioners can be acknowledged by the House of Commons." R. to H. Dundas, May 3, 1793.

burgh reform agitation was thereupon suspended.[1] At the same time, the county reform movement came to an end. The decision of the House of Lords in 1790 had failed to abolish nominal and fictitious voters. Consequently another convention of county delegates assembled in December, 1792.[2] A committee was then appointed, which in February, 1793, drafted another Bill. This Bill was discussed at a convention in July of the same year. Lord Chief Baron Dundas presided, and the Lord Advocate attended as a representative of his native county. It was proposed not only to abolish nominal and fictitious votes, but also to extend the franchise to those who held property valued at £100 Scots. The convention, after approving simply of the preamble, which affirmed that all landowners originally possessed the right to be represented in Parliament, referred the whole matter back to the county meetings. These dilatory tactics were due to the Lord Advocate, and to bar further progress more effectually, he called a meeting of his "friends" in Midlothian, who drew up a report giving a circumstantial account of the convention. It stated that "the minds of many members of the community were filled with most delusive and dangerous doctrines with respect to civil government," and it

[1] Fletcher, *Memoir*, 125.

[2] "I am not a little anxious as to the result of to-morrow's meeting of delegates on the Election laws. Harry Erskine is playing off the business on party motives. Sir Thomas Dundas is led by him, and they will drive their schemes through so as to bring it before Parliament this winter. We shall resist it. But whether successfully or not, I am sorry to say, is uncertain. Berwickshire from excess of zeal refused to countenance the scheme at all, which, however right some months ago, is in fact depriving us now of five votes." R. to H. Dundas, Dec. 9, 1792, *Scot. Corr.* vol. vi. Three days later, the Lord Advocate reported that the Bill was so ridiculed that he believed Erskine and T. Dundas would drop it themselves. "I repent much of my ever having set my face there," he wrote on Jan. 15, 1794. Margarot and Gerrald (*infra*, ch. vii.) did not fail to remind him that he also had attended a reform convention.

recommended the more conservative Bill of 1785. Even this recommendation was of little value, for in April, on the hint of the Lord Advocate, Midlothian withdrew its delegates and informed the other counties of its decision. An obviously inspired letter appeared in the press during the same month advising them to return "to the known track of constitutional procedure" and denouncing delegation as dangerous. In May, various counties recalled their delegates, and county reform became moribund.[1]

To the astonishment of the Lord Advocate, the Friends of the People still gave signs of vitality.[2] To answer a long-standing complaint that "there was nothing to do," the Edinburgh Society instituted political debates.[3] The affairs of the *Edinburgh Gazetteer* also provided a topic for discussion, with the result that the newspaper became, in a sense, the official organ of the societies.[4] Most of the provincial associations, forsaking their original programme, were now engaged in protesting against the war. The delegates of all the societies of the County of Renfrew issued a further manifesto pointing out that the prolonging of the war—its professed object of throwing open the Scheldt being accomplished—afforded the strongest and most

[1] *Cal. Mer.* April and May, *passim.*

[2] "I had no idea they would have stuck so long and so well together." R. Dundas to Nepean, June 21, 1793, *Scot. Corr.* vol. viii.

[3] The first discussion was whether men of property ought to be represented in Parliament. "The chief speaker quoted largely from Croix's book on the government of Europe and the United States of America." *Ibid.*

[4] Captain Johnston's offer was made in a general committee of the Friends of the People meeting as individuals. He was willing to hand over the type, etc., if paid simple interest on the money he had sunk in the concern, and provided £500 was subscribed to continue the paper upon the principles on which it had started. The sum raised was to be entrusted to a committee and not uplifted for three years. It was agreed to get subscription papers ready at once. Spy's reports, June 16, 18, 21, *Scot. Corr.* vol. viii.

melancholy proof of the absolute necessity there was of a speedy and thorough reform in the representative system of Great Britain.[1] Though the Glasgow societies did not take any steps in their collective capacity, a petition against the war, said to be drawn up by Professor Millar, was largely signed.[2] "You may rest assured," wrote the Lord Advocate to his uncle, "from the accounts I have received from Glasgow and from Perth and Angus, that those rascals have laid a plan for exciting the country again to discontent and disorder on account of the war, and that this is the topic on which they are to dwell."[3] He enclosed an address on the subject, printed at Dundee and circulated in Edinburgh. "Palmer, the Methodist clergyman who lately went over to Dundee, is strongly suspected. If he is the man, I shall doubt not his being got hold of; which he was artful enough to keep clear of last winter." J. B., the chief Government spy, was sent to trace the suspect on the understanding that this would be considered "extra" and rewarded accordingly. The hunt was successful; Palmer's Edinburgh agent was discovered along with some incriminating documents relating to the handbill. "He is the most determined *rebel* in Scotland," wrote the Lord Advocate.[4]

His letter contained the additional news of Muir's return and arrest. After his examination before the sheriff, Muir had left for London, where he had been received by Fox, Grey, and other Whig leaders, and welcomed by the Friends of the People. At a meeting of the society over which Thomas Erskine presided, Muir recounted the oppression to

[1] *Ibid.* July 5. They further voted "thanks to the *Edinburgh Gazetteer* and the *Caledonian Chronicle* for the impartial manner in which they disseminated truth and political knowledge."

[2] *Ibid.* July 2 and 12, 1793.

[3] *Ibid.* July 29.

[4] *Ibid.* Aug. 2, 1793. This aspect of Palmer's case has not hitherto been noticed, *e.g.* in *Dict. Nat. Biog.*

which he and his friends in Scotland were subjected, and he was heard " with murmurs and marked signs of contempt of the agents in power." On the motion of Mr. Taylor, Member of Parliament, a committee was appointed to take the situation into consideration. A few days later, Muir set out for Paris " to try what could be done with the Convention to save the life of a certain great personage, and to circulate it as the opinion of the people in Britain that the death of the king would disgrace the cause of freedom for ever." [1] Muir arrived at his destination the day before the execution, and he lingered in Paris cultivating the friendship of Barras, Condorcet, and Lafayette. He wrote to his friends in Edinburgh, asking them to warn him of the date fixed for his trial, as he was determined to plead his cause in person. The day appointed was February 11, but Muir was unable to leave France owing to the outbreak of hostilities. He therefore failed to appear, was outlawed, and his name struck off the roll of advocates. Extraordinary stories were current in Edinburgh as to his doings abroad.[2]

[1] *Resumé* of Muir's letter to Skirving, Jan. 20 (?), 1793, *Scot. Corr.* vol. viii. It was therefore not only "at his trial," as Dr. Holland Rose is inclined to believe (*Pitt and the Great War*, p. 175), that Muir gave his reasons for the journey.

[2] In his letter to Skirving, Muir said that if it was determined to bring him to trial, his stay in Paris would be short, as he intended to plead his own cause in person. A letter of James Smith, who had fled to France on being cited for sedition in connection with an advertisement in the *Glasgow Advertiser* (*State Trials*, xxiii. 33), was opened at the Glasgow Post Office. It was dated Paris, February 15. The writer stated that he had met Muir accidentally in Paris. Muir told him that he had only received notice of his indictment on the 8th, and that he was making arrangements to return as soon as he got his passport, a matter of some difficulty. "Mr. Muir," he added, "makes a great sacrifice in coming so soon back as he has already made a very great proficiency in the language, has made valuable and dear connections, and is enchanted with the climate." On March 1, J. B. reported that he had learnt the contents of a letter of Muir to his father from one who had seen it. Seven manufacturers in the west of Scotland had asked him to purchase £50,000 worth of land in France where they meant to set up a factory. " Mr. Muir

Now it was rumoured that he had enlisted in the National Guard of France; now, that his return to his native country would be "like Coriolanus with an army of the enemy at his back."[1] Nothing definite was known until his arrest at Stranraer, when it transpired that he had left France in an American vessel which touched at Dublin. There he had been received by the Society of United Irishmen, of which he had been enrolled a member in January, 1793. Thence he had made his way to Scotland. These peregrinations did not tend to increase Muir's chance of acquittal, for the Lord Advocate had now no doubt that he was "an emissary from France or the disaffected in Ireland."[2]

His trial, which began on August 30, has been exhaustively examined by Lord Cockburn, who remarks: "This is one of the cases the memory whereof never perisheth, history cannot let its injustice alone."[3] Most of the injustice was due to the panic pervading all classes, including the bench.[4] When, in the beginning of the year, the Lord Provost of Edinburgh paid a state visit to the Court of Session, the Lord President delivered a violent speech against the reformers, which was printed, and scattered broadcast over

adds that he would have come over and stood his trial and paid any fine, however high, if he had been certain that he would not have been condemned to imprisonment or sent to Botany Bay." *Scot. Corr.* vol. vii.

[1] Spy's reports, Feb. 16, 21, 1793.

[2] R. to H. Dundas, Aug. 2, 1793, *Scot. Corr.* vol. viii. The Government dreaded a coalition of the reformers of the three kingdoms. "I understand," wrote Major Hobart to Nepean, "that Mr. Archdeacon from London and Mr. Muir from Scotland are expected here in the course of a short time for the purpose of establishing a more intimate correspondence between the societies of England, Scotland, and Ireland." *Irish Corr.* vol. xxxviii. Dec. 19, 1792. Hobart enclosed a copy of the Address of the United Irishmen which Muir had defended in the Convention.

[3] Cockburn, *op. cit.* i. 144-184; *State Trials*, xxiii. 117 *et seq.*

[4] This is hit off in the amusing speech of Lord Eskgrove in the skit entitled, "The Diamond Beetle Case," reprinted in Dean Ramsay's *Reminiscences*, ch. v.

the country.[1] But the trial also exemplified some characteristic defects of the Scottish courts. The judges had practically the selection of the jurymen in their own hands.[2] When a trial took place in Edinburgh, the sheriff of each of the Lothians sent in a list of forty-five names. From these hundred and thirty-five, the justiciary clerk chose forty-five, from which, on the day of hearing, the judge picked the fifteen jurymen without challenge on the part of the accused. In Muir's case, the bench exercised its rights to the full, and there is no doubt that care was taken to select those whom the Lord Advocate, with reference to Tytler's trial, had described as men of "proper principles." [3]

[1] *Cal. Mer.* Jan. 24, 1793. Col. Macleod seized the occasion to lay before the court a letter to the Lord President asking if the speech was as reported. "If your Lordship is ready to avow it, I am equally ready to counteract several propositions in it as perfectly unconstitutional, in the quality of a member of the British Legislature, and I mean to publish my sentiments as quickly as possible, but certainly not till your Lordship has sufficient time to honour me with an answer." The macer was instructed to inform Macleod that no notice was to be taken of his letter, but Ilay Campbell, the Lord President, wrote an account of the incident to H. Dundas. "I should wish you would take the trouble of stating the thing to such authorities in the law as you may think proper to consult with, and give us the satisfaction of knowing whether we have actually done anything wrong or not." *Scot. Corr.* vol. vii. Jan. 25, 1793.

[2] In addition, the bench was also accused of browbeating the jury. V. *The Rights and Powers of Juries* by a Member of the College of Justice, Edin. 1791. *Thoughts on the Privileges and Powers of Juries, suggested by the case of James Robertson and Walter Berry, Printer and Bookseller*, Edin. 1793.

[3] *Scot. Corr.* vol. vii. Jan. 7, 1793. Four years later, a Mr. Lockhart wrote a begging letter to the Lord Advocate supporting his claims by affirming that he and a friend "went through the jury lists previous to every seditious trial, and, after making enquiries respecting those they did not well know, . . . were at length enabled to furnish the Lord Justice Clerk with fair and honest juries." W. Lockhart to Ld. Adv. Nov. 20, 1797. *Edin. Univ. Laing MSS.* No. 501. Lockhart seems to have been depute sheriff clerk. *State Trials*, xxiii. 1256. Even in the United States of America, regarded by the Democrats of the time as the land of ideal liberty, Cobbett's trial, according to his own story, was delayed for two years owing to the difficulty of packing the jury. E. I. Carlyle, *Life of Cobbett*, 71.

The jurymen were all members of the Goldsmiths' Hall Association, which had not only struck Muir's name off its roll, but had even offered a reward for the discovery of any persons circulating Paine's works—the very offence of which the prisoner was now accused.[1]

Muir's indictment contained three main charges: exciting disaffection by seditious speeches, circulating Paine's *Rights of Man* and other seditious works, and reading and defending the Address of the United Irishmen in the first General Convention of the Friends of the People. The first charge, as the public prosecutor knew full well, could not have been substantiated even by the spy's reports. The second depended for the most part on the evidence of a suspiciously learned servant who had been in Muir's household. Of the third Muir was undoubtedly guilty,[2] though only one witness brought this fully home to him, and the address itself, intemperate as it was, could hardly be described as seditious. It was enough, however, for the Lord Advocate and the judges that the accused was a "French emissary," had been outlawed, had a seal inscribed with the words "Ça ira," and was a member of a society which was playing the same part in Ireland as the London Corresponding Society in England.[3] "Demon of mischief," "pest of

[1] Cockburn takes this as certain because Muir's assertions were never contradicted; but in the *Cal. Mer.* Dec. 27, 1792, will be found the advertisement of the association offering a reward of five guineas to any one giving evidence that "any bookseller in Scotland, had, after this date, sold or distributed gratis, Paine's Rights of Man, or any abridgment of that pamphlet, or who shall give evidence of any other person having . . . circulated among the working people of Scotland copies of that libel on the Constitution. . . ."

[2] With Cockburn's examination of this part of the evidence must now be compared the minutes of the Convention in Appendix A.

[3] It was not till two years later that the societies of United Irishmen became revolutionary in character. E. Guillon, *La France et l'Irlande pendant la Révolution*, chap. iv.

Scotland," "diabolical conduct," were the mildest expressions which Robert Dundas used in his address to the jury. Muir, in an eloquent and powerful speech which lasted three hours, pled guilty to one offence, and that not in the indictment—the advocacy of Parliamentary reform. "What has been my crime?" he exclaimed. "Not lending a relation a copy of Mr. Paine's works; not the giving away to another a few copies of an innocent and constitutional publication; but for having dared to be, according to the measure of my feeble abilities, a strenuous and active advocate for an equal representation of the people in the House of the People." Braxfield, the Lord Justice Clerk, in speaking to the jury,—for, according to Cockburn, it would be an abuse of the term to say that he made a judicial charge,—corroborated Muir's view. "I leave it for you to judge," he said, "whether it was perfectly innocent or not in Mr. Muir, at such a time, to go about among ignorant country people, and among the lower classes of people, making them leave off their work, and inducing them to believe that a reform was absolutely necessary to preserve their safety and their liberty, which, had it not been for him, they would never have suspected to have been in danger." With brutal frankness he summed up the position of himself and his friends: "A government in every country should be just like a corporation; and, in this country, it is made up of the landed interest, which alone has a right to be represented. As for the rabble, who have nothing but personal property, what hold has the nation on them? What security for the payment of their taxes? They may pack up all their property on their backs, and leave the country in the twinkling of an eye. But landed property cannot be removed." Muir was found guilty, and sentenced to transportation to Botany Bay for fourteen years, to the consternation of the jury who intended to send in a petition for leniency. But one of their number produced a letter threatening him with assassination for concurring in the verdict, and this, they considered, rendered it "impossible for them to interfere."[1] Next month, Palmer, as the result of an equally outrageous trial, was punished with transportation for seven years, ostensibly for being art and part guilty of writing the address against the war issued by the Dundee Friends of Liberty, really because of his record as a reformer.[2]

These trials evoked widespread indignation. Jeffrey and Sir Samuel Romilly, who were present in court, were horrified at the conduct of the judges. In France, the account of the proceedings published in the press deepened that hatred of England to which Kersaint had given expression in the National Convention in January, when he eulogised the zealous Scottish defenders of the principles of the French Revolution "who were meriting the honour of being persecuted by the British Government."[3] In America, where discussion of the French Revolution had still further provoked the animosities of Royalist and Republican, Muir was regarded by many as a martyr; and it was in an American vessel, specially despatched for the purpose, that he eventually effected his escape from Botany Bay.[4] In England, the London Corresponding and other democratic societies publicly avowed their admiration for Muir and his fellow victims.[5]

Though the Friends of the People in London did not collectively express an opinion on the trial, their leaders

[1] Cockburn, *op. cit.* i. 182.

[2] *State Trials*, xxiii. 237 *et seq.*; Cockburn, i. 184 *et seq.*

[3] *Moniteur*, Jan. 3, 1793; Eng. trans. Lond. 1793.

[4] In later years, Muir's address to the jury was a favourite piece for declamation in New England schoolhouses. "Thomas Muir" by B. Drew, art. in *Old and New*, a Boston periodical, vol. ix. 1894, 316-321.

[5] *Brit. Mus. Add. MSS. Place Coll. of Newspaper Cuttings*, vol. xxxvi.

had soon an opportunity of doing so. In October, the Lord Advocate reported that the Earl of Lauderdale had visited Muir in prison in Edinburgh. Two months later, in company with Grey and Sheridan, he waited on Henry Dundas and pointed out that the judges had exceeded their legal powers by punishing leasing-making (verbal sedition) with transportation.[1] This view they put in writing, at the request of the Home Secretary, who referred the whole matter back to the Lord Justice Clerk and his colleagues for their opinion.[2] Braxfield reported that the cases of Muir and Palmer had nothing to do with leasing-making. "Upon the whole," he wrote, "as I am perfectly clear that the court have full powers to transport for the crime of sedition, so I am equally clear that in this case the punishment is not greater than their conduct merited, and that any mitigation, by the interposition of the royal mercy, would in the present conjunction be a most inexpedient measure. In the course of two or three weeks, there will be no less than five different trials before the Court of Justice for the crime of sedition."[3] The Whigs next proceeded to bring the sentences before Parliament, where they were discussed on four different occasions.[4] The debates were on party lines, all reconsideration being refused by the Government; but they drew from Fox words long remembered in Scotland: "God help the people who have such judges!"

[1] The punishment itself was illegal, according to one authority. The Act relating to the removal of offenders from Britain expired in 1788, and when it was renewed, Scotland was omitted. "Muir and Palmer were actually removed from Scotland, and transported to Botany Bay, though there was no statute then in force to warrant it." *Diary of Lord Colchester*, i. 50.

[2] Memorial, Dec. 14, 1793, *Scot. Corr.* vol. ix.

[3] *Scot. Corr.* vol. ix. Dec. 27, 1793.

[4] Cockburn, *op. cit.* ii. 133 *et seq.*

CHAPTER VII.

THE BRITISH CONVENTION.

THE severity of Muir's sentence, instead of extinguishing the spirit and vigour of the Friends of the People, gave them new life and activity.[1] The Canongate Society met to declare that, though the "*Accuser of the Brethren*" might brand Thomas Muir as the "*Pest of Scotland*," they exulted in the hope that the time would come when Scotland would regard him as her glory.[2] The two hundred members who attended the September monthly convention resolved that "so far from fainting in the day of evil, . . . they would immediately proceed to renovate their various societies before the sitting down of Parliament, on purpose to make up their minds about another application for redress of grievances and restoration of rights: that, with the same purpose, they would also immediately proceed to cultivate a more intimate correspondence with all the societies of Parliamentary reform in the kingdom."[3] The last clause was probably due to Skirving, the secretary, who, in the preceding April and May, had been in communication with the Sheffield, the Leeds, and the London Corresponding

[1] Spy's report, Sept. 6, 1793, *Scot. Corr.* vol. ix.

[2] *Ibid.* Sept. 3, 1793.

[3] *Ibid.* Sept. 5 and 7. The *Edin. Gazetteer* refused to print the resolutions as being "too dangerous," and they were ordered to be sent to the *Morning Chronicle*.

Societies.[1] Hitherto the Scottish Friends of the People had only maintained a connection with the parent association in London; now, unrestrained by the more moderate section who had withdrawn early in the year, they were entering on a more dangerous course.

A letter from the London Corresponding Society, dated May 17, 1793, requested a "renewal of correspondence."[2] "Our petitions," it ran," have been all of them unsuccessful; our attention must now therefore be turned to some more effectual means. From your society we would willingly learn them." Skirving, nothing loth,[3] replied with characteristic self-importance, hinting at an international convention. In July, he wrote to the secretary of the London Friends of the People definitely proposing a "plan of delegates," but in a private letter that official gave it as his opinion that such a meeting would be "very improper."[4] The other English political associations welcomed the idea enthusiastically, though only three took action. On October 17, the London Corresponding Society elected "Citizens Margarot and Gerrald" to represent them.[5] Similarly the London Constitutional Society appointed Charles Sinclair and Henry York,[6] and the Sheffield Society, M. C. Brown.

[1] Second Report of the Committee of Secrecy. *Parl. Hist.* xxxi. 727, 815 *et seq.*

[2] *Ibid.* 729. The *Journal* of the London Corresponding Society does not reveal much previous correspondence. In addition to those communications given *ante*, chap. v., there is only this entry previous to the above date. "Dec. 6, 1792. A correspondence was ordered to be opened up at the first opportunity with Bath, Glascow (*sic*), Durham, Bamf (*sic*), Dundee." *Place Coll. Brit. Mus. Add. MSS.* 27812.

[3] An international convention had long been one of his ideas; v. Appendix A.

[4] *Parl. Hist.* xxxi. 842.

[5] Their instructions are in *State Trials*, xxiv. 41, 42.

[6] For their instructions v. *State Trials*, xxiv. 342. York fell ill on the way, and did not attend the Convention.

"There is a Convention of the Friends of the People to be held here to-morrow," wrote the Lord Advocate on October 28, in a letter urging Muir's removal to London. Though no respectable persons had as yet appeared amongst them, almost all the clubs of the previous year had been revived. Lord Lauderdale had visited Muir, and the case was to be brought before Parliament. This had already encouraged the clubs, and the bad news from the Continent was not likely to depress them.[1] The Convention, which duly assembled on the following day, was attended by about one hundred and sixty delegates, those from the Edinburgh and Glasgow districts forming the majority.[2] Although the English deputation had not arrived, business was at once proceeded with.[3] Much time was spent, as usual, in appointing committees, and it was not till the evening of the second day that, amid signs of enthusiasm, the assembly declared for universal suffrage and annual Parliaments, the individual societies being subsequently instructed to make this vital change in their original constitutions. It was further resolved to petition Parliament for removal of grievances, and to address the Crown against the war. The Convention then adjourned till April, having sat for four days.

Shortly afterwards, the English delegates arrived in

[1] Omond, *Arniston Memoirs*, 237.

[2] Glasgow, Oct. 27, 1793, J. Dunlop to H. Dundas: "The Friends of the People . . . are still indefatigable . . . but I do not think the people here have *confidence* in the leaders of the party, although I believe the general principles of it have taken very deep root and are making daily progress." *Scot. Corr.* vol. ix.

[3] The minutes of this Convention and its successor are printed in *State Trials*, xxiii. 391 *et seq.* The original documents will be found in *Scot. Corr.* vol. ix.; v. also *An Account of the Proceedings of the British Convention*, by a Member, Lond. 1794 (?). The Earl of Lauderdale, though in Edinburgh at the time, refused to act as delegate of the Portsburgh Friends of the People. *State Trials*, xxiv. 1111.

Edinburgh. On November 6, they attended a general committee meeting of the Edinburgh associations, when approval was given to the advertisement which Skirving had inserted in the *Edinburgh Gazetteer*. It recalled the members of the late Convention to another on November 19.[1] In the interval the Englishmen were not idle, Margarot inaugurating a new society at Broughton, now a part of Edinburgh, and Gerrald visiting the reformers at Penicuik.[2] Of the new Convention which met on November 19, it is difficult to give any precise account. The Government spy was unable to take shorthand notes, and he had to be content with borrowing the minutes from one of the assistant secretaries and making a hasty copy.[3] One thing is evident: Gerrald and his companions soon justified the fears of the secretary of the London Friends of the People, that they would import into

[1] A. Hamilton Rowan and the Hon. Simon Butler, members of the United Irishmen, having arrived in Edinburgh on November 4, were present at this meeting. They did not come as delegates to the Convention as Dr. Holland Rose states (*Wm. Pitt and the Great War*, 180), but were admitted as such by the committee. *State Trials*, xxiii. 416. Hamilton Rowan's mission was to challenge the Lord Advocate for having characterised the United Irishmen as "wretches" in his speech at Muir's trial. A long correspondence on the matter, beginning on September 14, is preserved in the *Edin. Univ. Laing MSS.* No. 500. Even Pitt was twice consulted as to the course to be pursued by the Lord Advocate, who was inclined to accept the challenge. At last, Hamilton Rowan, having been examined before the sheriff, left Edinburgh without having attended the British Convention. He was entertained to dinner at Belfast on November 14, the toasts including "the Scotch Convention," "Mr. Muir," and "the swine of England, the rabble of Scotland, and the wretches of Ireland." *Edin. Gazetteer*, November 26, 1793. Hamilton Rowan and Butler were subsequently arrested for having signed a paper issued by the United Irishmen denouncing the Irish Parliament. Lecky, *Hist. of Eng.* vii. 9; Kay, *Orig. Ports.* ii. 169; Omond, *Arniston Memoirs*, 239.

[2] Spy's report, Nov. 16, *Scot. Corr.* vol. ix.

[3] Letter of J. B., accompanying his copy of the minutes, Oct. 29, 1793, *Scot. Corr.* vol. ix. "They are meagre, abrupt, desultory and confused." Cockburn, *Exam. of Trials for Sedn.* i. 223.

Scotland "that intemperate spirit which had brought blame on the moderate and sincere friends of reform in England." [1] They quickly took the lead; for of former prominent members of the Scottish societies, Lord Daer, owing to ill-health, was present only for a few days, and Macleod, who had guardedly expressed his approval of the earlier Convention, openly withdrew his support from its successor.[2] In a week, the assembly had assumed the title of the "British Convention of the Delegates of the Friends of the People associated to obtain Universal Suffrage and Annual Parliaments"—all joining hands to celebrate "this important epoch in the history of their country." Other topics discussed included the diffusion of knowledge in the Highlands, the affairs of the *Edinburgh Gazetteer*, and the Convention Bill recently passed in Ireland. The last led to the appointment of a secret committee of four, including the secretary, to fix the meeting of a "Convention of Emergency," the signal for which was to be the first announcement of a similar Bill for Britain, the suspension of the Habeas Corpus Act, the invasion of the country, or the admission of foreign troops; and it was finally determined on December 4, "that the moment of any illegal dispersion of the present Convention" was also to be considered as a summons to the delegates to repair to the appointed place.

These proceedings, as printed in the *Edinburgh Gazetteer*, appeared "so strong" to the Solicitor General and the Lord Advocate that they "agreed to take notice of them." [3] Margarot, Gerrald, Skirving, and some others were

[1] *Parl. Hist.* xxxi. 868.

[2] His letter is printed in the *Edin. Gazetteer*, No. 80, Dec. 10, 1793, Brit. Mus. Cf. *State Trials*, xxiii. 406.

[3] R. to H. Dundas, Edin., Dec. 6, 1793, *Scot. Corr.* vol. ix.; Omond, *Arniston Memoirs*, 242.

apprehended early on Thursday, December 5, and their papers secured. In the evening, the Lord Provost, attended by thirty constables, compelled the Convention to disperse. The delegates re-assembled later the same evening; but on the following night, while Margarot and Gerrald, who had been liberated on bail, were giving an account of their examination before the authorities, the sheriff-substitute of Edinburgh again broke up the gathering. "Behold," cried Gerrald, as he saw the lights of the attendants, "the funeral torches of liberty!"[1] Scott, Sinclair, Skirving, Margarot, and Gerrald were subsequently indicted on a charge of sedition.[2] Scott, the editor of the *Edinburgh Gazetteer*, sought safety in flight. Besides publishing the minutes of the Convention, he had printed an account of "the heroic lunacy of public spirit" shown by the Cobbler of Messina, who had secretly assassinated the oppressors of his country. "What if the Cobbler of Messina should revive?" was the daring comment. Sinclair, according to his counsel, Archibald Fletcher, became a Government spy, and his case was dropped. Skirving, Margarot, and Gerrald were tried and found guilty. Each received the same sentence as Muir. They had all played a prominent part in the British Convention, the object of which, the Lord Advocate said, was "not a reform but a subversion of Parliament, not a redress or cure of grievances, imaginary or real, in a legal, peaceable, and constitutional way, but a determined and systematic plan and resolution to subvert the limited monarchy and

[1] *Political Martyrs of Scotland*, 23. The last attempt to assemble the Convention was made by Skirving on December 12. *State Trials*, xxiii. 479.

[2] *State Trials*, xxiii. *passim*; Cockburn, *op. cit.* i. and ii. *passim*. Of the others arrested, Callender was outlawed for non-appearance, and Wm. Moffat (Muir's solicitor), Geo. Ross and Wm. Ross were not brought to trial. *Account of Proceedings of the British Convention.*

free constitution of Britain, and substitute in its place, by intimidation, force, and violence, a republic or democracy. . . ." [1]

There can be no doubt that these individuals did agree as to the necessity of a national convention. According to their view of constitutional history,[2] universal suffrage and annual Parliaments dated from the time of Alfred,[3] when every man had a vote and the people obeyed the laws which they themselves had made. In the process of time this original purity of the constitution had been lost. To regain it, the precedents of early history had to be followed. The people must be enlightened. "Then," said Gerrald, "the people assembled in the different departments of the country will resemble the ancient folk-motes, and will speak in language too reasonable to be confuted, too peremptory to be refused." It was thus by the force of public opinion, and not by arms, that Parliament was to be overawed. Such an idea was chimerical. According to this reasoning, the convention could only become "national" by such an accession of numbers as would include all the inhabitants of the country. Yet during the sittings of the British Convention not more than one hundred and fifty had been present, and the funds raised during its session, as Thomas

[1] *State Trials*, xxiii. 545.

[2] V. Gerrald's speech at his trial, also his pamphlet, *A Convention the only Means of saving us from Ruin* . . . (1793), new edn. Lond. 1796, and *The Address of the British Convention to the People of Great Britain*, Lond. n.d.

[3] Alfred's was the golden age of political reformers.

"A single jail in Alfred's golden reign
Could all the nation's criminals contain,
Fair justice then, without constraint ador'd,
Held high the steady scales, but dropp'd the sword.
No 'spies' were paid, no 'special juries' known,
Blest age, but ah! how different from our own!"

Ask and You Shall Have, Lond. 1795.

Erskine carefully calculated, did not exceed fifteen pounds, including two bad shillings. But the proceedings of the delegates naturally lent themselves to the construction put on them by the Lord Advocate. In imitation of the French, they had called each other "citizens," divided themselves into "sections," received reports from these sections, some of which were headed "Vive la Convention!" and ended with "Ça ira." They had also appointed committees of "organisation," of "instructions," of "finance," and of "secrecy," designated their meetings "sittings," granted "honours of sittings," dated their minutes the "First Year of the British Convention," and made "honourable mention" of patriotic donations.[1] The French Convention had led to a regicide rebellion, to "scenes of anarchy, scenes of rapine, scenes of bloodshed, of cruelty and barbarity, hitherto unknown to the world," and the British Convention, "by showing a wish to adopt this model," was aiming at the same results.

The trials were as unjust as those of Muir and Palmer. Braxfield, owing to the exasperating insolence of Margarot, excelled even his former conduct. Margarot and Gerrald both asserted in open court that he had pre-judged them by venting the opinion, at a private dinner-party, that the members of the British Convention deserved whipping as well as transportation, and that "the mob would be the better for the spilling of a little blood." "For the judicial spirit of this court," says Cockburn, "we must go back to

[1] *State Trials*, xxiii. 815. For the impression produced on Beattie of Aberdeen, v. M. Forbes, *Beattie and His Friends*, 282. Skirving averred that such terms were used as a mark of contempt "by holding up such empty bugbears to the deluded as nurses do to children to frighten them to sleep." *State Trials*, xxiii. 579. Gerrald said that one of the secretaries, George Ross, had inserted them without his knowledge. *Ibid.* 984. In Kay, *Orig. Portraits*, ii. 177, M. C. Brown, the Sheffield delegate, is credited with suggesting the obnoxious phraseology.

the days of Lauderdale and Dalzell." [1] Such cruelty created a deep and lasting impression at home. Margarot became the hero of the populace. His friends escorted him from the Black Bull Inn, in the Grassmarket, to the court room, bearing a Tree of Liberty, "shaped like the letter M," with a scroll inscribed, "Liberty, Virtue, Reason, Justice and Truth." [2] Thomas Campbell, the poet, then in his sixteenth year, tramped from Glasgow to Edinburgh to be present at Gerrald's trial. "By heavens, sir, that is a great man," he remarked to a stranger beside him as Gerrald closed his defence. "Yes, sir," was the answer, "he is not only a great man himself, but he makes every other man feel great who listens to him." [3] "It was an era in my life," wrote the poet afterwards. In England, all the democratic societies passed resolutions of sympathy with the "martyrs," the London Corresponding Society ordering one hundred thousand copies of Margarot's indictment to be printed.[4] Southey, then an ardent republican, begged the "exiled patriots" to accept "one Briton's grateful song." [5] In other quarters the action of the authorities in Scotland was viewed with approval. "You get great credit here for your attack on the Convention," Dundas wrote from London to his nephew on December 11. "I desired Nepean to send you a perusal of the King's note to me on the subject." [6]

[1] *Memorials*, 88. Cf. *The Defence of Joseph Gerrald . . . to which are added Parallel Passages between the Speeches of Lord Chief Justice Jeffries in the case of Algernon Sydney, and of the Lord Chief Justice Clerk in the trial of Joseph Gerrald.* Corrected by himself. Lond. 1794.

[2] *Scot. Corr.* vol. x. Jan. 13 and 15; *Scot. Reg.* i. 145-6; *Moniteur*, Jan. 26, and Feb. 1, 1794; Cockburn, *Exam. of Trials for Sedn.* ii. 23.

[3] W. Beattie, *Life and Letters of Thomas Campbell*, i. 85-8.

[4] E. Smith, *Story of the English Jacobins*, 92; *Place Coll. of Newspaper Cuttings*, vol. xxxvi. Brit. Mus.

[5] *Place Coll. Brit. Mus. Add. MSS.* 27817, f. 432.

[6] G. W. T. Omond, *Arniston Memoirs*, 240.

The Manchester Church and King Club toasted "The Lord Advocate and the Court of Justiciary in Scotland."[1] No series of trials in Scottish history ever created such world-wide interest. In America they provided fresh material for the discussion which Muir's case had provoked.[2] The French press devoted ample space to the British Convention and the subsequent prosecutions.[3] The Government itself took action. The Committee of Public Safety ordered the French Admiralty, to intercept, if possible, the vessel bearing Margarot and his companions into exile.[4]

Few of the Scottish societies survived the dispersion of the British Convention. In Edinburgh, where the year before twenty societies of the Friends of the People had met, it was now difficult to find one.[5] The Stirling reformers ceased to meet except in private gatherings.[6] The Glasgow Association adopted the terms "citizens," "divisions," and "sections," thereby offending many of

[1] Trial of Walker of Manchester, *State Trials*, xxiii. 1116.

[2] *The Trial of Joseph Gerrald*, New York, 1794. It has an engraving of Gerrald as a frontispiece, with the motto, "Omne solum forti patria." V. also W. Cobbett, *Observations on the Emigration of Dr. Priestley*, Phila. 1796.

[3] *Moniteur*, Dec. 1793—April, 1794, *passim*.

[4] "Copie de l'Arrêté du Comité du Salut-public du 30e pluviôse, an 2e de la République, une et indivisible. Le Comité du Salut-public conformément aux principes de la constitution qui offre un asile en France aux hommes persécutés pour la cause de la liberté; arrête que le Ministre de la Marine prendra toutes les mesures nécessaires pour délivrer Muir, Palmer, et Margarot et intercepter le vaisseau qui les conduit en exil. Signé au registre: St. Just, B. Barère, Jeanbon St. André, C. A. Prieur, R. Lindet, Carnot, Collot d'Herbois, Billaud-Varenne. Pour copie conforme." Archives, French Foreign Office, *Correspondance Politique* (*Angleterre*), No. 588, f. 139.

[5] W. Scot to H. Dundas, Jan. 24, 1794, *Scot. Corr.* vol. x.

[6] Declaration of J. Forrest, surgeon, Stirling, June 19, 1794, *ibid.* vol. xi.

its members, and sank into insignificance.[1] While the Dundee Friends of the Constitution had refused to send delegates to the British Convention,[2] the Friends of Liberty in the same town carried out its instructions, as did also the Perth Society.[3] In the country districts, such as Strathaven, the numbers of the Friends of the People were sadly thinned by local prosecutions.[4] Yet below the surface discontent was rife. Thomas the Rhymer's prophecy regarding 1794:

> "A mild winter, a cold spring,
> A bloody summer, and no king"

was on many lips.[5] The seditious spirit was said "to be reviving" in the west, and barracks were erected to overawe the malcontents.[6] Occasional disturbances, such as a riot in the Edinburgh theatre, revealed the latent irritation. In April, a play entitled *The Royal Martyr* was staged,[7] and the public was invited to compare "the similarity of circumstances which attended the two kings [Charles I. and Louis XVI.] . . . a proper lesson at this juncture to be held out to warn mankind from stepping out of the paths of virtue and religion."[8] Such an advertisement was a challenge to the Democrats who mustered in force. Cries for "Ça ira," "The Sow's Tail to Geordie," and "God save the People," drowned the strains of "God save the King";

[1] Declaration of J. Sinclair, Reedmaker, Glasgow, June 11, 1794, *ibid.*

[2] Letter of Rev. Neil Douglas in *An Address to the Judges and Jury*, Glasgow, 1817.

[3] Declaration of G. Mealmaker, Weaver, Dundee, June 18, 1794, *Scot. Corr.* vol. xi.

[4] *State Trials*, xxiii. 1255.

[5] Report of J. B., Jan. 24, 1794, *Scot. Corr.* vol. x.

[6] Lord Provost Hamilton to Henry Dundas, Jan. 19, 1794, *ibid.*; H. Dundas to Ld. Adv., Feb. 8, 1794. *Entry Books*, vol. i.

[7] Alex. Fyfe, *The Royal Martyr*, Lond. 1709.

[8] *Cal. Mer.* April 5, 1794.

and in the fight which ensued the denizens of the gallery claimed the victory.[1]

To cope with the prevailing unrest, Dundas, in March, laid before the king a proposal to appoint Lords-lieutenant and Sheriffs Principal in Scotland, and by May the scheme was in full working order.[2] One of their duties was to make arrangements for the defence of the country against invasion.[3] As this was considered to have been secured two years before by the establishment of Fencible Corps (troops raised for service in Great Britain only), special emphasis was laid on that part of their instructions which dealt with "internal tranquillity." For this purpose the Lords-lieutenant were to organise into companies those who offered themselves as Volunteers. Care was to be taken that no one likely to enlist in the army or navy was enrolled, and all were to be men of known loyalty to His Majesty's Government. Suitable individuals, of the same unimpeachable principles, were to be nominated deputy-lieutenants, and they were "to

[1] Report of J. B., April 18, 1794, *Scot. Corr.* vol. x.; *State Trials*, xxiv. 82, 83. Scott took part in the fray, Lockhart, *Life of Scott*, ch. vii. For an account of a similar disturbance at Dumfries in October, 1792, in which Burns was implicated, v. Chambers's *Life and Work of Burns*, ed. W. Wallace, iii. 384. *The Last Days and Execution of Louis XVI.* was acted at Musselburgh in 1793, Philo-Scotus, *Reminiscences of a Scottish Gentleman*, 31. In June of the same year the Dublin Theatre Royal Company produced *Democratic Rage or Louis the Unfortunate*, *Irish Corr.* P.R.O. vol. xliv. Cf. Dr. John Moore's description of the contemporary French stage: "Kings and princes are represented as rapacious, voluptuous, and tyrannical; nobility as frivolous and unfeeling, fawning to the sovereign and insolent to their fellow subjects; priests as hypocritical, artful and wicked. To inspire a hatred to monarchical government and a love of republicanism is one great object of almost every new piece." *Journal* (Nov. 18, 1792), 392-3; v. also W. T. Wolfe Tone, *Life of Wolfe Tone*, ii. 11.

[2] Henry Dundas to the King, March 6, 1794, *Scot. Corr.* vol. x. Lords-lieutenant had been appointed after the 'Forty-Five in April, 1746, *Pelham Corr. Brit. Mus. Add. MSS.* 33049. Probably the office had fallen into abeyance.

[3] Draft Circular to Lords-lieutenant, *ibid.* May 14, 1794.

inform themselves respecting the dispositions of those living in their districts," and to prepare lists of such as were willing to assist the civil magistrate in quelling tumults or illegal meetings.

In England, the harsh treatment of the members of the British Convention had led to emphatic protests from the "Jacobins," as their enemies called them. In January, the London Corresponding Society resolved to call another convention should the Government proceed to further repressive measures. After communicating with the Constitutional Information Society, it held an open-air meeting on April 24, 1794, at Chalk Farm, London, when a joint-committee was appointed to take the necessary steps. Thereupon the Government decided to suspend the Habeas Corpus Act, and to justify this momentous step, a secret committee of both Houses of Parliament was elected by ballot on May 15 to examine certain papers of the Corresponding and Constitutional Information Societies, whose prominent members had been arrested some days before. On the presentation of the first report, Pitt brought in a Bill to suspend the Habeas Corpus Act, and it became law on May 23. Subsequently a second report was presented by the Committee of the Commons, and two by that of the Lords.[1]

These committees, in spite of the ballot, consisted entirely of supporters of the Ministry. It would be futile, therefore, to look in the reports for an impartial account of the aims of the Democrats. The papers disclosed little that was not already known to the public—intemperate resolutions, addresses to the French Convention, and the minutes of the British Convention. But the second report appeared to substantiate the assertions made in the first, that an armed insurrection had been planned. It contained the following startling intelligence, communicated by Henry

[1] The reports are printed in *Parl. Hist.* xxxi.

Dundas in a series of letters to Pitt during the investigations of the committee. While a search for embezzled goods was being made in Edinburgh, twelve pike or spear heads had been discovered in the house of a certain Robert Watt and some twenty more in the smithy of a man named Orrock. These had been made to the order of the Committee of Ways and Means of the late British Convention. Though orders had been received for the weapons from the west, their manufacture was confined to the Capital, where the Friends of the People had hatched a regular conspiracy to seize the authorities, the castle, the banks, and the public offices, and set up a provisional government. Attempts had been made to incite the troops to mutiny. In Paisley the intention to arm and hold nightly meetings had been ascertained. A meeting of several hundreds of the townsfolk had elected a citizen president, and passed resolutions in favour of the assembling of another convention to redress all grievances.

In connection with this conspiracy, numerous arrests were made, and in August and September, Robert Watt and David Downie were brought to trial on a charge of high treason.[1] This grave indictment brought about a much needed change in the bench. Since 1709, the Court of Justiciary in Scotland had exercised a jurisdiction, according to the forms of English law, in trials for high treason.[2] This Act of Queen Anne likewise authorised the sovereign to issue a special commission of Oyer and Terminer in such cases. The Lord Advocate was extremely anxious that the latter procedure should be adopted. "*Entre nous*," he writes to his uncle on June 20, "I would prefer a commission were it only for this reason, that the President or Chief Baron would, in that way, fall to preside in place of the violent

[1] *State Trials*, xxiii. xxiv.

[2] R. to H. Dundas, June 21, 1794, *Scot. Corr.* vol. xi. He cites the trials of 1748 and 1749.

and intemperate gentleman who sits in the Justiciary, and whose present state of health and spirits is such as to afford no chance of his being more soberly inclined in his demeanour than he was last winter."[1] Henry Dundas agreed, and for the first time since the prosecutions began, the prisoners had a fair trial.

The evidence of the witnesses considerably modified the account of the conspiracy given in the second report of the Committee of Secrecy, where it was stated to be part of a far-reaching scheme originating with the London Corresponding Society. When the British Convention was dispersed, a few of the members and other sympathisers in Edinburgh, to the number of about one hundred, continued to meet in a school-room in Simon Square. Of this society, Robert Watt, the first spy to be employed by the Lord Advocate at the beginning of the political excitement, became the leading spirit.[2] Under his guidance, it drew up a new set of rules, printed as "Fundamental Principles." According to these regulations a Committee of Union was appointed. This body, consisting of delegates from four surviving societies in Edinburgh and the neighbourhood, elected on March 5 a permanent secret committee of seven—the Committee of Ways and Means. Watt was on both of these, and thus the control of the whole policy and funds of the society fell into his hands.[3] In April, circulars were received from the secretary of the London Corresponding Society asking the Scottish Friends of the People to take part in another convention. After despatching these to Perth,

[1] *i.e.* Braxfield. R. to H. Dundas, June 21, 1794, *Scot. Corr.* vol. xi.

[2] V. *ante*, ch. v. p. 89.

[3] J. B.'s report, April 19, 1794, *Scot. Corr.* vol. x.: "The Simon Square meeting last night was as crowded as ever. . . . The Fundamental Principles were discussed. . . . In several parts the Committee of Union and of Ways and Means were thought to arrogate too much power to themselves."

Paisley, Strathaven, and Dundee, the Committee of Ways and Means met to choose a delegate. By this time two of its members had prudently withdrawn, and to the remaining five Watt disclosed his nefarious schemes. On his own initiative, he then sent John Fairley and other "collectors" to various parts of Scotland, to ascertain the "sentiments" of the Friends of the People; but, judging from Fairley's report, they would have nothing to do with the violence which was vaguely hinted at. Self-deluded as to the amount of support to be expected, Watt then gave instructions for the manufacture of pikes and halberts, but his plans were discovered before fifty had been made. Two months later the same evidence was largely used in the trial of Hardy, the secretary of the London Corresponding Society,[1] but the Lord Chief Justice in summing up declared that "he did not see anything that made it probable that Hardy, personally, was concerned in this part of the conspiracy, or that he knew anything about it." [2] Reduced to its true proportions, the proposed insurrection is to be regarded as the work of Robert Watt. Since July, 1793, his services as a spy had been dispensed with, and he probably hoped, should his plans prove successful, to find a readier means of filling his purse. He was found guilty, and hanged at the Tolbooth of Edinburgh. His body was then cut down and laid on a table. The head was cut off, the executioner exclaiming

[1] Those arrested with Watt turned king's evidence, and were ultimately pardoned. "Most of my seditious friends are safely arrived and will be liberated under the Privy Council warrant this day or to-morrow. I wish to God you had kept them with you." Letter of Lord Advocate, Dec. 19, 1794, *Scot. Corr.* vol. xi.

[2] *State Trials*, xxiv. 1347. Regarding Watt, Hardy wrote to Francis Place: "I had no knowledge of, nor had I any communication with him whatever." "The London Corresponding Society as a Society," says Place, "never gave any countenance to the use of such instruments [the pikes]." *Place Coll. Brit. Mus. Add. MSS.* 27817, f. 127. *Memoir of Hardy*, Append. p. 119.

as he held it up to view, "This is the head of a traitor."[1] Downie, the treasurer of the society, was pardoned, to the regret of the Lord Advocate, who wrote: "I am convinced from anything I have heard since my return here, that the respite to Downie will be generally disapproved, but after the report of the President it was impossible for you to act otherways."[2]

The supporters of the Government, however actuated by genuine feelings of alarm, did not fail to profit by the crisis. "Everything," says Cockburn, speaking of the Reign of Terror, "rung and was connected with the Revolution in France. . . . Everything, not this or that thing, but literally everything, was soaked in this one event."[3] The Tories had confidently affirmed that the reformers were but revolutionaries masquerading in disguise. Watt's plot was now triumphantly cited as a conclusive proof, and a host of pamphleteers drove the lesson home.[4] "The miseries and dissensions by which that city was ruined," said one in a *Narrative describing the Siege of Lyons*, "arose in a manner so very like to that in which the seditious in Great Britain have lately attempted to introduce confusion, dissension, and treasonable insurrection in some of our great towns, that this narrative will be found to afford a most awful and instructive lesson for our present use." Thousands rushed to join the Volunteers, so that by July, 1796, forty-one

[1] Omond, *Lives of the Lord Advocates of Scotland*, ii. 204.

[2] R. to H. Dundas, Oct. 13, 1794, *Scot. Corr.* vol. xi.

[3] *Memorials*, 70.

[4] Literary men who held Government posts were expected to lend their aid. Some years afterwards, Gillies, who succeeded Principal Robertson as Historiographer Royal for Scotland, claimed an increase of salary. He had published, by request, an edition of Aristotle's *Politics*, "as peculiarly calculated to counteract the wild and dangerous principles afloat," and thus had been unable to undertake more profitable labours. *Banks Corr. Brit. Mus. Add. MSS.* 33982, f. 294.

districts in Scotland had either a regiment or a company.[1] Though a haunting fear of invasion had existed since the outbreak of the war with France, it was rather the expected blow from the "accursed dagger of domestic treachery" that now swelled the ranks. In the articles of the Edinburgh Volunteers, nothing was said of serving against a foreign foe; but the members formally reprobated the doctrine of universal suffrage and Jacobin political principles, disapproved of the Friends of the People and the British Convention, and obliged themselves to prevent such societies being formed and such meetings being held in the future.[2] For those who now prudently renounced their democratic zeal, the uniform of Windsor blue was a conspicuous sign of repentance. Burns, like many others threatened with the loss of their post, sought thus to reinstate himself in the good graces of his employers.[3] Those who clung stubbornly to their opinions were distinguished, like the Roundheads of old, by having their hair closely cropped. Attired in trousers and gaiters, of a stuff known as "rap rascal," these "Crappies" were as obnoxious to Government Men who stuck "to the constitution and to buckles," as the "Black Nebs" who refused to join the volunteers.[4]

[1] *List of Officers of Militia and Volunteers, War Office*, 10*th July*, 1796. P.R.O. Library.

[2] *A View of the Estab. of the Corps of Royal Edin. Volunteers, June* 15, 1795. Edin. 1795. 735 were on the roll. At least 50 per cent. of these were connected with the law courts.

[3] Chambers's *Life of Burns*, ed. Wallace, iii. 375, iv. 206 *et seq.*; Chambers's *Hist. of Peebles*, 270.

[4] Cockburn, *Memorials*, 60. Philo-Scotus, *Reminiscences of a Scottish Gentleman*, 22. Even a French refugee in Edinburgh, M. de Latocnaye, was regarded with suspicion because he refused to join, and he was reproached with "having the abomination" of eating with equal relish the dinners of Whigs or of Tories. *Promenade d'un Français dans l'Irlande*, Dublin, 1797, p. 260.

Cockburn's account of the intolerance pervading all ranks of society is amply confirmed from other sources. Tradesmen of "Jacobinical" sympathies had their credit stopped at the bank.[1] Housewives refused to buy unless from shopkeepers of approved loyalty. Even Nasmyth, who could ill conceal his politics, gave up painting the portraits of Tory clients to devote himself to those landscape studies which had such an important influence on the evolution of Scottish art.[2] Manufacturers did not scruple to dismiss workmen suspected of disloyal opinions. Combinations or strikes were put down with a ruthless hand,[3] and philanthropic work was regarded with distrust. Archibald Fletcher's wife, who was credited with guillotining hens in her backyard, in order to be prepared for higher game when the time came, with the greatest difficulty obtained official permission to establish a Female Benefit Society.[4] Education was considered a dubious advantage for the lower classes, and as late as 1812 a Lancastrian school, founded by the Edinburgh Whigs, had to be erected on the Calton Hill, "where it was the fashion to stow away everything that was too abominable to be tolerated elsewhere." [5] Among the professional classes there were a few who refused to give up their convictions. In Glasgow, though Reid bowed to the

[1] In a letter to the Lord Advocate in 1797 (?) Col. Johnstone warns him that the Bank agent at Dunfermline had countenanced an opposition meeting. "It will be of consequence to have this man dismissed from the employment he holds." *Edin. Univ. Laing MSS.* No. 501. Sir Wm. Forbes' bank in Edinburgh refused to cash the drafts remitted by Hardy through the London banks to Margarot and Gerrald. *Place Coll. Brit. Mus. Add. MSS.* 27814, f. 63.

[2] J. L. Caw, *Scottish Painting Past and Present*, 48.

[3] A. Fergusson, *Henry Erskine*, 401.

[4] *Autobiography*, 70, 86. Rule 20 of the *Regulations of the Canongate Society* (Edin. 1798) enacted that "any member guilty of attending any seditious or illegal meeting should be expelled."

[5] Cockburn, *Memorials*, 233.

storm,[1] Professor Millar was venerated by a band of ardent disciples, one of whom was Thomas Campbell, the future poet-laureate of the Whigs.[2] Even in St. Andrews University, where the influence of Henry Dundas, its Chancellor, was paramount, Dr. James Brown was the inspirer of such youthful enthusiasts as Thomas Chalmers and John Leslie, who fed their minds on Godwin's *Political Justice* and aired their opinions in the Political Society.[3] The leading figure in the academic world was Dugald Stewart, the fame of whose teaching attracted students from England and abroad. Yet as an ardent Whig he was a marked man, whom "not a few hoped to catch in dangerous propositions." [4] Jeffrey, whose father had forbidden him to attend Millar's lectures in Glasgow, found, on his return from Oxford, the same veto put on Dugald Stewart's; [5] and he had to be content with the congenial company of the professor's admirers in the Speculative Society, which, in like manner, was looked upon as a hotbed of Whiggery and sedition.[6]

The full weight of public disapproval, however, was felt in legal circles. Most of the leading Whigs were advocates. "Even the Whig lawyers who had secured their footing at the Bar . . . had hard enough work to keep their places," says Cockburn.[7] "There being no juries

[1] V. *Sketch of the Career of the late Thomas Reid, D.D., . . . with Observations on the Danger of Political Innovation, from a Discourse delivered on Nov.* 29, 1794, *by Dr. Reid before the Literary Society in Glasgow College.* Glasgow, 1796. A. Campbell Fraser, *Thomas Reid*, 115-6.

[2] W. Beattie, *Life and Letters of Thomas Campbell*, i. 206.

[3] W. Hanna, *Memoirs of Thomas Chalmers*, Edin. 1863, i. 11, 16.

[4] Cockburn, *Memorials*, 153-4. [5] Cockburn, *Life of Jeffrey*, i. 52.

[6] Cockburn, *Memorials*, 65; Atkinson and Jackson, *Brougham and His Early Friends*, i. 11; *Hist. of the Speculative Society*, 28, 29, 38. Three members of the society were sentenced to be reprimanded by the Principal of the University "for disseminating French principles and sedition." *Life and Times of Henry, Lord Brougham*, written by himself, i. 53.

[7] *Memorials*, 80.

in civil cases," writes Mrs. Fletcher, "it was supposed that the judges would not decide in favour of any litigant who employed Whig lawyers . . . We were often at that time reduced to our last guinea." [1] The case of the younger men, such as Jeffrey, Millar, Cranstoun, Thomson, Brougham, and Horner, seemed almost hopeless. Millar, who had been a prominent Friend of the People in 1792, retired to America, where he died shortly afterwards.[2] Cranstoun refused to subscribe a written test of political orthodoxy, and found it advisable to serve for a time as an officer of a Fencible Corps in Ireland.[3] Jeffrey saw so little prospect of success that he thought of settling in London. The fate of Thomas Muir, they were often reminded, was intended as a warning to his brother advocates, and in 1796, an opportunity occurred of making another striking example.

Though all open democratic activity had died down in Scotland, the condition of the poorer classes was such as to lead to frequent disturbances. A succession of bad harvests created such a dearth in Great Britain that the price of corn, which in 1792 had been 43s. a quarter, rose to 75s. In 1795, one-eighth of the population of Edinburgh, according to Cockburn's estimate, had to be fed by charity.[4] The cost of living rose in proportion. The Government, while upholding the corn laws, tried to mitigate their evil effects.[5] For a certain period all exportation was pro-

[1] *Autobiography*, 66. [2] *Ibid.* 71.

[3] Cockburn, *Memorials*, 80. "Deed, Mr. George, ye wad be muckle the better o' being whuppit," said Lord Swinton, whom he consulted about joining the Austrian army, where, it was said, officers were liable to be flogged. *Memorials* (1909 edn.), 104, fn.

[4] *Memorials*, 63.

[5] "It does not occur to me that any step could with propriety be taken to prevent the legal exportation of grain coastways to and from any part of the kingdom. The farmer and the landholder might too with justice

hibited, and importation was allowed free of duty.[1] Local dues were remitted by the magistrates, and public subscriptions were opened to buy grain in order to re-sell at a cheaper rate. Yet discontent was rife, and the people were further incensed by the ever-increasing load of taxation and the enforcement of impress warrants. Riots broke out in Dundee and other places, and would have been more numerous but for the high rate of wages in Glasgow and the west.[2]

In England the same conditions prevailed. Prospects of peace were therefore eagerly discussed in Parliament and in the press. On October 26, 1795, a huge meeting was held at Copenhagen Fields, Mary-le-bone, under the auspices of the London Corresponding Society, which had resumed its activities. Resolutions were passed demanding peace, Parliamentary reform, and the dismissal of Ministers. Three days later a mob pelted the carriage of the King on his way to open Parliament. Cries of "Bread!" "Peace!" "No Pitt!" rose on every side. Repressive measures were at once proposed by the Government. Two Bills were introduced; one, the Treason Bill, extended the law of treason to include mere words, spoken or written; the other—to prevent seditious meetings—forbade all political assemblies unless previously notified to the authorities, powers being

complain of their property being subjected to the pleasure of the Baker and Corn Dealer." Ld. Adv. to J. King (an official of the Home Office), Feb. 7, 1795, *Scot. Corr.* vol. xii. Cf. letter of J. Craig to Ld. Adv.: "I gave it as my opinion that however admirable the measure might be at a proper period, surely the present was the most unseasonable time for proposing or making any change in the Corn Law, as it would only tend to waken the jealousy of the lower class of people, and create a contention or misunderstanding between them and the said proprietors which above all things at this time should be avoided." He advised importation of grain at the lowest duty till the beginning of the following July. *Ibid.*

[1] Feb. 20, 1795, *Entry Books* (*Scot.*), vol. i.

[2] *Scot. Corr.* vol. xiii. Glasgow, March 14, 1796.

granted to the Justices to dissolve such a gathering without reading the Riot Act. These Bills caused wide-spread indignation. Whigs and Democrats united to denounce such an invasion of the liberty of the subject. Fox asserted that the "pretended law of Scotland regarding sedition" was being thus introduced into England, while Sheridan endeavoured to limit the discretionary power of the Scottish judges to the punishment laid down in the new Bill. Both parties made strenuous efforts to prove that their views were supported by the people at large. Dundas flooded the House with petitions from Scottish town councils and other corporate bodies, the value of which, as expressions of public opinion, Thomas Erskine and Colonel Macleod duly exposed. Against the Bills, the Glasgow petition was signed by 10,000 inhabitants; that from Paisley by 2500. On Novembei 28, Henry Erskine presided at a meeting in Edinburgh, which resulted in a petition containing 8000 signatures. It was laid before the House of Commons on December 10, by Thomas Erskine, who animadverted on the proceedings that were being taken against his brother. Alarmed by the growing opposition, the Edinburgh supporters of the Government had hastened to take action. In 1785, Henry Erskine, though a Whig, had been elected to the dignified position of Dean of the Faculty of Advocates. Yet two days after the meeting against the proposed Bills, eight of their number had signified their intention of opposing his re-election, on the ground that his action had compromised the loyalty of the Faculty.[1] Erskine's refusal to join the Friends of

[1] "We are all, except Dr. Adamson, who never speaks of the subject, perfectly sound in relation to the Dean's conduct. I cannot conceive a greater degradation for a man of family, of abilities, and at the head of a respectable profession, than to stand forth as the gatherer and instigator of a mob assembled to judge of a Bill intended to prevent the evils arising from such mobs. The Faculty has shown a becoming spirit; and whatever he may talk of persecution for opinions, and of attachment to

the People now stood him in little stead, and on January 12, 1796, he was deposed from office by a majority of ninety-five as an additional warning to Whig lawyers of the danger of attending public meetings "on the wrong side."[1] But such an act had an unlooked-for result. An even closer sympathy now bound together his thirty-eight supporters, and "The Independence of the Scottish Bar" became one of the rallying cries of the young Whig party.

Administration, I have no doubt the country feels that he suffers deservedly, not for his opinions, but for his conduct." Rev. Geo. Hill to Dr. Carlyle, St. Andrews, Jan. 5, 1796. *Edin. Univ. MSS. Letters of Dr. Carlyle*, No. 79.

[1] *The Hist. of Two Acts*, Lond. 1796, gives a full account of the Parliamentary debates, the petitions, and the particulars of Erskine's deposition. V. also A. Fergusson, *Henry Erskine*, Append.; Cockburn, *Memorials*, 81.

CHAPTER VIII.

FRENCH PROJECTS OF INVASION.

THE hopes of peace entertained in 1795 were doomed to disappointment, and, with the advent of the Directory to power in November, an invasion of the British Isles was at last seriously contemplated in France. Ever since the relations with Great Britain had become strained, the chances of the success of such a project had been tentatively discussed, and the favourable symptoms in the political conditions of England, Scotland, and Ireland, carefully noted. The rise of the British democratic societies seemed at first to preclude the very possibility of war. They would form, it was supposed, a means of communication between the two peoples; the new ideas would triumph on both sides of the Channel, and fraternity would be established between sister republics. Thus in the Jacobin Club in August, 1792, Oswald, a native of Edinburgh, whose presence gave a piquancy to its deliberations which was duly appreciated in his native land, showed how "the glorious 10th of August" had been misrepresented by the Ministerialist press in England. He proposed that a circular should be sent to all the popular societies in England, Scotland, and Ireland, giving a true account of the facts.[1] Condorcet, in

[1] Aulard, *Société des Jacobins*, iv. 220. A circular was accordingly drawn up. *Ibid.* 356-9. On June 4, Oswald had maintained that the neutrality declared by the King of England was due to the firmness of

an article in the *Chronique de Paris* of November 23, 1792, drew further attention to the importance of these clubs. " Popular societies," he wrote, " have been established in the three kingdoms. . . . It is well known what a number of persons there are who think rightly, and daily enlighten the people of England whose opinions furnish useful subjects for disputation. This people, who at once fear and desire a revolution such as ours, will necessarily be drawn along by these courageous and enlightened persons who always determine the first steps : the opening of the session of Parliament which approaches will infallibly become the occasion of reforms which are most urgent, such as those which regard the national representation. From thence to the establishment of a republic, the transitions will be less tedious, because the foundations of liberty have long existed in England." [1]

the English clubs, which had forced the Government to listen to reason. *Ibid.* iii. 653-4. The proceedings of the Jacobin Club were fully reported in the Scottish press ; v. *Cal. Mer.* Sept. 6, 1792, where Oswald's biography is given. The *Glasgow Courier*, Sept. 8, 1792, says : "When last in Edinburgh, Oswald made a conspicuous figure in the Pantheon debating society." V. also *Hist. MSS. Com. Reports*, *Dropmore MSS.* ii. 309, and Lichtenberger, *Le Socialisme Utopique*, chap. viii. : John Oswald, Écossais, Jacobin, et Socialiste.

[1] *A Collection of Addresses of Eng. Clubs to the Nat. Convention*, 2nd edn. Lond. 1793, p. 22. The same ideas are expressed in the following report : "Malgré l'influence du gouvernement, il existe en Angleterre des germes puissans de mécontentement et un parti assez fort pour nos principes ; ce parti est à la veille d'être étouffé, mais nous pouvons augmenter sa vigueur. Ne nous flattons point : l'Angleterre n'a point à présent le désir de nous reconnaître parcequ'elle craint que nous ne voulions propager nos principes chez elle. La démarche de nous faire la guerre est hardie ; car si elle ne trouve pas les moyens de la faire nationale, elle deviendra bientôt une République elle-même. Eh bien, négocions ; elle paraît vouloir nous parler ; causons avec elle. Voyons l'avenir, flattons ses espérances, ne heurtons pas ses préjugés, et faisons traîner la chose en longueur pendant un mois ou deux, car pendant cet intervalle, la question de la réforme sera entamée au Parlement. Si les esprits ne sont pas occupés ailleurs, vous verrez cette réforme être réellement le commencement d'une révolution sérieuse. Déjà l'Écosse paraît

Such dreams were rudely dispelled by the outbreak of hostilities. "Never was there so feeble an opposition to the Government, and never was public opinion so unanimous for war with France," wrote an official in March, 1793.[1] Yet in the British democrats, whose proceedings were fully reported in the newspapers, the French still professed to see a growing body of sympathisers, and, in the event of invasion, of possible allies. Thomas Muir, who was in Paris during the winter of 1793, wrote afterwards that he heard men whose names were unknown in his native land, declaring in the cafés, in the clubs, and even to Ministers, that England only awaited the descent of the French to welcome them with affection, and conjointly with them to destroy their detestable government, and establish a republic on the principles of the Rights of Man.[2] Scotland and Ireland, it was thought, would be only too willing to profit by such an occurrence. "The English people," Kersaint had said, addressing the Convention in January, 1793, "like all conquerors, have long oppressed Scotland and Ireland; but it should be noted that these two nations, always restive, and secretly in revolt against the injustice of the dominating race, have acquired at different epochs concessions which have engendered the hope of ultimately regaining their entire independence. . . . Since the Union, Scotland has been represented in Parliament, but out of such proportion to its wealth, its extent, and its population, that it does not conceal the fact that it

imbuë de nos principes. Voyez à Dundee M. Dundas brulé en effigie; voyez-y l'arbre de la liberté planté par le peuple; voyez-le abattu dans la nuit par deux aristocrats, et voyez enfin le lendemain leurs maisons rasées par le peuple. Voilà vraiment qui désigne une révolution prochaine." Archives, French Foreign Office, *Mémoires et Documents* (*Angleterre*), 53, f. 144. Vues sur la Situation Intérieure de l'Angleterre et sur Sa Position envers la France. Dec. 12, 1792.

[1] Aulard, *Études et Leçons sur la Révolution Française*, Paris, 1892-1907, 3e sér. 75.

[2] *Correspondance Politique* (*Angleterre*) 592, f. 161.

is nothing but a dependent colony of the English Government. Yet the Scots know their rights and their strength: the principles developed by the French nation have there found zealous defenders who have been the first to merit the honour of being persecuted by the British Government; but these persecutions have made proselytes, and nowhere is more joy caused by your victories than in Scotland, the principal towns of which have been illuminated to celebrate them." [1]

The reports of spies conveyed the same impression to official minds. In October, 1792, Citoyen Pétry had been appointed "agent de la marine et du commerce" in Scotland, and in this capacity had spent a few days in Glasgow.[2] The authorities, however, had had timely notice of his arrival, and he had been ordered to leave.[3] The account of his visit, which he laid before the French Minister in March, 1793, justified the opinion of the Sheriff of Glasgow that he "had come to Scotland with no good intentions." Pétry described the enthusiasm for the Revolution evinced by the people in the west of Scotland, the subscription raised in Glasgow on behalf of the National Assembly, the rise of the Friends of the People, and of the counter constitutional associations. He explained the difficulty experienced by the latter in promoting loyal addresses, the spread of pamphlets defending the French Revolution, and the prosecution of their authors and printers. The death of Louis had further strengthened the Government, who had adroitly used the catastrophe to render the war popular. Yet it was long after other towns that Glasgow had voted bounties to seamen, for the manufacturers were adverse. "In a word," he sums up, "if Ministerial influence has

[1] *Moniteur*, Jan. 3, 1793; also published, London, 1793.

[2] *Corr. Polit.* (*Angl.*) 584, f. 16.

[3] *Scot. Corr.* vol. vii. Jan. 28, 29, Feb. 16, 1793.

reduced to silence nearly all the societies for the rights of the people, the members of which they were composed are still alive. The slightest thing will awaken them from the state of lethargy they appear to be in. I even dare to state that, if success crowns the efforts of the Government against us, it will be obliged to obtain popularity for the consequent additional taxes by granting reform so often demanded, and then it can hardly be doubted that these changes will be but the beginning of many others." [1] Three months later, another spy, Colonel Oswald, an American, who had been sent to Ireland by Le Brun, returned with an even more optimistic report of his eight or ten days' sojourn in Scotland. The people were incensed against Pitt and Dundas. They were meditating a decisive blow, and though the time and the circumstances were not yet propitious, a foreign enemy would soon cause a revolution.[2]

A month after Oswald's return, the Convention renewed the powers of the Committee of Public Safety, which entered at once on a more strenuous foreign policy. "The extermination of England" became the subject of its most secret deliberations. In a document ascribed by Aulard to this period, two means of accomplishing this end were laid down.

[1] *Corr. Polit.* (*Angl.*), Supplément 21, f. 108.

[2] *Ibid.* 587, f. 167, June 11, 1793. Lecky, *Hist. of Eng.* vii. 2. In a report to the Ministre de la Marine, dated May 23, 1793, the writers state that, according to their instructions, they had distributed the address to the English sailors in the maritime towns and villages and in London. They then go on to describe the political situation in England and Scotland: "Depuis plusieurs années, les Écossais se plaignent des abus qui se sont glissés dans leur gouvernement. Les mêmes dissensions politiques qui règnent en Irlande règnent aussi en Écosse. Ils viennent de demander le rappel du Test Act . . . Il s'est formé à Édimbourg une Convention, composée des députés de divers sociétés d'Écosse, sous le titre des Amis du Peuple. Il y a été arrêté que la société ne se dissouderoit, et ne cesseroit ses sollicitations auprès du parlement, que quand il auroit acquiescé à sa demande." A list of the resolutions of the second Convention of the Friends of the People follows. Rapport et Observations données au citoyen Ministre de la Marine. *Ibid.* 587, f. 125.

An endeavour was to be made to raise, in the British Parliament, a discussion regarding the Rights of Man, and at the same time negotiations were to be opened with the people of Ireland and Scotland by the offer of alliance should they revolt.[1] It was rumoured that the Committee had resolved, on December 14, to spare no expense in trying to raise an insurrection in these countries, so that, according to Robespierre, England would be forced either to withdraw from the coalition or drive Pitt from office. Barère, according to another *Bulletin*, stated in the Convention that such a host of spies was being employed in England, Scotland, and Ireland, that the Minister, Forgues, would have been afraid of being accused of squandering the public money, had he not been certain of being able to prove the utility of each.[2] One Jackson had been sent on a mission to the United Irishmen,[3] but no secret agent seems to have been despatched to Scotland. The proceedings of the British Convention were possibly regarded as affording sufficient evidence of its intentions.[4]

[1] "La Politique Étrangère du Comité du Salut Public," art. in *La Révolution Française*, vol. xiv. (1888), p. 1111.

[2] *Dropmore MSS.* ii. 480, 538 (*Bulletins* 5 and 14).

[3] Lecky, *Hist. of Eng.* vii. 27.

[4] In the *Moniteur*, 10 nivôse, an ii. (Dec. 30, 1793), five columns out of twelve are devoted to the British Convention. It was proposed in the Jacobin Club that a letter of sympathy should be written to the London Corresponding Society regarding the treatment of its delegates, but the motion was dropped. *Moniteur*, 6 pluviôse, an ii. (Jan. 25, 1794). In *Bulletin* No. 5, dated Dec. 20, 1793 (*Dropmore MSS.* ii. 480), "Brower and Hastee" are said to have been the Scottish correspondents of Rabaut St. Etienne, who was executed on Dec. 3, as a *Girondin*. These were Brown and Hastie of the British Convention, for their names are so misspelt in the *Moniteur* (Dec. 30, 1793). In *Bulletin* No. 8 (*Dropmore MSS.* ii. 514), it was reported that "their friends in Scotland" were asking from the Bishop of Autun, then supposed to be in Ireland, a loan of 120,000 francs to prevent the entire ruin of the work of "sieurs Brewer et Margarot," *i.e.* Brown and Margarot. But the *Bulletins* are so full of such palpable absurdities that they may be disregarded as statements of facts. In this case the source of information is shown by the misspellings.

As Dorat-Cubières expressed it in his *Prophétie Républicaine* :[1]

> "Édimbourg ressaisit les droits sacrés de l'homme,
> Édimbourg s'est levée : à sa puissante voix,
> Albion va bientôt voir refleurir les lois,
> Et les François vainqueurs secondant son audace,
> Elle va des tyrans exterminer la race."[2]

And it was in accordance with its declared policy that the Committee of Public Safety, as we have seen, took steps to rescue Muir, Margarot, and their companions.[3] Disorders in France and negotiations for peace suspended more decisive action,[4] but the Directory, to which the government was entrusted in November, 1795, at once took up the project of invasion.

This renewed vigour in the councils of the Republic coincided with the arrival in France of Wolfe Tone, charged with a message from the United Irishmen.[5] Since the

[1] 17 nivôse, an ii. (Jan. 6, 1794). A note is added here in the original : "D'après la Convention Nationale qui s'est formée à Édimbourg, on ne peut guère douter qu'une grande révolution ne couve dans la Grande Bretagne et qu'elle ne soit bien voisine de son année 1789."

[2] Cf. *Ode aux Français sur leur Projet de Descente en Angleterre*, par P—— C——, an xii. (1804) :

> "Oui ! Londres finira comme finit Athènes,
> Déjà de cet empire on voit flotter les rênes,"

where the following note appears : "Plusieurs insurrections se sont déjà manifestées en Irlande et en Écosse : elles sont ordinairement d'un mauvais augure, et finissent par précipiter la décadence des Empires."

[3] V. *ante*, chap. vii. p. 146. On Sept. 12, 1797, Windham wrote to Lord Grenville that they should retaliate by saving Pichégru from exile in Guiana. *Dropmore MSS.* iii. 374.

[4] The project was not lost sight of. Citoyen J. B. André, in a long memorial on England, dated 20 pluviôse, an iii. (Feb. 8, 1795), which he laid before the Committee of Public Safety, after describing the oppression in Scotland, summed up thus : "Tout fait résumer qu'elle reprendroit son ancienne indépendance si l'on aidoit à secouer le joug." *Corr. Polit.* (*Angl.*) 588, f. 313.

[5] Lecky, *Hist. of Eng.* vii. ; E. Guillon, *La France et l'Irlande pendant la Révolution*, *passim*.

missions of Oswald and Jackson, this society had been completely reorganised, had abandoned the advocacy of constitutional reform, and become definitely revolutionary. Tone laid a long memorial before the Directory, in which Ireland was represented as ready to welcome assistance from France. On the strength of this and other information, active preparations were made for sending a force to Ireland. But Tone was apprehensive lest this expedition should only be part of a general scheme of invading Britain. In April, 1796, in conversation with Aherne, who was to be sent to Ireland, he learnt to his dismay "that there was something going on regarding Scotland." "My opinion is," was Tone's comment, "that nothing will ever be done there, unless we first begin in Ireland." A fortnight later, a French general asked his opinion of *chouannising* England. Tone replied that "perhaps in Scotland, which, however, he was not sure of, it might do, but in England never." [1]

The Directory, however, wished to base their plans on more particular knowledge of these countries. As Delacroix pointed out to his colleagues, they were already acquainted with the troubles agitating England, Scotland, and above all, Ireland, and it was their duty to neglect nothing that would render them a source of profit to the Republic and of confusion to the most cruel of its enemies. Yet the fullest knowledge must be obtained of their extent and of the open or secret means of stimulating them. He proposed, therefore, that secret agents should be sent to England, Scotland, and Ireland, for this purpose.[2] The Directory concurred, and Citoyen Mengaud was selected for this service in Scotland. Elaborate instructions were drawn up for his guidance. During his stay in London he was to make inquiries as to

[1] W. T. Wolfe Tone, *Life of Wolfe Tone*, Washington, 1826, ii. 90, 99. Aherne, Tone notes, had already been employed in Scotland.

[2] *Corr. Polit.* (*Angl.*) 589, f. 241, 12 floréal an iv. (April 30, 1796).

the state of the funds, public opinion on the war, and other matters. He was then to proceed to Scotland, where he was to try to discover how far the discontent prevailing there might influence the actions of the people, and how far, should they be disposed to revolt, they would be willing to trust the French nation and take advantage of the efforts it would make on their behalf. After getting cautiously into touch with sympathisers, he was to question them as to their resources and the number of their supporters in the different classes of society. If they were not already in communication with the United Irishmen, he was to offer himself as an intermediary. He was also to find out in what ports and bays the Scottish revolutionaries would carry out their operations, so as to induce the French to show themselves. He was also to urge that persons enjoying the confidence of the people at large should be sent as delegates to France. These were to make their way with credentials to Hamburg, there to wait till the French Minister was informed of their arrival, when the necessary passports would be sent. Afterwards Mengaud was to cross to Ireland and make similar investigations.[1]

These plans of invading the British Isles were considerably modified after an interview with other envoys from the United Irishmen towards the end of the year. The expedition was limited to Ireland, and under General Hoche, preparations were pushed rapidly forward. On December 16, the flotilla sailed from Brest, only to return reduced in numbers in the following January without having landed a single troop. The Irish, contrary to all expectation, had not availed themselves of the opportunity, and this fact alone should have discredited the report of Mengaud, who arrived in Paris in July, " after running the greatest risks,

[1] *Corr. Polit.* (*Angl.*) 589, f. 215, 18 germinal, an iv. (April 6, 1796).

and having escaped as if by a miracle." [1] But the Directory was occupied with another project of invasion, and formally expressed satisfaction with his conduct.[2] His statement is couched in such general terms as to lead one to suspect that he never quitted London, though he avers that he "saw both Edinburgh and Glasgow." The Scots, he found, were more disposed to a revolution than the English, and the Irish to a still greater degree. This feeling, which had existed since the Union of England and Scotland and the conquest of Ireland, could be used to excite a civil war. He had not been able to accomplish much, as he had been recognised in London, but he had learnt enough to be persuaded that the policy of the Directory, strengthened by the triumphs of the French, would overthrow Great Britain sooner than was supposed.[3]

The new expedition was organised by the Dutch. But contrary winds prevented the sailing of the fleet at the very moment when the mutiny at the Nore rendered success probable. "All is ready," Tone noted in his diary on July 17, "and nothing is wanting but a fair wind." [4] By the time the weather had changed, the British fleet, restored to order, was mustered in force under Admiral Duncan at the mouth of the Texel. Every day strengthened Duncan's position, and the Dutch had to change their plans. Various alternative schemes were discussed. According to one, the fleet was to issue forth to fight. If the action was successful, fifty thousand men were to be sent to Scotland "in everything that would swim." After Edinburgh and Glasgow

[1] *Corr. Polit.* (*Angl.*) 591, f. 168, 25 messidor, an v. (July 12, 1797).

[2] *Ibid.* f. 218.

[3] *Corr. Polit.* (*Angl.*) 591, f. 174 *et seq.* Yet Nettement had written from London to Delacroix in July, 1796: "On se fait illusion, citoyen Ministre, lorsqu'on pense que nous trouverions ici des amis puissans. L'Écosse est parfaitement tranquille." *Ibid.* 589, f. 330.

[4] Tone, *op. cit.* ii. 421.

had been seized, the invaders were to maintain themselves along the line of the canal between Falkirk and Dumbarton. The vessels in the Clyde were then to be collected, so as to enable them to pass over into Ireland, which, by that time, would probably be denuded of troops for the defence of England. A later idea was to land all the Dutch soldiers in order to give the appearance of having abandoned the enterprise, and when Duncan's vigilance was relaxed, to make for Scotland.[1] In October, all such schemes were overturned by the defeat of the Dutch at Camperdown.

Yet so elated was Tone by the formation of the *Armée d'Angleterre* in the same month that he almost forgot to record this disaster.[2] Bonaparte, fresh from his victories in Italy, was put in command. The new project was highly popular in France, and it revived the hopes of the little colony of "Patriots" in Paris, mostly Irish and English, but including some Scots, who had been driven into exile by prosecution at home.[3] Tone had several interviews with Bonaparte as to the feasibility of co-operating with his countrymen in Ireland.[4] Somewhat later, another member of this community, a Scot named Watson, published a typical "Address to the People of Great Britain," inviting them to welcome the French. "Think of Ireland bleeding before you," he wrote to the Patriots of Scotland, "and be assured that the same fetters are being forged for you." Had Wallace died, had Buchanan and Fletcher written, had Ossian sung in vain? he asked. The name of their country could scarce be found on the map of Europe, but it was about to regain its pristine glory. Its forsaken hamlets, its heather-clad mountains, would resound with joy, and

[1] *Op. cit.* ii. 439, 441. [2] *Ibid.* ii. 452.

[3] V. J. G. Alger, *Englishmen in the French Revolution* and *Paris in 1789-1794*.

[4] *Op. cit.* ii. 455, 456.

Scotland would be free.[1] Pamphlets appeared describing former *Descentes en Angleterre,* and Hume and Robertson, whose histories had enjoyed an immense vogue in France, were cited to prove the tyrannical government of Scotland in the seventeenth century, which, it was calmly assumed, still prevailed at the end of the eighteenth.[2]

Public interest in this country was further stimulated by the arrival in France of Thomas Muir. On February 11, 1796, he escaped from Botany Bay in an American vessel. On reaching the west coast of North America, Muir, afraid of being recaptured by a British Man-of-war, set sail in a Spanish schooner and landed at Acapulco on the western shores of Mexico.[3] The viceroy sent him to Vera Cruz, whence he made his way to Havannah. There the governor detained him as a prisoner of war, and finally put him on board one of two frigates about to escort the viceroy's suite to Spain. While nearing Cadiz, the vessels fell in with two of Jervis's squadron. A fierce fight ensued, in which Muir was wounded,

[1] *Moniteur*, 4 frimaire, an vii. (Nov. 24, 1798). Alger, *Englishmen in the Fr. Rev.* 271-2. Cf. Théo. Mandar: "Ô Calédonie, Ô Fingal ! héros chantés par Ossian, vos épées seraient-elles tombées entre les mains des femmes, de ce sexe timide ! " etc. *Philippique adressée au Duc de Norfolk* in *Adresse au Roi de la Grande Bretagne*, 3e édn. Paris, an vii.

[2] *Précis Historique des Principales Descentes qui ont été faites dans la Grande Bretagne*, par le c. Peyrard, 2e édn. Paris, an vi. ; *Des Suites de la Contre-Révolution de 1660 en Angleterre*, par Benjamin Constant, Paris, an vii. ; *Tableau Historique et Politique de la Dissolution et du Rétablissement de la Monarchie Anglaise depuis 1625 jusqu'en 1702*, par le c. J. Chas. Paris, an viii.

[3] His biographer, P. Mackenzie, makes his hero traverse "a distance of over 4000 miles" on foot. This is taken from a contemporary, but for biographical purposes, worthless narrative entitled, *Histoire de la Tyrannie exercée envers le Célèbre Thomas Muir*, Paris, an vi. The more probable account of David in the *Moniteur* has been followed, supplemented by a letter from the French agent in the Windward Islands to Delacroix announcing Muir's escape and subsequent imprisonment at Havannah. *Corr. Polit.* (*Angl.*) 570, f. 260.

losing one eye and part of his cheek-bone.[1] It is said that he was about to be cast overboard as dead when he was recognised by one of the doctors of the British fleet who had been his school-fellow.[2] The doctor concealed his countryman's identity, and Muir was handed over to the Spanish authorities along with the other wounded. On his recovery he was again threatened with imprisonment. Fortunately, he found means of communicating with the Directory, and after some delay he was liberated as a French subject. An enthusiastic welcome awaited him at Bordeaux. He was entertained at a public banquet, where five hundred guests drank to the health of "The Brave Scottish Advocate of Liberty, now the Adopted Citizen of France." An immense crowd assembled in front of the illuminated building in which the celebrations took place, and his appearance on the balcony was greeted with shouts of "Long live the Defenders of Liberty!" In a few days the portrait of "Le Célèbre Thomas Muir" was everywhere on view.[3] An article by David in the *Moniteur* heralded his approach to Paris.[4] "He arrives in France," it concluded, "at the very moment when the *Grande Nation* is menacing England,

[1] V. Cobbett, *Political Register*, vii. 162-266: "The miscreant Muir has lost one eye, etc." These remarks were paraphrased in the *Porcupiniad* addressed to Cobbett by M. Carey, Philadelphia, 1799:

> "Muir the rascal's lost one eye,
> So far so good, or may I die.
> . . . .
> A thousand blessings on the ball
> That caused his wounds. Such fate befall
> All Jacobin traitors, great and small."
>
> (Cited in *Notes and Queries*, ser. 4, iii. 365.)

[2] P. Mackenzie, *Life of Thomas Muir*, 39 *et seq.*, also his *Reminiscences*, pt. i. *passim.*

[3] F. Michel, *Les Écossais en France, Les Français en Écosse*, ii. chap. xl. where the references to the *Moniteur* are given.

[4] *Moniteur*, 12 frimaire, an vi. (Dec. 2, 1797).

and is taking steps to realise the project which he had conceived. Let this apostle of philanthropy come among us, let him find in his new fatherland friends and brothers, and may our victorious cohorts call him back to the country which gave him birth there to establish liberty. . . . It would be impolitic as well as inhuman to leave in oblivion and expose to penury those illustrious strangers to whom we offer a place of refuge." Muir was not disposed to let himself be either forgotten or neglected. The Directory provided him with funds; he set up a carriage and lived in considerable style.[1] Nevertheless he continued to pester the Government with demands for money.[2]

As his health did not permit him to serve in the army of the Republic, he determined to aid it with his pen.[3] He made friends with Napper Tandy, and published articles on behalf of the United Irishmen, which roused the wrath of Wolfe Tone.[4] More interesting are the memorials on the state of England and Scotland which he laid before the French Minister for Foreign Affairs. In one he pointed out that there was no foundation for the belief current in France that the English lower classes would welcome an invader.[5] The case of Scotland was quite different, as he showed in

[1] Some glimpses of his life in Paris are given by the present writer in an article entitled *Two Glasgow Merchants in the French Revolution* (based on documents in the P.R.O., London, and F.O., Paris) in the *Scot. Hist. Rev.* Jan. 1911.

[2] In one letter he wishes to be put in immediate possession of a *Domaine National* valued at 150,000 francs, so as not to be obliged to abuse their kindness any longer. *Corr. Polit.* (*Angl.*) 590, f. 321. In another he desires to be informed at once of the intentions of the Directory. Other nations, he says, had offered him a place of retreat, and frigates had been despatched to find him, as the Minister for Foreign Affairs well knew. But he had sacrificed all for the sacred cause of the Republic. *Ibid.* 592, f. 144.

[3] *Ibid.* 590, f. 321.

[4] *Life*, ii. 461.

[5] Mémoire de Muir sur l'état d'Angleterre. *Corr. Polit.* (*Angl.*) 592, f. 161.

another, where he discussed at length the political condition of the country, the moral character of the people, their physical strength, the means of rendering a revolution successful, and how best it could be supported abroad.[1] His sketch of Scottish history was on the lines of French pamphleteers. "The pen of posterity would leave an indelible mark on the pages of Robertson and Hume." The Union between England and Scotland had been accomplished, in spite of Fletcher, by English bribes, and since then English influence had been paramount in its Parliamentary representation, in the universities, and in the Church. Commerce had been sacrificed to English interests, and in 1748 the country had been disarmed. Scotland was asking liberty, justice, and vengeance, from the French Republic, and the people were not unworthy of their assistance. They were well educated and industrious.[2] The artisans had been inspired by the French Revolution, and had held a solemn convention in 1792, which was to be carefully distinguished from the British Convention of 1793, "a miserable plaything of the English Government." But its members had been without arms, without money, without means of defence. In France the storms of liberty were then about to burst. "They could but expose their hearts and

[1] *Mémoires et Documents* (*Angl.*) ii. 153.

[2] In a document entitled, "Idées sur la Situation en Angleterre," dated brumaire, an v. (Oct.-Nov. 1796), the writer, who professes to have been obliged to flee from Scotland for taking part in the first Convention of the Friends of the People, concludes thus: "The Scots are all democrats because they read good authors. Rousseau, Montesquieu, etc., are in the hands of the workmen." *Mémoires et Docs.* (*Angl.*) 53, f. 215. It is a fact that the *Edinburgh Gazetteer*, which was largely circulated among this class, contained numerous advertisements of French works. V. No. 28, March 8, 1793, in the Brit. Mus. Cf. also *Mémoire Historique et Politique touchant la Conduite du Ministère de la Grande Bretagne à l'égard de la France*, Paris (?) an ii., *Corr. Polit.* (*Angl.*) 588, f. 213. "L'Écosse offrit encore un moyen de nuire au gouvernement britannique. Le peuple y est beaucoup plus instruit qu'en Angleterre; il estime les Français, il aime leur révolution."

their virtues." But since that time liberty had marched with giant steps. In case of invasion fifty thousand enlightened Highlanders would be ready to come forward. According to English newspaper reports, the Highland regiments had lately refused to fire on the United Irishmen. There had also been opposition to the enrolment of militia in Scotland. Altogether the French Government might count on the support of one hundred thousand patriots. The Scots would not be provoked by the Government into any partial rising; when they struck (and the time was soon coming), the blow would resound in every quarter. He suggested three ways in which they might be helped. The Republic should send officers, munitions of war, and money; a proclamation should be issued allowing freedom of worship and the right of every class to choose its own pastors; and the French troops should be warned to conduct themselves circumspectly. A provisional government could then be set up and an independent republic finally established.[1] Such was the extraordinary document that Muir, diseased in body and mind, submitted to his benefactors.[2]

In January, 1798, the British Government received secret intelligence that the Directory had determined, if successful,

[1] There is another memorial proposing an insurrection (1) in Scotland, (2) in England, (3) in the British fleet. The writer, a Scotsman, says he could carry out these plans "if he had a safe and confidential messenger to go to London and arrange to meet Muir *not in Paris*, but in some other place less suspicious." One part of the scheme was to seize the Castle of Edinburgh. The memorialist knew of a secret passage by which it could be surprised. The letter accompanying this document is dated 19 brumaire, an ix. (Nov. 10, 1800), but it should probably be an vii. *Corr. Polit.* (*Angl.*) 594, f. 53 *et seq.*

[2] Muir's account of the convention in which he took part is obviously false. Allowance must be made for the sufferings he had since undergone, and for his desire to increase his influence with the Directory. Tone says of him, "Of all the vain, obstinate blockheads that ever I met, I never saw his equal." *Life*, ii. 461. This description, and the tone of his correspondence at this period, show how far the character of the popular advocate of early days had changed.

to set up separate republics in England, Scotland, and Ireland, and that the " Scotch Directory " was to consist of Muir, Sinclair, Cameron, Simple, Lauderdale, and " a Sorbelloni," with Ferguson, Macleod, and Campell (*sic*), as Ministers.[1] A month later, Bonaparte reported adversely on the whole plan of invasion, and the energies of France, for some years to come, were turned into other channels. Before the projects were renewed, Muir had been laid to rest in the land of his adoption. He died in January, 1799, and was interred at Chantilly.[2]

[1] Secret Intelligence from France, January, 1798, *Dropmore MSS.* iv. 69 and 70. Sinclair was one of the delegates of the British Convention; Simple was probably Lord Sempill. Macleod was the M.P. for Inverness. For Cameron v. *infra*, chap. ix. *passim*. Campbell may have been the person mentioned *infra*, chap. ix. p. 188.

[2] Later accounts (*e.g. Dict. of Nat. Biog.*), following Mackenzie, give Sep. 27, 1798, as the date, but the *Moniteur*, 11 pluviôse, an vii. (Jan. 30, 1799), reports that he has just died as the result of the wounds he had received in the engagement near Cadiz. Mackenzie either suppressed, or was ignorant of Muir's dealings with the Directory, and all subsequent writers have derived their knowledge from him.

CHAPTER IX.

THE MILITIA RIOTS AND THE UNITED SCOTSMEN.

WHILE the Directory had been engaged in such schemes, Great Britain, "destitute of efficient allies, threatened with invasion, short of money, burdened with debt and taxation, with public credit at a low ebb, and its fleets in mutiny," had been passing through one of the most critical periods of its history.[1] The condition of Scotland had increased the anxiety of the Ministry. Since the trials of Watt and Downie, all democratic agitation had subsided, but in 1797 new causes of irritation against the ruling classes brought it once more to the surface.

During the wars of the eighteenth century, Scotland had been peculiarly open to attack, and the year 1760 had witnessed a demand for a Scottish militia on the lines of the English Act of 1757. In spite of a characteristic outburst of national feeling, it was refused on party grounds by the Newcastle Government.[2] During the American War the question was raised again, but no action was taken. "I recollect nothing more worth communicating at present," wrote John Hope to Townshend in October, 1782, "except the opinion of my father and some of the old Whigs in Scotland concerning their Militia so much talked of, that it would be rather dangerous to put arms in the hands of the fanatics in the west of Scotland; and I found, when I was lately in

[1] *Polit. Hist. of Eng.* x. 395. [2] Hume Brown, *Hist. of Scot.* iii. 341.

the neighbourhood of Edinburgh, that though most people were affronted at being refused a Militia, very few would exert themselves in it if it were really granted."[1] In December, 1792, Dundas had proposed bringing in a Scottish Militia Bill, but it was dropped, probably for similar reasons.[2] In 1797, however, the measure could no longer be delayed. It was known that the French had designs on Scotland, and privateers began to appear off the coasts. Internal tranquillity was secured by the Volunteers, and it was thought that the people could now be safely trusted.[3] In March, Dundas formulated his ideas on the subject in a long letter to the Lord Advocate.[4] Orders were given to suspend the enrolment of Volunteers except in the maritime counties,[5] and in June an Act was passed for embodying a militia force in Scotland.[6] By its provisions, 6000 men were to be called out in the following manner. The schoolmaster in each parish was to make a list of all the able-bodied men between the ages of nineteen and twenty-three. The names were to be posted up at the church door on the Sunday preceding the day fixed for the meeting of the deputy-lieutenants of the district, where complaints were to be heard, the lists revised, and a date appointed for the ballot. Married men with more than two children, and all Volunteers, privates as well as officers, were to be exempt. Among other advantages, the militiamen were to receive 1s. 1½d. a day,

[1] *Scot. Corr.* vol. i. Oct. 18, 1782.

[2] "The idea of a Militia is giving serious uneasiness to many people in this town and its neighbourhood, and I am fully convinced that it would be highly improper to trust arms in the hands of the lower classes of people here and in Paisley." Ld. Prov. Dunlop, Glasgow, July 16, 1793, *Scot. Corr.* vol. vii.

[3] Ld. Adv. to Home Secy. Feb. 15, 1797, *Scot. Corr.* vol. xiv.

[4] Appendix C.

[5] Draft Letter, March 1797, *Scot. Corr.* Supp. vol. lxii.

[6] 37 Geo. III. c. ciii.

and, on being disbanded, would be free to set up in business in any town without paying the customary dues.

In May, Robert Dundas had warned the Duke of Portland [1] that the Militia Bill was likely to be so much opposed and was so late in being brought forward, that it could not be counted on that summer as part of the national defence ; [2] but the authorities were totally unprepared for the fierce popular clamour that the enforcing of the Act provoked. From every quarter came reports of disorder.[3] The most serious disturbance occurred on August 29 at Tranent in East Lothian.[4] On the day preceding the statutory meeting for revising the lists, rumours reached the deputy-lieutenants that messages were passing from colliery to colliery, and from parish to parish, urging the people to resist. In the evening a crowd of some two or three hundred from Tranent made a tour of the neighbouring villages, beating drums and shouting " No Militia ! " " To Tranent ! " The lives of the schoolmasters were threatened until they handed over the parish registers to the mob. The officials took their precautions, and arrived in the village escorted by some of the local yeomanry and a detachment of the Cinque Ports Cavalry. They were received by a large crowd, composed chiefly of irate wives and mothers, who openly declared

[1] In July, 1794, he had been appointed Home Secretary in succession to Henry Dundas, who became Secretary of State for War and the Colonies. The new arrangement was very distasteful to the latter, and the Records show that he still continued to exercise a great influence on all matters pertaining to Scotland. Stanhope, *Life of Pitt*, ii. ch. xviii.; Holland Rose, *William Pitt and the Great War*, 271.

[2] Ld. Adv. to J. King, May 19, 1797, *Scot. Corr.* Supp. vol. lxii.

[3] Sir Henry Craik, the only historian who refers to this subject, minimises the opposition. *A Century of Scot. Hist.* ii. 166.

[4] An excellent account of the riot will be found in J. Miller's *The Lamp of Lothian*, new edn. Haddington, 1900, pt. i. ch. xix. The deputy-lieutenants' version was printed at the time as a handbill entitled *A Narrative of the Proceedings at Tranent.*

that they would never let them leave the town alive. Most of the soldiers, reinforced by two troops of the Pembrokeshire Cavalry, were posted at one end of the village, and the deputy-lieutenants made for the inn, where a guard was set and business proceeded with. A "round robin" against the Act, presented to them on behalf of the inhabitants of Prestonpans, was held to be highly seditious and was rejected, and the crowd, which had meanwhile been pelting the house with stones, redoubled the attack. An attempt was made to read the Riot Act, and the streets were cleared by the troops. The rioters, however, made a fresh onslaught from the fields behind the inn. The soldiers opened fire, and the cavalry, exasperated by the treatment they had received, threw off all restraint. Charging across the fields, they continued their mad career for a distance of two miles, shooting or cutting down all who crossed their path. Eleven people were killed and about twelve wounded, most of whom had taken no part in the riot.[1] Such brutality created an immense sensation in the eastern districts, and the *Scots Chronicle*, with which Morthland, a former Friend of the People, was connected, published a violent letter on the subject.[2] In the west and south the authorities experienced the same difficulties.[3] At Carstairs in Lanarkshire the schoolhouse was set ablaze, and the fire was only extinguished when the parish registers were given up to the people. In Kirkintilloch and the neighbourhood similar outbreaks took

[1] Miller, *op. cit.* His statement as to the number killed is corroborated by a letter of the parish minister of Tranent to the Marquis of Tweeddale: "I can be positive," he writes, "because I visited the families of the dead and wounded." *Edin. Univ. Laing MSS.* No. 500, Sept. 2, 1797. The Lord Advocate maintained that only seven had lost their lives. *Scot. Corr.* vol. xv. Dec. 26, 1797.

[2] *Scots Chronicle*, Sept. 1797.

[3] Correspondence in *Scot. Corr.* vol. xvii. and *Edin. Univ. Laing MSS.* Nos. 500 and 501.

place. At Freuchie in Fife, and Strathaven in Lanarkshire, delegates assembled to take joint action. Trees of Liberty were set up at Galston and Dalry in Ayrshire. The Duchess of Montrose, whose husband was Lord-lieutenant of the County of Stirling, had to be protected by a squadron of dragoons on her journey to Glasgow. From the south the unrest spread to the north. In Aberdeenshire "people's minds were set against the Act." In every district of Perthshire there were mobs and riots, according to the Duke of Atholl, who was forced to sign an obligation that he would do nothing further "until the general sentiments of the country were fully known." It was said that a Mr. Cameron was encouraging the resisters by issuing arms, and that nocturnal drills were taking place.

Various explanations were given of the general upheaval. The Lords-lieutenant held that the Act had been sprung upon the people so quickly that it was imperfectly understood. But there were other reasons. In the past the Government had not kept faith with the fencible corps raised especially in the Highlands. Pressure had been brought to bear upon the men to "volunteer" for service abroad, where they had been detained for an indefinite time. As no period of service was mentioned in the Act, the same fears were now entertained.[1] The age limit told more heavily on the sparsely populated districts than on the towns; and as all Volunteers were exempt from the ballot, the lower classes felt that they were being made to pay for either their poverty or their former disloyalty.

[1] In a petition in favour of John Christie, who had been condemned to seven years' transportation for taking part in a riot in Fife, it was stated "that uncommon pains had been taken by men of anarchical principles to inflame the minds of the people against the Militia Act by pretending the men were to be sent to the West Indies, etc." *Scot. Crim. Corr.* vol. liii. Aug. 1797. For the same difficulties experienced in enforcing the corresponding Act in Ireland, v. Lecky, *Hist. of Eng.* vii. 14, 15.

The *Scots Chronicle* and various handbills did not fail to point out these objections to the obnoxious measure.[1] The officials were afraid to act. "There is no end of alarm and requisitions for troops," wrote the Commander-in-Chief. The Duke of Portland deemed the crisis so serious that he thought a meeting of the Cabinet should be summoned—a proposal deprecated by Dundas as likely to increase resistance by emphasising its importance. On the other hand, he urged that no efforts should be spared to carry out the law, and 1400 men were at once drafted into Scotland. As an object lesson, these reinforcements included two regiments of English militia. Explanations of the Act were issued, and its advantages set forth. Subscriptions for substitutes were raised. The Volunteers co-operated with the Regulars in attending the lieutenancy meetings, and the ringleaders of the malcontents, including Cameron, were apprehended.[2] Overawed by the military, and cowed by the punishment that had overtaken the Tranent and other rioters, the people submitted to their fate, and on October 3, word was sent to the Secretary of State that all was quiet.

Yet it was some time ere the soreness of feeling caused by the repressive measures passed away. Morthland, though threatened with expulsion from the Faculty of Advocates, prepared to champion the cause of the relatives of those killed at Tranent by indicting for murder the soldiers who

[1] In forwarding precognitions regarding Cameron, Mr. A. Campbell (Perthshire) wrote to the Ld. Adv. on Oct. 16, 1797: "The *Scots Chronicle*, I have found, is worth a hundred Camerons." *Edin. Univ. Laing MSS.* No. 501.

[2] "It is clear that in all places where resistance has been made or is expected, they should not proceed till they are seconded by such an overpowering force as will ensure success. The yeomanry and every other person are much mistaken if they think their barnyards or anything else will be safer by timidity in taking care of themselves and their property." H. Dundas to Ld. Adv. Sept. 3, 1797, *Edin. Univ. Laing MSS.* No. 501.

had taken part in the affray.[1] But one of the deputy-lieutenants raised an action for damages against him and his colleague of the *Scots Chronicle,* for publishing the letter of the brother of a girl who had been killed in the riot, and for five years the case dragged on in the Court of Session and the House of Lords.[2] The Lord Advocate endeavoured to stop the proceedings against the troops. He lodged a complaint in court that the agent of the plaintiffs, a Writer to the Signet, had instigated the unfortunate people to take action; but the Court of Justiciary dismissed the plea as incompetent.[3] Thereupon the Lord Advocate, as Public Prosecutor, refused to indict the military, and this method of evading the difficulty, having been submitted to English counsel, was approved of by the Government.[4] Cameron and others were charged with mobbing and rioting. The former fled the country, and four were sentenced by Braxfield to fourteen years' transportation to Botany Bay for participating in a disturbance at Eccles in Berwickshire. This harshness defeated its purpose, for the jury, in subsequent trials, acquitted the accused, from a feeling that the punishment likely to be inflicted was too severe.[5] Eventually it

[1] Charles Hope published a motion which he intended to bring before the Faculty, *Edin. Evening Courant*, Sept. 21, 1797; *Scots Chronicle*, Nov. 21-24, 1797, where Morthland's correspondence with the Ld. Adv. is given. Fox in a speech on the anniversary of his election to Westminster denounced the treatment of Morthland and H. Erskine.

[2] Miller, *op. cit.*; *Scots Chronicle*, Mar. 9-13, 1798; Couper, *Edin. Period. Press*, ii. 212-8.

[3] *Scots Chronicle*, Nov. 21-24, 1797.

[4] A large number of declarations were taken, and a plan of Tranent was prepared showing the places where the victims had been shot. The Lord Advocate admitted that one case warranted a charge of murder against the individual who might be proved to have fired. *Scot. Corr.* vol. xv. Dec. 26. Counsel's opinion was "that he did not think it a case which called for a prosecution when the whole of the provocation was taken into consideration." Vol. xvi. Jan. 3, 1798.

[5] "Truth is the Lord Justice Clerk was too violent and hasty in

was found advisable to pardon most of the culprits as the best means of conciliating the people, with the result that future embodiments of the militia gave little trouble.[1]

Though the manner in which the Militia Act had been promulgated, and the methods employed to enforce it, were sufficient in themselves to account for the general disorders that ensued, the authorities both in Edinburgh and London were convinced that deeper causes could be assigned. "I am satisfied," wrote Henry Dundas to the Duke of Portland, "that the Advocate is right in believing that Jacobinism is, to a certain extent, at the bottom of it." [2] These views of the recent crisis were based not only on the reports of the Lords-lieutenant, but also on information regarding certain secret societies known as "United Scotsmen." The trials for High Treason in 1794, as has been indicated, had been a fatal blow to the Democrats, but there were a few individuals who still maintained a secret propagandism. In July, 1796, for example, Alexander Leslie, an Edinburgh bookseller, wrote to the London Corresponding Society offering to act as their representative. He stated that he had agents all over Scotland, and that he would be pleased to receive any of their publications, more especially medals like half-pence, for which there was a demand.[3] Other

pronouncing sentence, though at his age, and with the respect we all bear him, I should be sorry if he thought either your Grace, or those whose opinion he values, disapproves of his judgment in that case." Ld. Adv. to Home Secy. April 27, 1798, *Scot. Corr.* vol. xvi. Braxfield died on May 30, 1799.

[1] *Scot. Criminal Corr.* April 11 and June 5, 1799, vol. liii.

[2] *Scot. Corr.* vol. xiv. Aug. 27 and 30, Sept. 5, 1797.

[3] *Place Coll. Brit. Mus. Add. MSS.* 27815, f. 74. Some of these medals are preserved in the Coin Department of the Brit. Mus. In the same collection there are also loyalist medals. One inscribed "The Three Thomases, 1796" represents Thomas Paine, Thomas Spence (a publisher of Paine's works), and Thomas Muir, hanging on a gibbet. On the reverse is the legend, "May the three knaves of Jacobin Clubs never get a trick." *The Writings of Thomas Paine*, ed. M. D. Conway, iii. 11.

letters in the Place Collection prove that the London Corresponding Society tried to keep up communication with their sympathisers in Scotland.[1] In May, 1797, a Mr. Jameson arrived in Edinburgh. His conduct aroused suspicion; his letters were opened at the post office, and it was discovered that he was one of their emissaries. He was followed to Glasgow and other places in the vicinity, where he met with select parties of former Friends of the People.[2] Jameson seems to have made little progress among them, and learning that he had been found out, he entered the Government service as a spy to watch the ramifications of another organisation among the cotton spinners and weavers in the west.[3]

The members of the new societies adopted the name of United Scotsmen, after the example of the United Irishmen, many of whom had crossed over to Scotland owing to the troubles in their own country.[4] Like the latter, the United

[1] 27815, ff. 5, 16, 17, 136.

[2] *Scot. Corr.* vol. xiv. May 7, June 26, Aug. 16.

[3] Sheriff of Glasgow to the Ld. Adv. Nov. 18, 1797, *Scot. Corr.* vol. xv. Some of Jameson's reports are in vol. xvi. May, 1798.

[4] As it was reported that the United Irishmen were in correspondence with the disaffected in Scotland, a watch was set on the boats crossing to Port Patrick. From April to June, 1797, as many as 912 individuals arrived there "in the hold." "We still have swarms from Ireland," wrote the Lord Advocate, "but have sent back as many, indeed more, persons than in strict law we are authorised to do. But we must not stick at trifles." *Scot. Corr.* vol. xiv. July 14, 1797; also *Irish Corr.* vol. lxix. May 9, 1797. There can be no doubt that the United Scotsmen learnt the details of the Irish organisation from these refugees. The Glasgow members "were mostly Irish," according to one of their number who made an official declaration on his arrest. *Scot. Corr.* vol. xvi. April 13, 1798. A society of United Scotsmen was formed in Glasgow on November 5, 1793 (*Glasgow Advertiser*, Nov. 11-15). It was represented at the British Convention, but it seems to have had no connection with the later societies, which were secret organisations. This explains Mr. Omond's erroneous account of the British Convention in his *Lives of the Lord Advocates*, ii. 194.

Scotsmen had an elaborate system of committees—parochial, county, provincial, and national—oaths of secrecy, and private signs and passwords. A few meetings of delegates were held in Glasgow and the neighbourhood during the summer and autumn of 1797, and it was reported that the central committee intended to send representatives to London, among other places, when they had sufficient funds.[1] The spread of the associations eastwards was facilitated by the discontent provoked by the Militia Act.[2] The chief organiser in that district was George Mealmaker, who had already brought himself within the grasp of the law in connection with Palmer's trial and the British Convention.[3] Under his direction, the *Resolutions and Constitution of the Society of United Scotsmen*, closely approximating to those of the United Irishmen, were printed, and distributed in the counties of Forfar, Perth, and Fife.[4] A meeting of four delegates from Cupar, Kirriemuir, Brechin, and Coupar-Angus, was subsequently held in the house of Mealmaker, who was appointed to represent them on a National Committee; but he was apprehended at Dundee in November,[5]

[1] Declarations taken at Glasgow, April, 1798, *Scot. Corr.* vol. xvi.

[2] "You will observe that the first step of this system (imported from Ireland) has been by threats to intimidate justice from acting on the Militia Bill; while a mob being once collected, and having effected that purpose, are by degrees to be carried by Cameron and other ring-leaders to purposes widely different." Duke of Atholl to Ld. Adv. Sept. 10, 1797. *Scot. Corr.* vol. xv.

[3] Mealmaker was the author of the address on the war for the revising and circulating of which Palmer had been transported. He had also been arrested in connection with Watt's conspiracy.

[4] *State Trials*, xxvi. 1138. In December, 1797, a spy reported that 17 "citizens were united" and 17 "supposed to be united" in Perth. *Edin. Univ. Laing MSS.* No. 501.

[5] A. Warrender to Ld. Adv. Nov. 10, 1797. "But what is to be done in the West country?" he adds. "Something must be; for there, I suppose, the business originated and is in chief force."

and further arrests were made at Perth, Dunfermline, and Edinburgh.[1]

Mealmaker was tried in January, 1798.[2] He was charged with sedition, with publishing inflammatory pamphlets, and administering unlawful oaths contrary to an Act passed in the previous year. His counsel urged that the sole aim of the United Scotsmen, as stated in their constitution, was to agitate for annual Parliaments and universal suffrage. The oath of secrecy, he said, covered no treasonable design, but had been rendered necessary by the intolerance of the times. The Lord Advocate contended that friends of good order would never have sought at such a time to inquire into the defects of the constitution. The United Scotsmen had declared that they would never desist until they had obtained their object. If they brought over the majority, rebellion, in the prisoner's opinion, would be a moral duty. He had sought to encourage his confederates by pointing to the existence of similar societies in England and Ireland, and Parliamentary reform was a mere pretext for " a total overthrow of the Constitution and Government, for which they were to substitute, at least what subsists in a neighbouring kingdom, murder, rapine, and all the enormities which can disgrace human nature." Mealmaker received the usual sentence of fourteen years' transportation. " It is of essential importance," wrote Robert Dundas, " that Christie, Campbell, and Mealmaker should be sent to Botany Bay as soon as possible. The discoveries we are daily making of what is going forward among the United Scotsmen warrant me in what I am now

[1] *Scots Chronicle*, Nov. 10-14, Nov. 14-17. Among those arrested was Leslie, the bookseller. He was "fugitated" for non-appearance in May, 1798. *Scots Chronicle*, May 25-29, 1798.

[2] *State Trials*, xxvi. 1138 *et seq.*; Cockburn, *Exam. of Trials for Sedn.* ii. 150 *et seq.*

stating."[1] Others were arrested at Glasgow in April, but none of the accused seem to have been brought to trial.[2]

These vigorous measures were prompted by the dread lest the rebellion which had broken out in Ireland should spread to Scotland, and the same fears had led to similar action in England. Two delegates of the United Irishmen, Arthur O'Connor and O'Coigley or Quigley, were apprehended at Margate in February, 1798, on their way to France, along with John Binns, who had been attempting to form societies of United Englishmen in London. The chief members of these associations were seized on April 18, and the committee of the Corresponding Society on the following day. As a result of information thus obtained, the suspension of the Habeas Corpus Act was immediately renewed, and in March, 1799, a committee of secrecy of the Commons presented a *Report relative to the Proceedings of Different Persons and Societies in Great Britain and Ireland engaged in a Treasonable Conspiracy*, which was followed by another from the Lords in May.[3] In these it was confidently asserted that all the "United" in Great Britain had been in the closest correspondence with the United Irishmen, whose acknowledged aim was to set up a republic in their country with the aid of the French. The treasonable designs of the original conspirators had been amply revealed by the recent events in Ireland, but there can be no doubt that the operations of their British associates were exaggerated. Francis Place, who was intimately acquainted with the extreme reformers in London, says that the United Englishmen consisted of some twelve

[1] *Scot. Corr.* vol. xvi. Feb. 13, 1798. Christie, and probably Campbell, had been sentenced in connection with Militia Riots in Fife. Braxfield reported adversely on a petition in Christie's favour. *Scot. Crim. Corr.* vol. liii. Aug. 1798.

[2] The declarations of the prisoners will be found in *Scot. Corr.* vol. xvi.

[3] *Parl. Hist.* xxxiv. 579 *et seq.* They were also published in pamphlet form.

enthusiasts, such as Binns and Evans, who had learned the details of the Irish organisation from O'Coigley.[1] With characteristic energy they had set to work, collecting adherents and preparing manifestoes. According to the Report, they had been so successful as to establish forty societies in London, but Place believed that not a single one existed, and that the April meeting where the agitators were arrested was the first that had ever been held.[2] He also maintained that the account of the London Corresponding Society was "a mass of exaggerations and falsehoods." "What remained of it," he says, referring to January, 1798, "was its refuse, with the exception of a few who, from what they considered conscientious motives, still adhered to it." Though these people voted an address to the United Irishmen—"a disgrace on those who passed it"—the society "had no secret whatever." Yet the same authority admits that Binns and his friends, connected both with this association and the United Englishmen, had aimed at a revolution, and it is not surprising that the Government, under the circumstances, regarded their operations as the culmination of designs which could be traced back to the year 1792.[3] Beyond their intercourse with O'Coigley and O'Connor, however, the United Englishmen appear to have had no communication with the United Irishmen in Dublin, who indeed disapproved of all such propagandism in Great Britain lest the attention of the French should be diverted from Ireland. For the same reason they had no dealings with the United Scotsmen.[4] It is true that, in a letter to

[1] *Brit. Mus. Add. MSS.* 27808, *passim.*

[2] Place was invited, but he refused.

[3] With much less reason the Committee of Secrecy attempted to connect the United Scotsmen with the Friends of the People of 1792.

[4] In August, 1798, O'Connor, M'Nevin, and Emmet, three leaders of the United Irishmen, gave evidence on oath before a secret committee of the Irish House of Lords. Lecky, *Hist. of Eng.* viii. chap. xxx. *passim.*

the French Directory, the Secret Committee of England stated that a delegate from the Irish and the Scots "was now sitting with them."[1] The Scots are said to have intended sending a representative, but it is unlikely that they ever had sufficient funds to defray the expense; and the person referred to may have been Cameron, or one of his associates who, having been outlawed in connection with the militia riots, came to London and assumed this rôle.[2]

In his examination O'Connor admitted that "there might have been some slight connection between the north and the Scotch and English societies, but that there was no close connection between them and the Executive Directory of the Union." "Any connection with them," he says in another passage, "was merely between individuals. The Irish Executive Directory wished to keep clear of them." *Report of the Secret Committee of the House of Lords (Ireland), August 30, 1798.* Dublin, 1798. Append. iv.; v. also the *Second Report*, Sept. 1798. These statements are corroborated by the documents in the *Irish Corr.* vols. lxii. and lxix. Thus on July 23, 1796, news came from Belfast that two delegates had been sent to Glasgow, and that they had returned in high spirits with the message that "the Scotch were willing and ready to act with the Friends of Liberty in Ireland." The same information was discussed three days later, at a Northern Provincial meeting of United Irishmen. In May, 1797, one Stephenson was said to be going on a mission to Paisley. The only paper which contradicts O'Connor's evidence states that three delegates from the United Britons had been sent to the *National* Committee at Dublin. This, however, may have been a mere rumour due to the publication of their address to the United Irishmen in January, 1798. *Parl. Hist.* xxxiv. 641; *Irish Corr.* vol. lxxv. Feb. 1 and 23, 1798.

[1] *Parl. Hist.* xxxiv. 646.

[2] There are two documents in the French Foreign Office Archives which throw some light on this point. In a letter, dated Paris, 13 vendémiare, an vi. (Oct. 4, 1797), O'Coigley and another United Irishman state that while in London they had become acquainted with members of the chief revolutionary committee of England, who had charged them to communicate certain information. They had also met a delegate from the United Scotsmen sent expressly to ascertain from the English patriots whether they were willing to assist their brethren in Scotland and Ireland. "He gave them to understand that the Scottish patriots were very powerful and ready to act with those of England and Ireland at any moment." *Corr. Polit.* (*Angl.*), 592, f. 43. The other document is a pretentious memorial, dated July 19, 1799, drawn up by "le citoyen Watson," probably the person mentioned *ante*, chap. viii. p. 171. He describes himself as "President of the Executive Committee

The organisation of the United Scotsmen existed largely on paper, and what Lord Rosebery says of the conspiracy of Watt in 1794 might be applied to theirs: "It was on so small a scale that it might well have been treated as venial." While the United Irishmen could be numbered by thousands, the United Scotsmen never amounted to more than a few hundreds of "the lowest order."

On July 12, 1799, an Act was passed suppressing all these societies by name. Continued dearth,[1] and the operation of the corn laws,[2] provided a fund of discontent upon which

of the London Corresponding Society, Member of the British Union, and Representative of the Associations of Bath, Bristol, etc., to the Directory of the French Republic." After giving an exaggerated account of the numbers and importance of the United Scotsmen, he goes on to say that the United Britons determined to send four delegates to the French Government. Williams and himself were selected as representatives of the English, and James Kennedy and Angus Cameron of the Scots. These plans were upset by the prompt action of the authorities. Five hundred patriots were arrested. He himself escaped to France, but the other delegates were still in London, and he adds a short sketch of their careers. Kennedy was assistant secretary of the British Convention, was arrested in 1794, and since his liberation, had been employed on various missions by the popular societies. Angus Cameron was a Highlander, and an orator of great importance among his countrymen, fifteen thousand of whom had risen at his call to oppose the Militia Act. *Mémoires et Documents* (*Angl.*), 53, f. 361. From these distorted statements the only deduction that can be safely drawn is, I think, the one given in the text. For Kennedy, v. *State Trials*, xxiii. 1181; for Cameron, *supra*, and *State Trials*, xxvi. 1170. Gray, one of Mealmaker's confederates who, according to the Report, had escaped to Hamburg, had never left Britain. *Scot. Corr.* vol. xviii. May 23, 1802.

[1] "Bread and corn are at a price high beyond all former experience." Ld. Prov. of Edin. to Duke of Portland, Mar. 11, 1800, *Scot. Corr.* vol. xvii. In Dumfries, a labourer's wage was one shilling a day, and oatmeal was selling at five shillings a stone. *Ibid.* Nov. 11, 1800.

[2] In a petition from the Friendly Societies of Dumfries, consisting of 2000 members, it was represented that the crop of 1799 had been bad, but that they had "calmly submitted to the will of Providence." Though the crop of 1800 was good, provisions were still dear. Dumfries was near Cumberland and Liverpool, and dealers exported. This had been prohibited, but the law was evaded by taking the grain to a southern Scottish port and thence by land to England. *Scot. Corr.* vol. xvii. Oct. 29, 1800.

agitators might still draw. The United Scotsmen continued to maintain a spasmodic activity, especially in Glasgow and the county of Fife, down to 1802. In that year, Thomas Wilson, a Fife weaver, was charged with sedition, a crime all the more heinous in his case as he had been a Volunteer.[1] But his comparatively lenient sentence of a month's imprisonment and two years' banishment showed that a calmer view of the situation was beginning to prevail in official circles, and from this date the United Scotsmen ceased to trouble the authorities.[2]

During the winter of 1800-1 there were meal riots all over the country, and the Volunteers and Regulars were in constant requisition to suppress them. *Scot. Corr.* vol. xvii.

[1] Cockburn, *Exam. of Trials for Sedn.* ii. 168. Wilson in March, 1802, acted as a delegate of the United Scotsmen. Copy of an examination taken by the Sheriff of Fife, March (?) 1802, *Scot. Corr.* vol. xviii.

[2] A good deal of uneasiness was caused by the fear of spies. The poet Campbell was suspected on his return home from a tour in Germany, and a warrant was issued against him. He cleared himself by a voluntary declaration before the Sheriff of Edinburgh, who reported: "He is a young man of some literary talents, and I understand supports himself by writing for the booksellers. Like many of his class he entertains rather free notions on political subjects, but I do not suppose he has carried them further than loose conversation." *Scot. Corr.* vol. xviii. May 19, 1801.

CHAPTER X.

THE CHURCH AND THE FRENCH REVOLUTION.

TOWARDS the close of the century, the forces brought into play by the French Revolution began to manifest themselves under new forms of energy in the Church. In 1784 the Moderates had secured a definite victory in the patronage controversy, and since then the same conditions that made for conservatism in the State had strengthened their position. The avowed aim of this party was to retain the governing and educated classes within its fold, and as the panic due to the ferment in France spread to Scotland, it was among the ministers of the Established Church that these sections of the community found their most efficient allies. The few who, like Somerville of Jedburgh, had evinced an early admiration for the Revolution, soon repented of their premature enthusiasm,[1] and joined those clerical pamphleteers who were inveighing against all innovation as not only dangerous but even impious. Paine in his *Rights of Man* had scoffed at Burke's idea of the indissoluble tie that bound together Church and State, and his *Age of Reason,* though originally intended to stem the flood of atheism in France,[2] confirmed the belief that

[1] Somerville, *Own Life,* 268. He published *Observations on the Constitution and State of Britain,* Lond. 1793; *Effects of the French Revolution,* Edin. 1793.

[2] *Works,* ed. M. D. Conway, iv. 21.

political reform and free-thinking went hand in hand. It is true that opinions not essentially different from those of Paine had long been fashionable among those ranks of society frequented by the Moderates,[1] but when the worship of the Supreme Reason was set up in Paris, when Paine's "bawbee blasphemies"[2] were found circulating among weavers and artisans, a cry of "The Church in Danger" was immediately raised. To such a cry even the Popular Party could not remain indifferent, and it was therefore with one voice that the clergy denounced all democratic aspirations.[3]

Their exertions in this direction were, in most instances, doubtless disinterested, but the Government, by a judicious distribution of its favours, did not fail to emphasise the importance it attached to their support. On the death of Principal Robertson, for example, the royal chaplaincies were increased to six,[4] afterwards to ten, and Dundas apparently went so far as to offer one of the new posts to Dr. Erskine, the venerable leader of the Popular

[1] Paine was a Deist. "I believe in God . . . I believe that religious duties consist in doing justice, loving mercy, and endeavouring to make our fellow creatures happy." *Ibid.* As early as 1746, Ramsay of Ochtertyre noted that "Deism, apparelled sometimes in one fashion and sometimes in another, was making rapid progress." Hume Brown, *Hist. of Scot.* iii. 363 and 373, where later evidence of free-thinking as a fashionable mental attitude is given. But whereas the Moderates who preached mere "heathen morality" were content with ignoring Christian mysteries, Paine openly attacked them.

[2] So Meg Dods characterises them in *St. Ronan's Well*, ch. xiv.

[3] Cf. Address of the Moderator of the General Assembly, 1794: "If designing men attempt to seduce the inhabitants of this country to sedition and rebellion by talking to them of the majesty and sovereignty of the people as Korah, Dathan, and Abiram of old . . . shall not ministers expose the enormity of such designs and set before men the terrors of the Lord that they may be prevented from 'perishing in the gainsaying of Core?'" *Scot. Reg.* ii. 273-4.

[4] Somerville, *op. cit.* 284.

Party.[1] On the other hand, this system of rewards tended to create sycophants like James Lapslie, minister of Campsie, the worst specimen of his class. For his officiousness in securing evidence against Muir, he received a pension for himself and his family,[2] and he continued to pester the Lord Advocate for even more substantial recognition of his services.[3]

Those outside the pale of the Established Church were not forgotten in the desire to preserve domestic peace. The Episcopalians were gratified by the removal of their religious disabilities in 1792,[4] and in the following year a Relief Bill conferred a similar boon on the Roman Catholics. To secure the good will of the latter, Henry Dundas exerted his influence to procure for them secret State aid.[5] Their resources had been much diminished by the loss of the Scots College in Paris during the anarchy in France, and in 1796 an application for pecuniary assistance was made on their behalf to the Home Secretary, on the ground that it

[1] At all events Erskine wrote to the Lord Advocate saying that he had explained to the brethren with whom he was most connected the Government's intention regarding "the new chaplaincies." He declined "what Mr. Secretary Dundas was so obliging as to offer to himself," but recommended two other divines, presumably of his own party. "I have only to add," he concludes, "I beg you would assure Mr. Secretary Dundas that the ministers with whom I have conversed on this subject and with whom I am accustomed to act on other occasions, may be entirely relied on as zealous friends to the constitution." *Scot. Corr.* July 25, 1793.

[2] "Rev. James Lapslie, The Pension Hunter," Kay, *Orig. Portraits*, ii. 113.

[3] *Edin. Univ. Laing MSS.* No. 500, June 27, 1798, Aug. 1799.

[4] Grub, *An Eccles. Hist. of Scot.* Edin. 1861, iv. ch. lxxxii. *passim.* "Fox remarked that the king's ministers were very ready to grant relief to one class of Dissenters in Scotland, although they had opposed a motion of his in favour of the English Unitarians."

[5] Life of Bishop Hay in the *Journal and Appendix to Scotichronicon and Monasticon*, J. F. S. Gordon. Glasgow, 1867. I. chaps. xxi. and xxii. The English Roman Catholics had already received a grant.

would prevent emigration. As an indication of their loyalty, the Scottish hierarchy issued a Pastoral Letter in February, 1798, in which they pointed out that while "everybody ought to bear his part in the common defence," Roman Catholics had special cause to arm against the French, since "their Holy Father had been banished from his Chair and become a prisoner in their hands."[1] When negotiations were renewed towards the end of the year, it was represented to Dundas that the subsidy "would secure friends to the great cause of subordination and allegiance to His Majesty's Government." Such arguments proved successful. £600 and a yearly allowance of £50 were given to the two Roman Catholic Seminaries in Scotland, as well as a sum sufficient to make up the salaries of the priests to £20. In addition, each of the Vicars Apostolic was to receive £100 a year, and their coadjutors £50. The profoundest secrecy had to be maintained regarding this grant from the public funds, and even the Roman Catholic laity were kept in ignorance.[2]

The attitude of various groups of Seceders with respect to the burning questions of the day caused much more anxiety to those entrusted with administration.[3] By this

[1] *Scot. Corr.* vol. xvi. May 7, 1798. Gordon, *op. cit.* 407. Hay's coadjutor Geddes, who shared in its composition, had already written *Carmen Seculare pro Gallica Gente*, an ode in praise of the French Revolution. It was published with an English translation, Lond. and Paris, 1790.

[2] The grant, which was never regularly paid, ceased in 1805. Gordon, *op. cit.* 416. "Nor can we doubt that the original concession was dictated by motives of political expediency rather than by any real sense of what justice required." Bellesheim, *Hist. of Cath. Church of Scot.* trans. Hunter Blair, iv. 256.

[3] Referring to an advertisement of the Unitarians in Edinburgh, the Lord Advocate wrote: "It should be treated as the raving of some mad man. My hope is the good people of Edinburgh will rise and pull down the house to pieces, and sure I am their conduct in doing so should be winked at." Ld. Adv. to J. Davidson, London, March 19, 1792. *Edin. Univ. Laing MSS.* No. 294.

time they had increased to about 150,000. Of these, one-fifth belonged to the Relief Church, which had been set up as a result of the second secession in 1761. The first Seceders of 1733 had eventually constituted themselves under the name of the Associate Synod. In 1747, the Burgess Oath led to a division within their ranks. The Anti-Burghers objected to the clause binding the subscriber to acknowledge that " the true religion " was " presently professed within this realm," and formed the General Associate Synod. The Burghers accepted the oath and retained the original name of Associate Seceders. Each branch now numbered about 50,000.[1] In November, 1792, Henry Dundas, writing from Melville Castle to Pitt, reported that while the clergy of the Established Church were loyal, the others were far otherwise.[2] This impression was probably due to the part played by some of the Seceding ministers in the reforming societies.[3] Pulteney, during his stay in Scotland,[4] was therefore commissioned to make further investigation regarding their sentiments. James Peddie of the Burgher Synod, with whom he communicated, assured him that there was no reason to suppose that the members of the Secession were otherwise disposed than their predecessors in 1745, when an official inquiry proved that not one of them had joined the Pretender. He himself had signed the resolutions lying at the Goldsmiths' Hall, and if his colleagues had not collectively expressed their attachment to the constitution,

[1] In 1799 the Seceders are said to have numbered 154,000—Reformed Presbytery, 4000; Anti-Burgher Synod, 55,000; Burgher Synod, 55,000; Relief Church, 36,000; Methodists, Independents, Baptists, etc., 4000. G. Struthers, *Hist. of the Relief Church*, 408.

[2] J. Holland Rose, *William Pitt and the Great War*, 77.

[3] V. lists of delegates to the various conventions of the Friends of the People.

[4] V. *ante*, ch. v. p. 103. Wm. Pulteney to H. Dundas, Dec. 3, 1792, *Scot. Corr.* vol. vi.

it was on account of a rebuff they had experienced in 1769, when their address to the King had not been accepted because "they were not known in law." [1]

The Anti-Burghers, however, were distinguished by the zeal with which they endeavoured to maintain the testimony of the historic covenants of 1638 and 1643. In 1795, they provided fresh grounds for the insinuations against the Seceders in general by characterising as unwarrantable, "all declarations or subscriptions expressive of an unqualified satisfaction with a government" of which the Anglican Church was a component part. At the same meeting of Synod, a formal complaint was preferred against one of their divines, John Young of Hawick, who, in his *Essays on Government*,[2] had come forward to defend the British Constitution and free his brethren from the aspersions cast upon their loyalty. In these vigorous publications he had condemned the Friends of the People, and justified the war with France and the measures taken to crush the sedition at home. They became so popular that they ran through several editions in a few months, and the author was even offered a Government pension, which he refused. He was now accused in his own Synod of making statements regarding the connection of Church and State which were not in harmony with the principles of the Anti-Burghers. A committee was appointed to examine his writings, but nothing came of its deliberations. The same scruples prevented the adoption of a report prepared by another committee to prove that, "consistent with their solemn engagements to promote reformation," they had always "inculcated obedience to the civil authorities of the country." [3] In 1798, the Burghers voted a loyal address,

[1] J. Peddie to Pulteney, Dec. 26, 1792, *Scot. Corr.* vol. vi.

[2] Edin. 1794.

[3] M'Kerrow, *Hist. of the Secession Church*, ii. ch. 2, *passim.*

and it seems to have been effectual in clearing the Seceders as a whole from the charge of disaffection.[1]

Meanwhile these discussions, together with the overthrow of the religious establishment in France, had revived in all branches of the Secession the question of the relation of Church and State.[2] Not a few ministers of the Relief seized the occasion to call attention to the distinctive principle of their own communion by publishing pamphlets advocating the abolition of a national system of religion.[3] But among the Burghers and Anti-Burghers a controversy arose which produced further schisms.[4] While the "New Lights" averred[5] that the power ascribed to the civil magistrate in the Confession of Faith was Erastian, the "Old Lights," professing an unwavering belief in the National Covenant and the Solemn League and Covenant, maintained that it was the duty of rulers to employ their authority in the active support of the interests of religion. The New Lights were successful in both bodies in retaining the adherence

[1] M'Kerrow, *op. cit.* ii. 356. After consulting the Lord President of the Court of Session, and the officials of the Church of Scotland, the Lord Advocate forwarded it to the Duke of Portland with the following explanation: "In this country the Seceders amount as nearly as can be calculated to 100,000 persons, and your Grace will recollect that it has been, with too much reason, hitherto believed that the great majority of their pastors are as hostile to the state as to the religious Establishment. Whether that belief has hitherto been erroneous and unjust, or that the danger of the country has opened their eyes to their real duty and allegiance, I cannot but warmly approve and recommend to your Grace's acceptance this spontaneous and unsolicited pledge of the loyalty of so large a portion of the people." *Scot. Corr.* vol. xvi. May 1.

[2] Struthers, *op. cit.* ch. xxi. "Effects of the French Revolution."

[3] Struthers, *op. cit.* p. 382.

[4] M'Kerrow, *op. cit.* ii. chaps. iv. and viii. "The Secession Church [Burgher and Anti-Burgher] did not escape the sifting and liberalising influence of the French Revolution." Struthers, *op. cit.* 384.

[5] "As one result of the spread of the so-called rational opinions which sprang from the French Revolution." D. Scott, *Annals and Statistics of the Original Secession Church*, Edin. 1886, p. 38.

of most of their congregations.[1] This adoption of Voluntaryism paved the way for the future union of the Seceding Synods, the members of which exercised a considerable influence on public opinion when the same controversy became acute within the Established Church at a later time.

The dangers to which a State Church is peculiarly exposed had been emphasised in the pamphlets of the period,[2] and were practically exemplified in the condition of the Church of Scotland itself. For there can be no doubt that the close alliance between the Kirk, more especially the Moderates, and the partisans of Dundas, had been hurtful to its true interests. In Burke's phrase it had rendered the clergy "culpably obsequious to every measure of Government."[3] However anxious the Manager of Scotland might be to secure their support, he could not afford to offend the landed interest, as was shown by his acquiescence in the rejection of a much-needed Augmentation of Stipends Bill in 1793.[4] Patronage, which, in the opinion of its more enlightened defenders, was to be a means of raising the social status

[1] The New Lights among the Burghers carried the day in the Synod of 1799. Their opponents, seconded by Dr. Porteous of Glasgow, one of H. Dundas's regular correspondents in Church affairs, accused them of sedition. The charge was so persistently made in a case which came before the courts regarding congregational property, that the Lord Advocate was asked by the judges to investigate the matter. After inquiry, he acquitted them publicly as the victims of groundless slanders. M'Kerrow, *op. cit.* ii. chap. viii.; W. Porteous, *The New Light Examined*, Glasgow, 1800; J. Peddie, *A Defence of the Associate Synod against the Charge of Sedition*, *Addressed to Wm. Porteous*, *D.D.*, Edin. 1800.

[2] Smith of the Relief Church wrote: "The alliance of church and state is an ancient political engine." Struthers, *op. cit.* 382.

[3] V. *ante*, ch. iv. p. 69 fn.

[4] The Bill was prepared by the Lord Advocate; Kay, *Orig. Portraits*, ii. 119. "Sorry don't agree with you on Ministers' Stipend Bill. All against it." Letter of Sir J. Inglis to the Lord Advocate relating to the action of the county gentlemen of Midlothian, March 22, 1790. *Edin. Univ. Laing MSS.* No. 500.

and culture of the clergy, had been far more successful as a political instrument. The livings in the gift of the Crown had been freely used for party purposes.[1] Thus there crept into the Church the evils predicted by Hutcheson, who may be regarded as the inspirer of the early Moderates. "Instead of studying sobriety of manners, piety and diligence, or literature," he wrote in 1735, "one or other of which qualities are now necessary to recommend the candidates to the favour of heritors, elders or presbytery, the candidate's sole study will be to stand right in politics, to make his zeal for the *ministry of state* conspicuous; or by all servile compliance with the humour of some great lord who has many churches in his gift, whether the humour be virtuous or vicious, to secure a presentation."[2] Men of such opposite sympathies

[1] "The Duke lost the election by two votes, but is pretty certain of it next time. At the same time, unless the country sees the Duke has the influence to procure these trifles the Country Gentlemen only can judge of, it is almost impossible for the Duke to bring in friends to administration." Letter of the Duchess of Gordon asking for a Crown presentation in favour of some protégé. H. Dundas, however, recommended Lord Sydney to support the nominee of Lord Findlater, the Duke's opponent. *Scot. Corr.* Supp. lix. Jan. 15, 1788.

[2] Quoted by J. M'Cosh, *Scottish Philosophy*, 66. There are numerous references in the official correspondence of the time to Crown presentations being made in favour of young men of unimpeachable political principles. On Dec. 29, 1792, Lord Ruthven writes as follows to H. Dundas in favour of a minister: "I assure you that both in a religious and political view he is to be depended upon. He appears to be thoroughly well affected to the present Constitution and Government, and has distributed many pamphlets to that purpose in his parish, and in his religious principles is quiet and remarkably temperate." *Scot. Corr.* vol. vi. Sir J. Colquhoun in recommending a young man who had been in his family for ten years, states that "his political principles are such that we need not be afraid of him." *Edin. Univ. Laing MSS.* No. 500, Dec. 19, 1795. On May 16, 1799, the Rev. Robert Moodie writes to the Rev. Dr. Finlayson regarding a vacancy in the parish of Denny. "We want a moderate man. You know the many struggles we have had in the Presbytery: we should not always be left in a minority as it is now in the power of the Crown to give us some relief, and the parish requires a firm, steady, loyal man to counteract that spirit of Sedition and Democracy which abounds there, more perhaps than in any other parish in this

as Cockburn and Carlyle of Inveresk agree that the policy of the Moderates had failed both to attract the aristocracy of rank or intellect, and to maintain among the clergy the standard of learning which had characterised their more immediate predecessors.[1]

Moreover, the stern enforcement of patronage and the political preoccupations of the pulpit tended to lower the Church in the eyes of the common people. Somerville confesses that his attempts to "counteract anarchical principles" among his parishioners "lessened his authority";[2] and other divines, animadverting on Dundas's conduct with regard to the Stipend Augmentation scheme, declared in the General Assembly that by their support of Government they "had risked the friendship of their flocks and their own usefulness as pastors."[3] The horror of French infidelity healed this breach to some extent, but there were still large masses of the population outside all Church influence, especially in the rapidly growing towns. This was partly due to defects in ecclesiastical organisation, but largely to the spirit of the age which deprecated all religious enthusiasm. The Church of Scotland did not lend itself to expansion.[4] It

neighbourhood." *Ibid.* Sometimes a mistake was made. A Mr. Garvie was recommended for the church at Brechin. His opponents insinuated that he was a man of "democratic principles," and he was set aside. Thereupon a chorus of protest was raised, and Dundas admitted that he had been misled. "A bad case," he observes. *Scot. Corr.* vol. xvi. and Supp. vol. lxii. Jan. 1798. For the same methods at work in Crown appointments to university chairs, v. D. Welsh, *Life of T. Brown*, 165, and an interesting letter of Dundas to Pelham in *Pelham Papers*, *Brit. Mus. Add. MSS.* 33, 108, f. 450.

[1] *Carlyle MSS.*, quoted by Graham, *Scottish Men of Letters*, 99, note; Cockburn, *Memorials*, 202-4.

[2] *Own Life*, 267.

[3] "Faithful Service Rewarded," a caricature depicting Dundas astride two asses, representing Carlyle and Grieve, who had made the above remarks. Kay, *Original Portraits*, ii. 120.

[4] Cunningham, *Church History of Scotland*, ii. 564.

was difficult to erect new parishes. A few Chapels of Ease had been built by manufacturers, but as others had their origin in the reluctance of the people "to attend the ministry of some unpopular presentee," the Assembly, in 1798, passed an Act regulating the granting of constitutions to these chapels, which, according to the Popular Party, discouraged further effort in this direction.[1] The parish ministers did little to cure the evil, for though probably faithful enough in discharging their prescribed duties, most of them were absorbed in other pursuits than what Shaftesbury called "the passion of saving souls."[2]

It was one of the results of the French Revolution, that, by effecting a change in the temper of the times, it ushered in an era of religious activity—an activity which displayed itself in missionary enterprise, first abroad and then at home. The current ideas of political freedom, according to Warneck, a recent historian, contributed to awaken this interest. "Connected with these was the idea of humanity which proclaimed the common rights of men. Revolutionary as those ideas were, and little based on religion as was the advocacy of common human rights, yet they rendered preparatory service to the missionary movement by bringing about, in connection with Rousseau's ideals of nature, a change in the estimate of non-Christian and uncivilised humanity, and by making it materially easier for Christian circles to assert the right of all men to the Gospel also."[3] Nowhere was the connection of the new religious developments with the upheaval in France more clearly indicated than in Scotland.[4]

[1] W. M. Hetherington, *Hist. of Church of Scot.* 229.

[2] Mathieson, *op. cit.* 211.

[3] G. Warneck, *Outline of a Hist. of Christian Missions*, 8th edn. trans. by G. Robson, 3rd edn. p. 77.

[4] Hume Brown, *Hist. of Scot.* iii. 392-3.

The Baptist Missionary Society was founded in England in 1792, and the London Missionary Society in 1795. The enthusiasm evoked in certain quarters spread to Scotland, and in 1796 missionary associations were established in Edinburgh, Glasgow, and other towns. In May the subject was brought before the General Assembly by the Synods of Fife and Moray, which sent in overtures advocating the participation of the Church in such work. In the debate which ensued, Dr. Hill, the leader of the Moderates, insinuated that the rules of the missionary associations lent themselves to political propagandism. An elder, David Boyle, afterwards Lord Justice Clerk, further developed this argument. "Observe," he said, "the societies are *affiliated*, they *correspond with each other*, they *look for assistance from foreign countries* in the very language of many of our seditious societies." The overtures were rejected by fifty-eight votes to forty-four, and a colourless resolution was adopted recommending the brethren to take "all competent measures of promoting within their sphere of influence the knowledge of the gospel and the inestimable blessings it conveys." [1] The fact that such prominent leaders of the Popular Party as Sir Henry Moncreiff and Dr. Erskine were members of the committee of the Edinburgh Missionary Society probably had some effect in bringing about this decision, and the charge of sedition was rendered plausible by the part played in the same organisation by James Haldane of Airthrey,

[1] *Account of the Proceedings and Debate in the General Assembly of the Church of Scotland, May 27, 1796.* Edin. 1796. Dr. Hill sent this pamphlet to the Lord Adocate on March 2, 1797, and it is curious to find him writing as follows: "Of Mr. Haldane and his associates I have no personal knowledge. I pretend not to judge their motives, or to insinuate that the political principles which that gentleman is said to glory in holding, have any connection with his present scheme." *Edin. Univ. Laing MSS.* No. 501. In 1829, the Church of Scotland sent Dr. Duff to India, and Warneck remarks that, with this exception, "in no Protestant State Church have missions been from their inception the concern of the church."

whose brother Robert had incurred the suspicion of being a Democrat.

Robert Haldane had been " awakened from the sleep of spiritual death " by the French Revolution.[1] As we have seen, the perusal of the works of Burke, Mackintosh, Priestley, and others, had led him to look forward to a speedy improvement in the affairs of mankind.[2] Though he did not become a Friend of the People, he protested against the raising of Volunteers at a meeting of the freeholders of Stirlingshire in 1794, when he expressed the opinion that they would be better employed in studying reforms. He was fond of airing his views, and, as a result of private discussions with some of the local clergy, he came to believe that nothing but a revival of evangelical religion could bring about the reign of happiness he desired. " When politics began to be talked about," he says, " I was led to consider everything anew. I eagerly clutched at them as a pleasing speculation. As a fleeting phantom, they eluded my grasp, but missing the shadow, I caught the substance." About the same time, James Haldane, who had retired from the command of an East India merchantman, adopted the same religious opinions, and the two brothers threw themselves with ardour into the cause of missions. Robert determined to sell his paternal estate and to conduct a band of missionaries to Bengal. As the East India Company had shown itself hostile to all such enterprises, he wrote to Henry Dundas, to whom he was distantly related, asking him to use his influence as President of the Board of Control to obtain the directors' permission.[3]

[1] The account which follows is based on A. Haldane, *The Lives of Robert and James Haldane*. Lond. 3rd edn. 1853.

[2] *Ante*, ch. iii. p. 60.

[3] In this connection there is a characteristic letter of R. Haldane to R. or H. Dundas in *Edin. Univ. Laing MSS*. No. 501, dated Sept. 28,

Dundas had already frustrated similar plans of his friend Wilberforce, and Haldane's politics provided a ready excuse in the present instance. "I could not persuade him," says Wilberforce, whose sympathies the brothers had enlisted, "though, as I told him, it is on your own grounds the best thing you can do. In Scotland such a man is sure to create a ferment. Send him therefore into the back settlements to let off his pistol *in vacuo*."[1] Permission was refused, and the energies of the Haldanes, turned into other channels, soon justified Wilberforce's worldly wisdom.

In 1796, James Haldane accompanied an English divine on a trip through the Highlands. On the way they distributed tracts, and so novel was this method of evangelisation, that the leaflets were occasionally refused lest they should prove to be some of Paine's. In the following year he set off to the west of Scotland, taking with him John Campbell, who afterwards made his name as an African missionary and explorer. Campbell had founded in Edinburgh a Sunday school, independent of clerical superintendence, and it was to further this movement that the tour was undertaken. Sixty Sunday schools resulted from this expedition. Haldane now began to preach, and started on a series of home mission journeys which extended as far north as the Orkneys. By forming the Society for the Propagation

1796: "We will bring it before the public, and we have not a doubt but we shall interest in our favour all the numerous friends of religion and of human happiness, and of every denomination in every part of the country. The lively concern they will feel for our success, the numerous petitions with thousands of signatures they will present, will so fully express the sentiments and wishes of the most virtuous and respectable part of the community, that we are confident Government will feel it a duty to comply with their request." From a letter of Dr. Porteous to the Lord Advocate, Haldane seems to have tried to carry out this threat. Feb. 20, 1797. *Ibid.*

[1] R. J. and S. Wilberforce, *Life of W. Wilberforce*, ii. ch. xiii; A. Haldane, *op. cit.* 112.

of the Gospel at Home he was instrumental in organising a body of itinerant lay preachers.[1] Meanwhile his brother, Robert, having sold his estate, had purchased the Edinburgh Circus as a temporary meeting place, and in 1798 he invited Rowland Hill to open it. The oddity and humour of this eccentric evangelist attracted great crowds. Sometimes he preached in churches, oftener in the open air. On his return to England he published a *Journal* in which he denounced the Established clergy as sceptical and lukewarm, and the Seceders as blindly intolerant.[2]

This brought to a head the ill-feeling engendered in all ordained preachers throughout the country by the Haldanes and their associates.[3] The correspondence of Dr. Porteous of Glasgow with the Lord Advocate reveals the causes of their resentment.[4] "Many of us have reason to believe," he wrote on January 24, 1797, "that the whole of this missionary business grows from a democratical root, and that the intention of those who planted it was to get hold of the public mind, and hereafter these societies may employ its energy as circumstances may direct." In February, 1798, he professed to be further alarmed. Ten years before, Sunday schools had been established to keep educated boys in the practice of reading and repeating the catechism.

[1] *An Account of the Proceedings of the Society for Propagating the Gospel at Home*, Edin. 1799, gives extracts from the journals of its agents.

[2] Cunningham, *op. cit.* ii. 573; Rowland Hill, *Journal of a Tour through . . . Parts of Scotland, with Remarks on the Present State of the Established Church of Scotland and the Different Secessions therefrom . . . also some Remarks on the Propriety of what is called Itinerant Lay Preaching*, Lond. 1799; *A Series of Letters occasioned by the Late Pastoral Admonition*, Lond. 1799; and *Extracts of a Second Tour . . . through Scotland*, Lond. 1800.

[3] J. Haldane, *Journal of a Tour through the Northern Counties of Scotland and the Orkney Islands.* Edin. 1798.

[4] *Edin. Univ. Laing MSS.* Nos. 501 and 500.

Those of the Haldanes were on a new plan.[1] In Glasgow, for example, old and young, men and women, boys and girls, were invited to attend, and " in place of the former simple exercises, a loquacious manufacturer preached and prayed with vehemence till a late hour." Though they had not directly meddled with politics, yet obliquely they attacked religious establishments. Lay preaching was another dangerous symptom. " The ministers of the Church of Scotland," Porteous confessed, " have enjoyed ease and quiet so long that few of them have directed their studies to subjects of this kind ; and as they are not prepared for the attack, so I am afraid they are in some danger of giving a handle against themselves by an ill-tempered zeal. If any method could be fallen on to direct attention to the subject of Lay Preaching in a way that would not irritate, it would be a very seasonable service, but I am afraid the difficulties and perils of meeting a set of enthusiasts will prevent it." This "seasonable service" the General Assembly of May, 1799, proceeded to perform. It passed an Act forbidding the ministers of the Established Church to hold communion with any but its authorised licentiates, and it also issued a Pastoral Letter to warn the people of the danger of religious novelties. " It is much to be lamented," so runs this missive, " that while we are assaulted by false principles imparted to us from abroad, there should of late have risen among ourselves a set of men whose proceedings threaten no small disorder to the country." Missionaries were going about acting as universal itinerant preachers, intruding themselves into parishes without a call, and erecting Sunday

[1] The first Sunday schools, founded in 1787 on the model of those of Raikes, were countenanced by the authorities. A procession of magistrates celebrated their institution in Glasgow. *Scots. Mag.* Dec. 1787 ; *Glasgow Advert.* Jan. 1, 1790. But they were not "independent of clerical superintendence."

schools, which they committed to the charge of persons notoriously disaffected to the civil constitution; and secret meetings were alienating the affections of the people from their own pastors.[1] A specially appointed committee further recommended the revival of certain obsolete statutes which placed all teachers under the supervision of the Church.

It is significant that the Seceders were equally antagonistic to the new movement. In 1796, the Anti-Burgher Synod expressed its disapproval of the lay element in missionary societies, and in 1798 "unanimously declared lay-preaching to be without warrant from the Word of God."[2] The Cameronians in Glasgow excommunicated some of their members who had attended a missionary service conducted by a pastor not of their own sect.[3] In 1797, the Relief Church selected two of its ministers for mission work in the Highlands.[4] They encountered the same opposition as the Haldanes.[5] One of them, Neil Douglas, had been a delegate to the third Convention of the Friends of the People.[6] Before leaving Dundee for his new duties, he was commissioned by a friend to arrange for the printing of a pamphlet. It was deemed seditious on publication, and its author prosecuted; and Douglas, on his return from his labours in Argyllshire, was astonished to find himself pointedly referred to by the Lord Advocate

[1] Cunningham, *op. cit.* ii. 573 *et seq.* There is a caricature of the Rev. Dr. Moodie dispersing a Sunday school in Kay's *Orig. Portraits*, i. 356.

[2] M'Kerrow, *op. cit.* ii. 49, 62.

[3] A. Haldane, *op. cit.* 260.

[4] Struthers, *op. cit.* ch. xxii. *passim.*

[5] N. Douglas, *Journal of a Mission to part of the Highlands of Scotland in 1797.* Edin. 1799.

[6] But not to its successor the British Convention, as Cockburn states in *Exam. of Trials for Sedition*, ii. 192. See *ante*, ch. vii. p. 147 fn. Douglas was tried for sedition in 1817. Cockburn, *ibid.*

as the real culprit. When three other missionaries were sent out by the Relief Church, this incident was used against them, and the Synod, probably to save its reputation, passed a decree against unlicensed preaching.[1]

Meanwhile, wider currency was being given to the political motives imputed to the Haldanes and their fellow-workers. In 1797, Professor Robison of Edinburgh University published his *Proofs of a Conspiracy against all the Religions and Governments in Europe*,[2] in which he endeavoured to prove that the general unrest was due to the machinations of the Illuminati, the Free Masons, and other secret societies. In surveying the progress of their opinions in Britain he studiously identified the Haldanes with the Unitarians. "I grieve," he wrote, "that Dr. Priestley has left any of his friends and abettors among us. A very eminent one said in company a few days ago that he would willingly wade to the knees in blood to overturn the establishment of the Kirk of Scotland." The reference to missions in India, with which the paragraph concluded, pointed to the laird of Airthrey. In the third edition, the author, owing to a vigorous protest from Robert Haldane, modified the statement, but it was singled out for comment in a notice of a book on religious establishments, which appeared in the *Anti-Jacobin Review*, May, 1799. The editor subsequently printed Haldane's indignant expostulation, but retaliated by quoting from James Haldane's *Journal* the invectives which he had directed against the Established Church.[3]

By sending a copy of the Pastoral Letter to the sheriffs-depute of counties and the chief magistrates of all royal burghs, the General Assembly had shown a desire to invoke

[1] Struthers, *op. cit.* 400-5.

[2] Edin. 1797, 3rd edn. corrected, 1798. For a criticism of the book, v. W. Beattie, *Life of Campbell*, ii. 117.

[3] *Anti-Jacobin Review*, iii. 341-5.

the aid of the civil power.[1] At the same time the Duke of Atholl appealed to the Home Secretary for more stringent measures. The new sectarians, he wrote, were engaged in even deeper plans than that of undermining established religion. They were filling the country with meetings under the name of Sunday schools, where the lowest of the people became teachers, and were instilling into the minds of the rising generation the most pernicious doctrines, both civil and religious. "I have no doubt," he concluded, . . . "that energetic measures will be taken under the authority of Parliament, to annihilate the further progress of unlicensed missionaries and free schools, whether under the auspices of Mr. Haldane or any other enthusiastic and designing man whatever." [2] The Bill which was being actually prepared by the Government to restrain the activities of the Methodists and other Dissenters in England, would have been equally disastrous to the followers of the Haldanes in Scotland. But the remonstrances which Wilberforce addressed to Pitt were successful in averting the threatened blow.[3] The proposed legislation thoroughly alarmed Robert Haldane, and while the General Assembly was sitting in May, 1800, he published his *Address to the Public concerning Politics and Plans lately adopted to promote Religion in Scotland.*[4] This candid explanation of his principles

[1] "[This] speaks a language too explicit to be misunderstood." Neil Douglas, *op. cit.* 29. J. Haldane and Campbell were actually arrested in Argyleshire in 1800. Escorted by a party of Volunteers, they were taken before the Sheriff, who liberated them. A. Haldane, *op. cit.* 287.

[2] Duke of Atholl to Duke of Portland, London, May 20, 1799, *Edin. Univ. Laing MSS.* No. 500. On May 24, 1799 (?), the former writes to the Lord Advocate: "An Act of Parliament is the only remedy to check and restrain practices which will otherwise lay a sure foundation for overturning in the minds of the rising generation every constitutional and loyal principle." *Ibid.*

[3] A. Haldane, *op. cit.* 279; *Life of Wilberforce*, ii. 361.

[4] Two editions, Edin. 1800.

disarmed criticism, and henceforth the evangelists were allowed to carry on their work, free from official censure.[1] Although internal dissensions robbed the movement of much of its original force, later ecclesiastical historians have traced to the rude shock communicated by the Haldanes to the Church of Scotland, the beginning of that evangelical zeal which was to be one of its chief characteristics in the nineteenth century.[2]

[1] It is interesting to note that Hans Nielsen Hauge, who is credited with the revival of evangelical religion in Norway, experienced the same difficulties as the Haldanes. Like them he began itinerant lay preaching in 1797, and so roused the indignation of the state clergy that they examined over six hundred witnesses with a view to prosecuting him. In 1804 he was thrown into prison for holding religious meetings contrary to law—the *Konventikel-placat.* Art. by M. J. Philip in the *Missionary Record of the United Free Church of Scotland*, April, 1911.

[2] Cunningham, *op. cit.* ii. 577. In 1816 Robert Haldane carried on religious work in Geneva and Montauban. Merle d'Aubigné, the historian, was one of his converts. In France, Haldane was denounced to the Minister of the Interior as a firebrand, but after inquiry the Minister declared that "it mattered not to him whether Mr. Haldane taught Calvinism or any other *ism*, provided it was not *Deism.*" A. Haldane, *op. cit.* 482-3. Deism was evidently associated in the minds of the now triumphant royalists with republican principles.

CHAPTER XI.

CONCLUSION. 1802–1832.

THE year 1802 marks the end of the direct influence of the French Revolution on Scotland. "Somewhat less was said about Jacobinism, though still too much, and sedition had gone out," Cockburn records in his *Memorials*. "Napoleon's obvious progress towards military despotism opened the eyes of those who used to see nothing but liberty in the French Revolution; and the threat of invasion, while it combined all parties in the defence of the country, raised the confidence of the people in those who trusted them with arms, and gave them the pleasure of playing at soldiers. Instead of Jacobinism, Invasion became the word." [1] This new preoccupation is reflected in the correspondence of Lord Advocate Hope, who, having suppressed the United Scotsmen, was now engrossed in schemes for opposing the landing of the French.[2] The Volunteers became a patriotic

[1] *Memorials*, 164.

[2] In 1801, Hope succeeded Robert Dundas who was appointed Lord Chief Baron of the Court of Exchequer. For his famous regimental orders of October 18, 1803, v. Cockburn, *op. cit.* Append. "I have the pleasure to add," he writes in one of his numerous letters to the Home Secretary, "that we have begun to fit out the Kinghorn Passage Boats (nine in number) to carry 18 pound Carronades and fifty Herring Boats to carry 12 pound Carronades at our own expense. If this shall be connected with a small squadron of larger vessels, and the whole placed under the command of an active and enterprising officer, I think we shall have nothing to fear." *Scot. Corr.* vol. xviii. Oct. 22, 1803.

rather than a political organisation, and Whig and Tory vied with one another in discharging military duties. The "False Alarm" revealed, among all classes of the community, a spirit of loyalty which put an end, for some time to come, to apprehensions of disaffection.[1]

In Scotland, as in England, the French Revolution had retarded the progress of liberal opinion. The dread of innovation had frustrated the efforts of the burgh and county reformers. This was caused partly by the horrors of the Reign of Terror abroad, and partly by the enthusiasm with which French principles had been welcomed by the industrial classes at home. Yet, as has been shown, it is with this momentous upheaval in France that the political awakening of Scotland begins. From 1792 there is no complete break in the political life of the nation. Until the victory of reform in 1832, the period from 1792 to 1794, during which the excitement had reached its highest pitch, was regarded by Tory, Democrat, and Whig, as marking an epoch in the history of the country. The Tories, strong in the belief that reform and revolution were identical, and presuming on a continuance of the national support extended to them during a time of crisis, sought to perpetuate the system of government associated with the name of Dundas. The lower classes, irritated by repressive and harsh laws, still based their hopes on universal suffrage and annual Parliaments, which, to them at least, were the legacy of the French Revolution; and the Whigs, sharing with these extremists their detestation of judicial cruelties and administrative abuses,

[1] Even Edie Ochiltree, the gaberlunzie in *The Antiquary* (chapter xliv.), was "as ready to fight for his dish as the laird for his land." There were probably few who shared John Younger's opinion that "only the rich had any reason to be patriotic." A. Lang, Border Edn. of *The Antiquary*, p. 33, Lond. 1898; *Autobiography of John Younger, Shoemaker, St. Boswells*, chap. xix. Kelso, 1881.

bent all their energies on effecting moderate and specific reforms.

As long as Britain was engaged in war abroad, there was little prospect of accomplishing reform at home. In the *Edinburgh Review,* however, the younger Scottish Whigs found an admirable medium for preparing the ground for the future triumph of their party. The first number appeared in October, 1802, at a time when the fear of Jacobinism had abated. The moderate tone of its politics tended at first to conciliate public opinion. "You will not be surprised," wrote Horner, "that we have given a good deal of disappointment by the temperate air of our politics. Nothing short of blood and atheism and democracy was predicted by some wise and fair ones as the necessary production of our set."[1] The "set" consisted, among others, of Jeffrey, Sydney Smith, Brougham, and Horner himself, and under their guidance the *Review* soon became an uncompromising advocate of Whig principles. To its influence on the younger members of the Scottish Bar, which provided most of the active politicians of both parties, none bore more striking testimony than the second Lord Melville. "The fact is," he wrote to Viscount Sidmouth in 1818, "that Mr. Jeffrey and the *Edinburgh Review* gang . . . gathered round them, by their talents and plausible jargon, a number of young men at the Bar of their own standing, and whose connections would have led them naturally into more proper society and modes of thinking."[2] But its real importance lay in its appeal to a wider public. Within a few years, it was an acknowledged force not only in Scotland but in England, and brought about the founding

[1] L. Horner, *Memoirs and Correspondence of Francis Horner, M.P.* i. 204.

[2] "Had gathered," he wrote, as he believed that the influence of the *Review* was declining. *Scot. Corr.* vol. xxix. June 19, 1818.

of the *Quarterly Review*, and later, of *Blackwood's Edinburgh Magazine*, in the interests of the Tories.

The success of these juniors was regarded with considerable jealousy by their seniors; and when, in 1806, the Whigs found themselves unexpectedly in office, the former complained that they were neglected. Jeffrey offended the Earl of Lauderdale, the new "Manager," by an article on his work on political economy; and a sinecure created for Dugald Stewart, and a proposed reform of the Court of Session, intended, according to Cockburn, to provide appointments for partisans, were condemned by the younger Scottish Whigs. Nevertheless, the change of administration was regarded by one of them as "a most salutary event for Scotland." The Whigs were roused from despair, and it convinced their opponents "that they were not positively immortal." [1]

The same lesson was more strikingly enforced in 1805 by the impeachment of Henry Dundas, who, in 1802, had been raised to the peerage with the title of Viscount Melville and Baron Dunira. Melville was acquitted of the charges of peculation preferred against him, and he was again sworn of the Privy Council from which his name had been erased. But he was never again in office, and shattered health and broken reputation prevented his further active participation in public affairs. Yet, as the future was to show, the rejoicing of his political adversaries was premature. The managership descended, as if by hereditary right, to his son. For the next twenty years Robert Dundas was to be consulted on every Government appointment in Scotland, and only his inferior abilities, political and social, were to prevent him from exercising over the destinies of his country as complete a sway as his predecessor. In 1807 he was President of the Board of Control, but it was not

[1] Cockburn, *Memorials*, 183-191.

till 1812, a year after his father's death, that his new office of First Lord of the Admiralty gave him Cabinet rank.

Three years before the peace of 1815, the industrial classes began once more to assert themselves. Baffled in their efforts to obtain Parliamentary reform, they now endeavoured to better their condition by means of the existing laws. At the beginning of 1812, the cotton spinners in Glasgow and the vicinity applied to the magistrates "to fix by their official capacity, reasonable prices for weaving fabrics of cotton cloth, agreeably to the spirit and letter of the Acts of Parliament stated in their petition." The magistrates, in order to avoid any turbulent demonstration, requested the workers to appoint a committee to present the petition and confer with their employers. Uncertain as to the law, the authorities took the opinion of counsel, who declared that the Justices of the Peace had no powers to regulate wages. Nevertheless, the spinners, acting on the advice of Jeffrey and other Whig advocates, asked the Justices to fix a list of prices. They agreed; but against this decision the manufacturers appealed. The Court of Session upheld the jurisdiction of the Justices, and remitted to them the task of drawing up the rates of wages. After a lengthy hearing of witnesses, a list of rates was prepared and declared by the Justices to be "moderate and reasonable." The manufacturers refused to pay according to these rates, and the employees, to the number of some 40,000, came out on strike.[1]

Justice now demanded that the employers should be forced to obey the law. Unfortunately the Government took quite a different view. Writing to Sidmouth on July 4, Lord Advocate Colquhoun had reported the existence of an association of weavers, who maintained a correspondence

[1] J. Dillon to Sidmouth, *Scot. Corr.* vol. xxii. Dec. 18, 1812. W. Cunningham, *The Growth of English Industry and Commerce*, iii. 638-9.

with similar organisations in England. Though no acts of violence had been committed, yet the societies "might easily be made instrumental for accomplishing seditious or treasonable designs." [1] During the strike it was discovered that Margarot, the only victim of 1794 who returned to his native land from Botany Bay, had paid a visit to Glasgow and other towns in Scotland, had been in touch with some of his former associates of the British Convention, and had been seen in the company of some of the weavers. His visit was connected in the minds of the officials with the propaganda of the Hampden Club, founded by Major Cartwright, the leading spirit of the former Society for Constitutional Information, to agitate for drastic measures of reform.[2] Under these circumstances, the Lord Advocate, whose anxieties were increased by rumours of intrigues and conspiracies artfully circulated by the manufacturers, determined to crush the whole movement. The houses of the delegates were entered illegally,[3] and search was made for incriminating documents. Finally the leaders of what Cockburn calls "the most extensive and peaceable combination of workmen that had ever appeared in this part of the kingdom" [4] were charged with contravening the Combination Acts of 1799 and 1800, and sentenced to eighteen months' imprisonment [5]—a punishment which could

[1] *Scot. Corr.* vol. xxii.

[2] *Ibid.* vol. xxii. Nov. 4 to Dec. 25, 1812. Margarot survived till 1815. Skirving died at Port Jackson on March 9, 1796, and Gerrald three days later. Palmer set out for England in January, 1800, but died at Guam, one of the Ladrone Islands, in June, 1802.

[3] Ld. Adv. to Sidmouth, "Private," Jan. 2, 1813.

[4] *Memorials*, 281.

[5] "In case of any dispute between masters and men, or of a strike, the employers were able to have recourse to this Act at any moment, and summarily crush all opposition." Cunningham, *op. cit.* 736. Moreover, sect. 17 of 39 and 40 Geo. III. c. 106 rendered combinations among employers also illegal. Cunningham, *op. cit.* 732.

not be reconciled with the recognition of the cotton spinners' association both by the Justices and the Court of Session. As a result of the strike, the clauses in the Statute of Artificers authorising magistrates to fix the wages of labour were repealed in 1815.

Nothing was more calculated to render the industrial classes conscious of their utter helplessness, and, in the same year, a new corn law increased the irritation. During the war the landed proprietors had benefited by the high price of corn, but the prospects of peace threatened to involve them in ruin. By the Corn Law of 1815, the importation of foreign corn was prohibited as long as the price of wheat did not exceed 80s. a quarter. "The policy was only in the obvious interest of a class," says Dr. Cunningham, "and as it could be depicted as demanding the sacrifice of the masses of the population, it was resented accordingly." [1] Riots broke out in Glasgow, Perth, Dundee, and other manufacturing centres. Inflammatory bills were posted up in Edinburgh.[2] The Glasgow petition to the Commons is said to have been forwarded to every town of note in Scotland. "Your petitioners," it ran, "were always led to consider your Honourable House as the Constitutional Guardian of our Rights and Liberties, and as the Organ of Public Opinion; but the marked disregard which, on this recent and momentous occasion, has been shown to the voice of the nation, constitutionally expressed, has excited in them sentiments of a very opposite kind, and demonstrated beyond the possibility of contradiction, that in your Honourable House, the Representation of the People is radically defective." [3]

Owing to the resentment caused by such partisan administration and legislation, and the distress occasioned by the

[1] *Op. cit.* 730. [2] *Scot. Corr.* vol. xxv. March 18, 31; April 21, 1815.
[3] *Ibid.* vol. xxv. April 21.

industrial crisis which followed on the close of the war, the extreme doctrines of Parliamentary reform which had been popular among artisans in 1793 received a fresh lease of life. The writings of Cobbett, now a Radical pamphleteer, were widely disseminated in the west. Major Cartwright, the agent of the Hampden Club, made a tour through the manufacturing districts of Scotland, advocating universal suffrage and annual Parliaments, and as a result of his exertions, numerous societies and committees were formed.[1] "I have no hesitation in saying," wrote the provost of Dunfermline to the Lord Advocate regarding an attempt to hold such meetings in the town, "that reform is merely a pretext, and that the present movement originates from the recent visit of Major Cartwright to this vicinity and other incendiaries employed by the Hampden Club, and that the object is nothing less than revolution or rebellion; and what strengthens this opinion—at least in the view of the people here—is that several of them who were particularly active in the seditious transactions of 1793 have been the *first* to step forward on this occasion."[2] In Renfrewshire, the leader of the reformers was said to be Archibald Hastie, a prominent member of the British Convention.[3] Richmond, a weaver who had been outlawed in connection with the troubles of 1812, now entered the Government service as a spy. As a result of his investigations, he reported that "secret committees of the disaffected, consisting chiefly of

[1] Cartwright visited Greenock and the coast of Ayr; Renfrew, Paisley, Stirling, and Alloa; Dunfermline, Newburgh, and Perth; Coupar-Angus, Forfar, Brechin; Crail, St. Andrews, and Aberdeen; was twice at Stonehaven, Inverbervie, Montrose, Dundee, Cupar-Fife, Kirkcaldy, Lanark, and Hamilton; and thrice at Edinburgh and Glasgow. *A Collection of Reports of the Proceedings of the Hampden Club.* (Lond. 1814-1822.) Brit. Mus.

[2] *Scot. Corr.* vol. xxvi. Dec. 9, 1816.

[3] *Ibid.* Dec. 22; v. *ante*, ch. viii. p. 166 fn.

the ringleaders of the combination in 1812, and of such members of the seditious societies of 1793 as were still alive, had been formed in different quarters of Glasgow, Ayrshire, Dumbarton, and Stirlingshire"; that delegates from England had visited the Glasgow committee; and that this committee, after discussing the organisation of the United Irishmen, and of the "traitors in Scotland in 1795," had resolved to adopt the plan of the former, so as to get together a disciplined force and all the arms within reach.[1] Yet the majority of the societies were quite open in their proceedings, and the meetings held under their auspices were for the purpose of preparing petitions in support of Sir Francis Burdett's motion in the House of Commons.[2] Nevertheless, the Lord Advocate, like his predecessors, was convinced that the reformers were revolutionaries, and further discoveries by his spies confirmed his suspicions. The members of the secret committees, he was informed, were being "initiated" by taking an oath which bound them "to try by all means in their power, moral and physical, to endeavour to obtain universal suffrage and annual Parliaments."[3]

Meanwhile, riots in London, and the insult offered to the Prince Regent on his return from opening Parliament on January 28, 1817, had created wide-spread alarm in England, and the Ministry proceeded, as Pitt had done under similar circumstances in 1795, to introduce repressive measures. One Bill suppressed seditious meetings and the other sus-

[1] *Scot. Corr.* vol. xxvi. Dec. 25, 1816.

[2] Ld. Adv. to Sidmouth, Jan. 27, 1817, *Scot. Corr.* vol. xxvii. At a meeting held in the Relief Church, Kilbarchan, on December 21, 1816, one of the speakers said: "A mental revolution has taken place which the *ratio regum*, the logic of legitimacy, the point of the bayonet cannot counteract. . . . A spark was kindled at the French Revolution which the enemies of freedom think they have extinguished, but still it burns, and every fresh occurrence fans the flame." Printed report forwarded to Sidmouth by the Lord Advocate, June 2, 1817.

[3] *Scot. Corr.* vol. xxvi. Jan. 26; vol. xxvii. Jan. 31.

pended the Habeas Corpus Act till the following July. These proposals aroused keen opposition, and during the debate on the latter Bill, the House seemed disposed to question its necessity, until the Lord Advocate of Scotland, in a maiden speech, read, at the request of the Cabinet, the secret oath of the Glasgow committee. A deep impression was made on the listeners, and the Bill was passed.[1]

Numerous arrests were made in Scotland in connection with the agitation. The first to be brought to trial were those who had openly committed what was then considered sedition. A weaver named M'Laren was accused of having delivered a violent speech in Kilmarnock, and Baird, a shopkeeper, of having printed it.[2] In the days of Braxfield, a sentence of transportation would have been a foregone conclusion; but Lord Gillies, who now occupied his place on the bench, was a Whig, and the Whig counsel who defended the prisoners were able to procure for them a satisfactory trial. Sentences of six months' imprisonment were imposed. The case against Neil Douglas, a prominent reformer of 1792, now a Universalist preacher, broke down completely.[3] Among other charges, he was indicted with having drawn a parallel between the Prince Regent and Belshazzar—in many respects only too true—but he was unanimously acquitted by the jury. The trial of M'Kinlay, a weaver, involved more serious issues. At first the Lord Advocate preferred against him a charge of high treason on account of his having administered unlawful oaths, but, owing to the learned attack of Whig counsel, he was forced to draw up another indictment. Again the Crown officials were defeated on points of criminal law, and again the indictment was

[1] Omond, *Lives of the Lord Advocates*, ii. 238; *Hansard*, xxxv. 729-30.

[2] *State Trials*, xxxiii.; Cockburn, *Exam. of Trials for Sedn.* ii. 177 *et seq.*

[3] *Ibid.* xxxiii. 633 *et seq.*; Cockburn, *op. cit.* ii. 192 *et seq.*; v. *ante*, chap. x. p. 210.

altered. "The delay which has arisen in these cases," wrote the Lord Advocate to Sidmouth on June 4, "has given me the greatest uneasiness, and my only consolation is that it has proceeded altogether from the Court, which, I cannot help saying, has shewn a want of nerve that, had it belonged to the Judges in the year 1795, would have gone far indeed to the destruction of the Government."[1] These proceedings led to a discussion in the Commons, even Finlay, the Tory member for Glasgow, denouncing the Lord Advocate for incompetence.[2] At last M'Kinlay was brought up for trial on July 23. After strenuous efforts, the law officers of the Crown had succeeded in inducing John Campbell, one of the prisoners lodged in Edinburgh Castle, to turn King's evidence. When his examination in court began, he was asked the formal question if he had been promised any reward for coming forward as a witness. "Yes," he answered. "By whom," was the next question. "By that gentleman," he replied, pointing to the advocate-depute. "The judges," says Cockburn, one of the nine Whig counsel for the defence, "frowned on the man as if they would have eaten him on the spot."[3] The case against the prisoners collapsed, and although the judges declared their conviction that a conspiracy had existed, there was a prevalent idea that the Government had grossly exaggerated it. This trial, like those of Muir and Palmer, occasioned debates in Parliament, but Lord Hamilton's motion that the record of the court be laid before the House was defeated by a large majority.[4]

[1] *Scot. Corr.* vol. xxviii. On July 18, he reported that only Gillies was against the relevancy of the indictment. "As his character was eulogised by Brougham in the House of Commons, I had no doubt that this result was to be expected."

[2] Omond, *op. cit.* ii. 243; *Hansard*, xxxvi. 1078-1081.

[3] *Memorials*, 285.

[4] Omond, *op. cit.* ii. 252-3.

Another "blunder" on the part of the Lord Advocate revived the whole question of burgh reform. In 1817, the election of the Town Council of Montrose was declared void, owing to a failure to comply with its "sett." Following the precedent established by Henry Dundas in the case of Stirling in 1781, Maconochie issued a new charter for the burgh.[1] According to its provisions, all the burgesses were to vote in the first election, and in future the corporation was to consist, among others, of the Deacon of the Trade Incorporations, and of six of the merchants who were to be appointed annually by the Guild Merchant. "The effect of this change," wrote the Lord Advocate to Sidmouth, "was to throw the election of the magistrates and council more into the hands of the corporation at large than it had been before, and as an enemy to all extension of this description, I certainly felt adverse to comply with the wish of the petitioners." But, not desiring to act in opposition to the "unanimous wish of the whole parties concerned," he thought it advisable to make the concession. The burgh reformers immediately seized the opportunity to renew their agitation. Meetings were held in Edinburgh and other towns to prepare petitions to the Prince Regent requesting alterations in their respective setts similar to those granted to Montrose.[2] It was at this juncture that Fletcher wrote his *Memoir* on the history of the movement since 1782, and that some of the official documents of the same period were reprinted. The Government, alarmed at the storm they had unwittingly raised, refused to grant a poll warrant to the burghs of Inverness and Aberdeen, whose elections

[1] Ld. Adv. to Sidmouth, Nov. 2, 1817, *Scot. Corr.* vol. xxviii.; Cockburn, *Memorials*, 275.

[2] The Guild Brethren of Inverness on Dec. 1, 1817, passed a vote of thanks to the Lord Advocate "for his recommendation of the liberal constitution recently granted to the citizens of Montrose."

were also declared invalid, and renewed their charters on the old principle of self-election; and the Court of Session upheld the action of the Crown.[1] In 1819, Lord Archibald Hamilton succeeded in obtaining a committee of the Commons to inquire into the state of the Scottish burghs, and its report showed that the contentions of the reformers were substantially correct. Three years later, he proposed the abolition of the existing system of municipal government. The Lord Advocate resisted this change on the ground that it would involve Parliamentary reform; but, as a concession to public opinion, he brought in a Bill authorising burgesses to call corrupt magistrates before the Exchequer Court. As the system of self-election was still maintained, this Act did not satisfy the reformers, and such piece-meal legislation only drew further attention to the reality of those long-standing abuses which were to be swept away by the Municipal Reform Act of 1833.[2]

This activity of the burgh reformers coincided with fresh signs of unrest among the industrial classes. By August, 1819, large numbers of artisans were out of employment. Numerous meetings in favour of universal suffrage and annual Parliaments were held throughout the manufacturing districts, especially in Glasgow and Paisley.[3] *Wooler's Gazette*, the *Black Dwarf*, and the pamphlets of Cobbett were reported to be widely circulated among the "Radicals,"

[1] Lord Melville, who, as usual, was consulted, wrote to Sidmouth on November 8, 1817: "The having been led into one error at Montrose is no reason why we should repeat it in the other burghs. . . . There is no part of the United Kingdom that has prospered more than North Britain for above a century past, with the exception of a small mistake we made in 1745, and I have no relish for experimental changes by wholesale." *Scot. Corr.* vol. xxviii.

[2] Omond, *op. cit.* ii. 270-1.

[3] At a Paisley meeting a Cap of Liberty was placed on the chairman's head. *Scot. Corr.* vol. xxxi. Oct. 30, 1819.

as the extremists were now beginning to be called.[1] To prepare for emergencies, additional troops were drafted into Scotland, and the former corps of Volunteers were re-organised. Yet the system of police in Glasgow was so defective, and the magistrates so prone to take alarm, that Lord Advocate Rae, Maconochie's successor, deemed it advisable to send Captain Brown of the Edinburgh force to investigate the situation. Writing to Rae on September 19, he stated that nothing serious was to be anticipated. The riots in Glasgow and Paisley, the immediate causes of apprehension, were " the entire work of a gang of resolute blackguards." The reformers disapproved of these disorders, according to two of his agents who had joined their committee. They wished to move with caution, as they did not think the country ripe for reform. There was no military training going on, and " no arming in general." The Radicals, however, were very much against the clergy, who were " looked upon as the tools of the Government in oppressing the people." [2] During the months of October and December, the Radicals in Scotland, as in England, organised huge open-air demonstrations, and on December 9, Captain Brown wrote to Rae that he had definite information that they were about to rise in revolt ; but although " there might be a bit of a brush—rather desirable than otherwise —it could not continue long or be on a very extensive scale." [3]

The uneasiness thus aroused in official circles both in England and Scotland, led to the passing of the repressive code known as the Six Acts, directed against the possession

[1] Ld. Adv. to Sidmouth, Sept. 27, 1819, *Scot. Corr.* vol. xxx. "*Wooler's Gazette* and *Black Dwarf* have created more disaffection than all others with the exception of Cobbett and Hunt." Anon. letter from Forfar, April 7, 1820.

[2] *Scot. Corr.* vol. xxx.

[3] *Ibid.* vol. xxxi.

of arms, the printing of seditious libels, and the holding of large meetings. In February, 1820, the authorities in Scotland arrested twenty-seven delegates of the Glasgow central committee, as they had received secret intelligence that arrangements had been made for a simultaneous rising in both countries. But it was not till April 1 that "An Address to the Inhabitants of Great Britain and Ireland," purporting to be issued by the "Committee of Organisation for forming a Provisional Government," heralded the revolt. "Roused from that torpid state in which we have been sunk for so many years," it began, "we are at length compelled from the extremity of our sufferings, and the contempt heaped upon our Petitions for redress, to assert our Rights at the hazard of our lives. . . . Let us show to the world that we are not that Lawless, Sanguinary Rabble, which our Oppressors would persuade the higher circles we are, but a Brave and Generous People determined to be free. Liberty or Death is our Motto, and we have sworn to return home in *triumph*—or return *no more*." All workmen were therefore called upon to desist from labour on and after April 1, so as to be able to "attend wholly to the recovery of their rights."[1] The bill was placarded on the walls throughout Glasgow, and for many miles around it, and the artisans, some 60,000 in number, obeyed its injunction. In Glasgow, where the military were mustered as if for a siege, everything pointed to a catastrophe. April 5, the day fixed for the rising, found thousands of troops drawn up in the streets, but the only disturbance that took place was an encounter in the evening between the cavalry and three hundred of the Radicals. On the morning of the same day,

[1] Ld. Provost to Sidmouth, April 2, 1820, *Scot. Corr.* vol. xxxii. P. Mackenzie affirmed that he proved in 1832 that the placard was printed by one Fulton, who received two pounds from Richmond the spy for doing so. *Reminiscences*, i. 135; ii. chap. xxxi.

between forty and fifty of the latter had left the city to escort a party of their friends expected from Carron in Stirlingshire. On the way they stopped one of the yeomanry then patrolling the country in large numbers. He immediately warned the officer commanding a detachment of Hussars stationed at Kilsyth. The Hussars and some of the local yeomanry set off in pursuit, and overtook the rebels at Bonnymuir. After a short skirmish, the Radicals fled, four of them being wounded and nineteen taken prisoners.[1] Two days later, Rae wrote to Sidmouth that the greater part of the operatives had returned to work. Thus ended the last attempt in Scotland to obtain redress of grievances by force of arms. A commission of Oyer and Terminer sat at Edinburgh, Glasgow, Dumbarton, Paisley, and Ayr, to try forty-seven persons who had been apprehended. Most of them were liberated, and only three, Wilson, Baird, and Hardie, suffered the extreme penalty of the law. The Government, as was natural, made the most of the "Radical War," as it was called, but did nothing to alleviate those hardships of the lower classes which had been the real cause of the desperate enterprise.

The Radical War was as fatal to the hopes of the extremists as Watt's conspiracy in 1794; but in 1820 there existed a growing body of moderate reformers whose efforts could no longer be thwarted by the bugbear of revolution. Their strength in "the very citadel of Toryism" was revealed by the famous Pantheon meeting held in Edinburgh in December of the same year, as a result of which, some 17,000 adult males signed a petition to the King to dismiss his Ministers. The ostensible cause of this, the first political gathering in the Capital since the "Reign of Terror," was the part played by

[1] *Scots. Mag.* 1820, new series, vi. p. 377. At Greenock an attempt to rescue five prisoners taken by the Port-Glasgow Volunteers led to a riot in which six persons were killed. *Ibid.*

the Government in supporting the divorce proceedings against the Queen ; but its real significance lay in the open hostility displayed towards existing powers. "A new day dawned on the official seat of Scotch intolerance," says Cockburn.[1] Further evidence of the influence exerted by public opinion is to be found in a series of law reforms, which, though eventually effected by the Tories, were due to the indefatigable crusade carried on by the *Edinburgh Review*. In 1808, the Court of Session had been reorganised in two divisions, and seven years later, a jury court for civil cases was established, thereby inaugurating an improvement which had been urged by many of the political societies in 1792. In State criminal cases, the Justiciary Court was still able to inflict excessive punishments. Thus in 1820, Gilbert Macleod, the editor of the Glasgow Radical organ, the *Spirit of the Union*, was convicted of sedition and transported for five years—a sentence impossible in England ; for an Act of 1819 only inflicted transportation for a second offence, and even then allowed the culprit forty days to put himself into voluntary banishment. Such a revival among the judges of the spirit of Braxfield, whose example was openly held up for veneration in court, alarmed the Whigs, and Cockburn, in the *Edinburgh Review* of 1821 and 1822, drew attention to the inequality between English and Scots law.[2] In 1821, Mr. Kennedy of Dunure, the Whig member for the Ayr Burghs, introduced a Jury Bill, whereby the jury was to be chosen by ballot, and the accused allowed the right of peremptory challenge. It was opposed by the Lord Advocate, who sent a circular letter to all corporate bodies in Scotland urging them to petition

[1] *Memorials*, 325.

[2] Cockburn, *Exam. of Trials for Sedn.* ii. 221. "Gillies held that the power to transport must be held to exist, but that it ought not to be exercised." All the other judges opposed him.

against it.[1] After much discussion and delay, two Bills embodying the principles of Kennedy's measure became law, one in 1822, the other in 1825; and in the latter year another was passed which made the punishment for sedition in Scotland the same as in England. Finally, in 1830, a Judicature Act simplified the forms of process in the Court of Session, which had hitherto been the cause of much delay and of innumerable appeals to the House of Lords.

During the halting progress of the Jury Bills through Parliament, a series of incidents, probably unique in the annals of British journalism, raised the wider question of the powers of the Lord Advocate, at which these law reforms were indirectly aimed. Most of the anti-Ministerialist newspapers established in 1791 and 1792 had been short-lived, but the first quarter of the nineteenth century saw a gradual growth of Opposition journals. The *Dundee Advertiser* was begun in 1801, and the *Ayr Advertiser* in 1803. The former, supported by Cockburn and other leading Whigs, drew largely on Cobbett for its material.[2] In 1816, the Glasgow Radicals, not content with importing *Wooler's Gazette*, the *Black Dwarf*, and the *Political Register*, set up the *Spirit of the Union*, while in January of the following year, the first number of the *Scotsman* appeared in Edinburgh to advocate radical reform. As in 1792, the administrators of Scotland took steps to counteract their influence. Writing to Sidmouth on April 2, 1820, the Sheriff Substitute of Lanarkshire enclosed the prospectus of the *Clydesdale Journal*, "which he had agreed to support,"[3] and in November, the Lord Advocate circulated a letter among his friends recommending it to their notice. Next year,

[1] Printed in *Letters on the Affairs of Scotland*, by Lord Cockburn and others, pp. 30-31.

[2] A. H. Millar, *The Dundee Advertiser, 1801-1901.* Dundee, 1901.

[3] *Scot. Corr.* vol. xxxii.

the *Beacon* was founded in Edinburgh under the same auspices. Both of these newspapers were distinguished, even at this period, by the virulence with which they attacked their opponents. Mr. Stuart of Dunearn, a prominent Whig, being grossly insulted in the *Beacon*, caned the printer in the street. Mr. James Gibson, another Whig, was then repeatedly attacked. At last, suspecting something more than Government patronage, he wrote to Lord Advocate Rae and asked if he were a partner. Rae replied that he was not; but he enclosed a copy of a document binding himself and other subscribers as security for the *Beacon* to the amount of £100. The names of the others soon transpired and were found to consist of Government officials. These disclosures ended the career of the *Beacon*, whose place was taken by the *Clydesdale Journal*, or, as it was now called, the *Glasgow Sentinel*. Stuart of Dunearn, being again scurrilously libelled in its columns, brought an action of damages against Borthwick and Alexander the publishers. Borthwick thereupon offered to hand over the originals of the articles if the case was dropped. Stuart agreed, and on examining the manuscripts he discovered that the bitterest libels had been written in a disguised hand by one of his kinsmen, Sir Alexander Boswell of Auchinleck, "Bozzy's" eldest son. Stuart challenged Boswell, the duel took place, and Boswell fell mortally wounded. Stuart was brought to trial for murder, and Borthwick, to prevent further revelations, was kept in custody by the Lord Advocate on a charge of having stolen the manuscripts from his partner. Stuart was acquitted, and Borthwick was at once released.[1]

In the House of Commons, in June, 1822, Mr. Abercromby moved for a committee of inquiry into the conduct of the Lord Advocate and other Scottish law officers of the Crown

[1] Cockburn, *Memorials*, 327-335, 338-347; Omond, *op. cit.* ii. 271-280.

in connection with these proceedings, but his motion was lost by a majority of twenty-five. Next year he returned to the attack, and on this occasion he scored a moral victory, as he was only defeated by six. Meanwhile, the former debate had induced the Government to take action, and in October, 1822, the Home Secretary consulted the Scottish judges as to the advisability of changing the method of selecting juries, and of curtailing the legal powers of the Lord Advocate. The judges seem to have been adverse to any change, but the Jury Acts of 1822 and 1825 removed some of the grievances complained of. They did not, however, satisfy the demands of the Whigs as stated by Cockburn in the *Edinburgh Review.* He pointed out that the Lord Advocate, besides being public prosecutor, was the dispenser of patronage and practically Secretary for Scotland, and he contended that nothing but the separation of the political from the legal duties of his office would restore confidence in the administration of Scotland.

Cockburn lived to modify his views when his own party came into power, and in point of fact it was against the principles of Tory government rather than the powers of the Lord Advocate that his criticism had been directed. For it was the second Lord Melville who, since the death of his father, had been the real "Manager of Scotland." It is true that he was never Home Secretary, and that during his time no member of the Dundas family filled the post of Lord Advocate. Moreover, Robert Dundas, the former holder of that office, since his appointment as Lord Chief Baron of the Court of Exchequer had been unable, partly through ill-health and partly through lack of opportunity, to co-operate with his cousin in maintaining the Dundas interest.[1]

[1] Referring to the early influence of the Edinburgh Reviewers, and of the necessity of rewarding and protecting those "fine young men of a subsequent growth who had not been inveigled," Melville wrote to

Nevertheless, the Scottish Correspondence in the Record Office shows that on all matters of importance relating to Scotland, and especially on all questions of patronage, Lord Melville was invariably consulted. In 1827 his management of Scottish affairs ceased. In that year the Ministry of Lord Liverpool was succeeded by that of Canning, and Melville, following the example of Peel and Wellington, resigned. Canning had therefore to turn to the Whigs for support. Lord Lansdowne was appointed Home Secretary, and, as a concession to the Scottish Whigs, it was agreed that he should be guided in the administration of Scotland by the advice of three of their party, Kennedy, Abercromby, and Lord Minto. The death of Canning in August, 1827, brought this arrangement to an end. The next Ministry, that of Goderich, only lasted four months; and in January, 1828, Wellington became Prime Minister, with Peel as Home Secretary. To the dismay of the Scottish Tories, Melville accepted the office of President of the Board of Control without a seat in the Cabinet. Although he succeeded to his former post of first Lord of the Admiralty nine months later, he never recovered the influence he had once possessed. Such at least was the inference which the Tories drew from an appointment made in 1830. Wellington and Peel, anxious to conciliate the Whigs, gave to Mr. Abercromby, the prominent reformer, the place of Chief Baron of the

Sidmouth on June 18, 1818: "When the present Chief Baron held the situation of Lord Advocate, his personal qualities, and the station of himself and his family in this part of the kingdom, kept together all those young men; his house was open to them, and they collected themselves from all parts of Scotland. But ever since he has been on the bench, and the state of his health compelled him to withdraw very much from the society in which he formerly lived, his place has not been supplied, and the Reviewing gang have been in full activity, administering fair and inviting poison. They must if possible be counteracted, however, and I have no doubt that with proper attention they may be successfully resisted." *Scot. Corr.* vol. xxix.

Exchequer, which, under ordinary circumstances, would have fallen to Lord Advocate Rae.

These Ministerial changes were but the outward signs of an approaching crisis. In June, 1830, George IV. died, and writs were issued for a new Parliament on the accession of William IV. During the elections came the news of the bloodless French Revolution, which gave a further impetus to the movement for reform. The opening Parliament of the reign was of a different complexion from its predecessors. Many of the Tories had been alienated from Wellington by the Catholic Emancipation Act, and the Whigs could no longer support one who had openly stated his determined opposition to reform. These conditions were fatal to the Wellington Ministry, which fell on November 16, 1830. In the Whig Administration formed by Grey, Jeffrey was Lord Advocate, and Cockburn, whose *Memorials* have been so frequently quoted, Solicitor General.

The advent of the Whigs to power had an immediate effect in Scotland. "Altogether Toryism seems dead in this place," wrote the new Solicitor General to Kennedy in December, " and our sole danger is from the Antipodes. . . . There is a good deal of Radicalism in the country, founded on long and absurdly defended abuses, excited by recent triumphs, and exaggerated by distress. But though the alarm that many people feel may be useful, I cannot say that I as yet discern anything that reasonable concession and a firm government may not overcome." [1] Cockburn's analysis of the situation proved to be correct. In the ensuing struggle, the Radicals joined forces with the Whigs. A common detestation of " absurdly defended abuses " was not the only bond of sympathy between the two parties. It was the Whig leaders of the Scottish Bar who had befriended the extremists in the courts of law. It was Jeffrey

[1] *Letters on the Affairs of Scotland*, 271.

and his Whig colleagues who had been their counsel in the sedition trials of 1817, and again in 1820. Jeffrey had long been of the opinion that the Whigs were too disposed to govern "without making the people a direct political element." "Let the true friends of liberty and the constitution," he wrote to Horner in 1809, "join with the people, assist them to ask with dignity and with order all that ought to be granted, and endeavour to withhold them from asking more."[1] The year 1830 witnessed the fulfilment of his hopes; and it is significant that when Peter Mackenzie, a noted Radical of his day, published the *Life and Trial of Thomas Muir* in 1831, the work was dedicated to Jeffrey, "one of the most esteemed and popular men in Scotland."

Mackenzie's preface was dated April 11, and the author anticipated that by the month of August the Reform Bill, then under discussion, would have received the royal assent. Such had been the general expectation in Scotland, the passing of the second reading having been made the occasion of public rejoicing.[2] But the Government was defeated on the third reading, and another appeal was made to the old constituencies. The country was thoroughly roused, and in Scotland, as in England, there was an almost universal demand for "The Bill, the whole Bill, and nothing but the Bill."[3] On the assembling of the new Parliament, the Reform Bill was immediately introduced and passed through the Commons. "What will the Lords do?" now became the burning question of the day. Alison, the historian, in an elaborate series of articles in *Blackwood's Magazine*, entitled "The Late French Revolution and Parliamentary

[1] *Life*, i. 195-7; v. also ii. 126-7, 199-200.

[2] Among the illuminations displayed in Glasgow was a transparency of Thomas Muir. *Scotsman*, Mar. 30, 1831.

[3] The phrase originated with Rintoul of the *Spectator*, a former editor of the *Dundee Advertiser*. A. H. Millar, *op. cit.*

Reform," tendered the advice of the Scottish Tories. It had been affirmed that the demand for an extended franchise must be satisfied or a revolution would inevitably ensue. A similar argument had been put forward in the days of Pitt. "But the clamour was *not* met by concession. Mr. Pitt resisted the popular cry."[1] Yet when the Peers justified the hopes of the Tories by rejecting the measure, there was every sign that the general fears of a revolution would be realised. "For God's sake keep the people quiet in Scotland," the Lord Advocate wrote to Cockburn. "Nothing in the world would do such fatal mischief as riot and violence, ending, as it *now* must do, in lavish bloodshed —from which my soul recoils."[2] Fierce as was the indignation in Scotland, however, it was vented in a constitutional manner, and no disturbance took place.

The apprehensions of disorder were finally dispelled by the passing of the English Reform Act on June 7, 1832. Inasmuch as the system of representation in Scotland was more irrational than that of England, the Scottish Reform Bill, which received the royal assent on the 17th of the following month, was a more revolutionary measure. According to its provisions, householders rated at £10 replaced the electorate of self-elected Town Councils. In the counties, the qualifications of Parchment Barons were abolished, and the franchise conferred on the proprietors of real property valued at £10 a year, and on tenants, with a nineteen years' lease, paying a rent of £50. Eight members were added to the representation of Scotland, two members being allotted to Edinburgh and Glasgow respectively, and one each to Paisley, Aberdeen, Perth, Dundee, and Greenock.

For several weeks after the passing of the Act, there were celebrations of the victory all over the country. One of the most imposing—the Reform Jubilee—was organised by

[1] Vol. xxix. 761.

[2] *Life of Jeffrey*, i. 324.

the Edinburgh Trades' Union Council. On the morning of August 10, a vast crowd assembled on the historic Bruntsfield Links, and voted addresses to the King, the Commons, and the Ministry. This was followed by a procession of the Trades. Of the numerous banners and insignia displayed on that occasion, two were of special significance. One, with the motto, " For a nation to be free it is sufficient that it wills it," recalled Lafayette's dictum, which had long been familiar to readers of the *Rights of Man*. The other, mounted in black, was carried by the chair and cabinet-makers, and was inscribed: " To the memory of Muir, Gerrald, and others, who suffered for reform."[1] The Whig Reform Bill would not have satisfied these advocates of manhood suffrage and annual Parliaments. Yet it was by a sure instinct that the artisans commemorated those who, in championing the principles of the French Revolution, had been the first to rouse the industrial classes from their political apathy. The abiding memory of their unjust punishment had been an impelling motive of all Scottish reformers, and even their political doctrines, for many years to come, were to be embodied in the programme of Radicals and Chartists.

[1] *Scotsman*, Aug. 11. "One most just placard." Cockburn, *Journals*, i. 53-4. But Cockburn was not in favour of the monument erected to their memory on the Calton Hill, Edinburgh, in 1844. He thought that if they had been properly tried, the idea of raising a monument would never have occurred to any one. Dislike of Radical enthusiasm had doubtless some influence on Cockburn's opinion.

APPENDIX A.

The Minutes of the Proceedings of the First General Convention of the Delegates from the Societies of the Friends of the People throughout Scotland, at their several sittings in Edinburgh on the 11th, 12th, and 13th December, 1792, as contained in the Spy's Reports, Public Record Office, London—*Home Office* (*Scotland*) *Correspondence*, vol. vi.—and in the Official Minutes published at Edinburgh, 1793, reprinted in *Parliamentary History*, vol. xxxi. 871-9.

Sederunt of the Delegates of the Associations of the Friends of the People met in Convention at Edinburgh, Tuesday, 11th December, 1792.

Mr. Hugh Bell in the chair,
Thomas Muir, Esq., Vice-President,
Wm. Skirving, Esq., Secretary, } *pro tem.*

Mr. Muir, after a short introductory speech, moved that the delegates verify their powers. Mr. Skirving then rendered the commissions. These were by letter, and some of them began "Citizen President."

Calton of Glasgow : Mr. David Russell.

Anderston : Allan M'Lean.

Glasgow : Colonel Dalrymple, Wm. Dalrymple, Esq., A. Riddell, George Crawford.

Canongate, No. 2 : John Stronach, Alex. Aitchison.

Canongate No. 1 : Thomas Muir, Esq., Geo. Malcolm, Wm. Campbell, Alex. Bell, John Buchanan, J. Fortune, J. Thomson Callender, John Thomson, Wm. Wallace, J. Taylor.

Dundee : Thomas Muir, Esq.

Anstruther Easter : James Darcy.

Kilbarchan, Lochwinnoch, and *two other societies :* Geo. Lee.

Pathhead of Kirkcaldy : Robert Cork, Matthew Shiells.

Stirling : Alex. Forrester, Wm. Clark, Wm. Gibson, Robert Marr, Wm. Patterson, Wm. Taylor.

Forfar : Rev. Thos. Fysche Palmer.

Paisley United Societies : James Alcie (?), David Graham.

Nine Societies in Perth : Wm. Bisset, Wm. Miller, Alex. Paul, Johnston, M'Nab, Pat. Grant, Rev. Mr. Wilson, Geo. Miller, Esq., Wyllie.

Cowgate, Edinburgh : John M'Intyre, Simon Drummond, John Gourlie, John Millar, Esq., Rev. Mr. M'Lean, and some others.

Portsburgh, Edinburgh : Lord Daer, Wm. Skirving, Esq., Robert Fowler, Allan, Hardie, and some others.

Dunbar : Thos. Mitchell, Sawers, Cowan.

Belhaven : Alex. Oliver, Kilgour.

Shotts : Rev. Ebenezer Hislop.

Hamilton : Joseph Miller, Esq., Bailie Vanie (?).

Lodge Room, Black Friars' Wynd, Edinburgh : John Reid, Alex. Crawford, and some others.

Gorbals, Glasgow : John Wilson, James Smith.

St. Cyrus : Wm. Christie, Wm. Walter.

Finnie : Wm. Wallace.

Strathaven : Wm. Aitken.

Dunfermline : James Boyd, Alex. Stewart.

Leslie : Wm. Skirving.

Candleriggs, Glasgow : Robert Smith.

Montrose : Wm. Robb, Jr.

Paisley : James Ellis (?), Dan. Blane.

Lawnmarket, Edinburgh : Wm. Romanes, John Grindlay, and three others.

Taylors' Hall, Potterrow : John Clark, Wm. Alexander, T. Ritchie, and other six.

Glasgow : John Gray.

Seven Societies, Kilmarnock : Wm. Wyllie, Wm. Muir.

Lodge Room, New Town : Gordon Murray, Kain, Walter Veitch, Phin.

Glasgow, High Street : John Bruce.

Glasgow, Balmanns Street : George Stayley.

Dundee : Wm. Bisset, Wm. Webster.

Penicuik: Smith, Tait.

Dovehill and Saltmarket, Glasgow: Geo. Hill.

Gallowgate, Glasgow: A. M'Vicar.

Dalkeith: Carfrae, Caldwalls, Moffat, Ritchie, Gray.

Musselburgh: Wm. Begg, A. Carmichael.

Grinston's Tavern, Glasgow: Wm. Hart, Wm. Riddell, Geo. Waddell.

Kirkintilloch: James Baird.

New Town and Calton of Edinburgh: W. Christie, White, Watt.

Abbeyhill: Alex. Nisbet.

Original Association, Edinburgh: Izett (?), Hugh Handyside, James Farquhar, Esq., Walter Russell, Sam. Paterson, Robert Forsyth, Esq., Lothian, Alex. Ritchie, James Inglis, Livingston, Berry, Mitchell Young, Galloway, Dr. Yuille, Taylor, Lancashire, Hutchison, Cleghorn, Dalrymple, Allan, [John Allen ?], Dunn, Smith, Campbell.

Pathhead No. 1.: } Letter congratulating the Convention, but
Pathhead No. 2.: } no delegates.

Campsie: Henry.

Water of Leith: A delegate, but not having his commission, was desired to bring it to-morrow.

New Society, Mather's Tavern, Edinburgh: Bartlet, M'Asline (?).

Linlithgow, and Linlithgow No. 2: Joseph Reed, Stephen Mitchell, Joseph Calder, Malcolm Ewan, Geo. Ross.

Mr. Muir moved that Mr. Henry, delegate from Saltcoats, should be admitted as a member of the Convention, although owing to the secretary's negligence the commission had not been made out.—Agreed.

A member of the Water of Leith Society claimed the same privilege, but not being known to the Convention, and being so near his constituents, was ordered to bring his commission to-morrow.

A letter from Saltcoats was read congratulating the Convention, and mentioning that, though newly erected, the society consisted of 60 persons, but, being yet in its infancy, had appointed no delegates.

Mr. Muir, after a short speech on the business they were met upon, proposed that the Convention should proceed to elect a President, Vice-President, Treasurer, and Secretary.

Lord Daer then rose, addressing the Convention by the familiar epithet of "Fellow Citizens," and insisted that there was no occasion for a formal election of office-bearers. That although there ought to be indeed some person in the chair, whom the speakers might address, there was no occasion for a president, vice-president, etc. That they were all met on the great principles of liberty and political equality, and therefore they ought to be jealous of all men set up in a permanent situation. He therefore moved that there should be no regular office-bearers or leaders. That it was proper, while Ministry had their eye upon those whom they considered as leaders, to divide the responsibility among many, and that at all events every appearance of establishing an aristocracy amongst us ought to be guarded against.

Colonel Dalrymple rose and seconded his Lordship's motion, and enforced the propriety of it. (Repeated applauses.)

Mr. Muir adopted the same idea and repeated what he had often observed formerly, viz. that no confidence ought to be placed in any man, but the Convention should keep constantly in their view the principles of liberty, political equality, and eternal justice. He concluded by moving that a daily election of office-bearers should take place.

Mr. Aitchison followed the last speaker. He agreed with the general ideas thrown out by the noble lord and the other speakers who had gone before him, but thought it necessary that the offices of treasurer and secretary should be permanent, to prevent the affairs of the Association from going into confusion. Lord Daer in a reply agreed that these offices should be permanent.

James Campbell, Esq., proposed that the election of a preses should be daily, and that Mr. Bell should now be called to the chair, which was agreed to by plaudits.

Mr. Muir and Lord Daer proposed that Colonel Dalrymple should be called to the chair, but the Colonel declined the honour, insisting that as a military man the Ministry might accuse him of an attempt to raise a rebellion in the country.

Mr. Muir replied and insisted on the Colonel's acceptance. The Colonel then accepted, saying he would not flinch from the service of his country. (Reiterated applauses.)

Mr. Muir moved that Mr. Skirving be elected secretary. (Agreed.)

James Campbell, Esq., moved that Mr. Muir be elected vice-president.

Mr. Muir insisted that according to what had now been resolved on there was no occasion for that office.

Mr. Fowler moved that, for preserving the order of business, no member should speak more than once on his own motion, and that all motions be put in writing.

Mr. Muir moved that a committee be appointed to draw up a solemn declaration of the principles of the Convention.

Mr. Morthland proposed some resolutions that were drawn up last night in Mather's by several members of the original association. Before reading them, he observed that placemen and pensioners load us with obloquy, accusing us of an intention to subvert the Constitution—that we are disloyal subjects—enemies to Kings, Lords, and Commons—that we wish to plunge everything into anarchy—that therefore it was necessary to refute their calumnies by full, fair, and free declaration of our principles. He then read the resolutions, and proposed that they should lie on the table for consideration on a future day.

Mr. Muir said that unless they were considered immediately, they might as well lie on Arthur's Seat.

Colonel Dalrymple agreed that they should be considered immediately.

Mr. Fowler insisted that all the motions should lie one day on the table.

A member from the country proposed that instead of petitioning Parliament, the Convention should present an address to the King.

Mr. Drummond opposed this measure.

Colonel Dalrymple, the Preses, called to the order of business.

Mr. Muir moved a committee on the declaration.

Mr. Bell moved that the committee should retire and report.

Colonel Dalrymple was against trusting a business of such importance to any committee.

Mr. Morthland on this proposed a committee of the whole house.

Lord Daer was against the immediate and precipitant consideration of a business of so much importance which might ruin the whole cause in twenty-four hours.

Colonel Dalrymple was against any delay, as he said that the whole association expected something to be done immediately.

Mr. Fowler said the declaration required caution. It was our sole business—we stake our reputation and character upon it. It therefore required time.

M. Campbell opposed any delay.

Mr. Muir insisted for an immediate determination in a committee of the whole Convention.

Mr. Buchanan proposed that the resolutions should be immediately printed and submitted to the consideration of the members.

Mr. Muir agreed to this, and proposed that the Convention should decide upon them to-morrow, which was agreed to and ordered.

Wednesday, 12th December, 1792.

Lord Daer, after an introductory speech directed to the establishing regulations for their procedure in business, read several propositions respecting the order of business, motions, etc.

Mr. Muir, in a speech of some length, opposed everything that had been proposed by Lord Daer.

A delegate from Glasgow then rose and expressed his surprise that the Convention should lose time debating about matters of form, and was followed on the same grounds by one of the Paisley delegates.

Lord Daer rose to explain, showed that forms were absolutely necessary, expressed his disapprobation of standing committees as tending to throw the powers of the Convention into the hands of a junto, insisted that every question should be discussed by the Convention, after being proposed in writing and lying on the table some time. That he had been in France, where the delegates at first were led into a labyrinth of business by particular motions made with the intention of interrupting or involving their proceedings, until they at last adopted the measure he was now proposing, of receiving a variety of motions, letting them lie on the table, then reading them all, and adopting the best.

The debate was interrupted by the reading of a commission just presented by the Bankhead Association in favour of Thomas Muir, Esq., A. M'Ewan, Bell, Farquharson, M'Coll.

A country delegate moved that the Convention should not be

bound by any fixed rules, but be at liberty to act as they should see proper at all times.

Mr. Muir moved for the order of the day.

Mr. Fowler spoke in favour of Lord Daer's propositions. He was against trifling about forms, said some people attempted to raise themselves from insignificance by advancing plausible arguments in favour of infamous measures.

Mr. Buchanan spoke in favour of Lord Daer's propositions, and insisted for a vote. Whereupon they were agreed to without a vote.

Lord Daer, called to the chair, declined on account of his having to attend a county meeting on the same business of Parliamentary reform, though he did not expect so much good from it. The Convention insisted by repeated plaudits. His Lordship accepted.

(Lord Daer in the chair.)

The minutes were read and corrected—the word "regularly" being inserted instead of "lawfully," as suggested by Lord Daer. It was agreed that no plaudits should be given in the course of the after proceedings.

Thomas Muir, Esq., presented a printed address from the Society of United Irishmen in Dublin to the Delegates for Promoting a Reform in Scotland, dated 23rd November, 1792, signed by Wm. Drennan, Chairman, Archd. Hamilton Rowan, Secretary.[1]

Colonel Dalrymple and Hugh Bell protested against its being read, as, in their opinion, it contained treason, or at least misprision of treason.

T. Muir, Esq., took upon himself the whole responsibility and the whole danger of the measure.

The cry to hear it was universal. Mr. Muir, after reading it and paying the author or authors many compliments, moved that it should lie on the table this day, and that to-morrow he would move that an answer be sent to it by the Convention.

Mr. Aitchison seconded the motion.

Mr. Forsyth gave Mr. Muir credit for his good intentions, but insisted by the motion he now made, and promised to make, he

[1] Printed in *Parl. Hist.* xxxiv. 615-7.

would render it no longer his own business but the Convention's. Mr. Forsyth added that in his opinion it was, *first*, very inexpedient for the Convention to answer it, that it bordered on an attack on the British Constitution, that the words "inviolability of the people" appeared to him in this view; to mend the Constitution was legal, to do more was to raise a standard against the Constitution. *Secondly*, with regard to the legality of the paper, it was not ascertained; in his opinion it was illegal, but at all events it was inexpedient. Hitherto Mr. Muir was responsible, but if the Convention should make it their own by approving and answering it, *they* became responsible. Therefore he cautioned the members against it.

Mr. Muir rose to explain—insisted that there was no danger: "The paper supports the Constitution—I am determined to act consistently."

Mr. Fowler insisted it was treasonable. He quoted the words, "Not by a *calm* contented secret wish for a reform, but by openly, actively, and urgently *willing* it, with the unity and energy of an *embodied* nation." He insisted that these words might be construed into high treason.

Lord Daer was against the paper being answered or even lying on the table.

A country delegate (who said he was also a member of the Royal Burghs) said that if such a paper was read before his constituents, they would withdraw themselves from the Association. An interruption issued from a call to "hear him, hear him."

The order of the day was called before he could proceed.

Mr. Muir, however, insisted on replying to Mr. Fowler.

A vote was called for. Upon a show of hands, a majority appeared for hearing Mr. Muir.

He rose and said that if he had made no reply to Mr. Fowler, the report would have gone out and been spread abroad by the enemies of reform that he had spoken high treason. He then read the pages objected to, and vindicated them, and added, "We *will* a reform, we do not, we cannot consider ourselves as mowed and melted down into another country. Have we not distinct courts, judges, juries, laws, etc.? I myself have studied the law, and am confident that the paper is perfectly constitutional. How ridiculous, then, will it appear if we send no answer to this address! Colonel Dalrymple, Lord Daer, and all the Honourable Gentlemen *will* a reform. But if the people of Ireland send us a congratulatory address in our spirit, it is immediately construed as treason. The people of Ireland *will* a reform, the Scotch *will* a reform. Is the Irish nation to be considered as the Scape Goat in this business ? Is it treason to petition Parliament ? "

Mr. Fowler said that Scotland and England were but one people.

Colonel Dalrymple, Mr. Forsyth, and Mr. Fowler opposed the paper lying on the table.

A vote was then taken whether the paper should lie on the table, or whether the Convention should pass to the order of the day. It was carried by a division for the latter.

Lord Daer said that he had got an anonymous letter addressed to him as a member of the *National* Convention. He took this occasion to caution the members against the use of this epithet, as the Convention could not merit that title unless all Scotland had sent up delegates.

Lord Daer, being obliged to go to the county meeting, Colonel Dalrymple was called to the chair.

(Colonel Dalrymple in the chair.)

The report of the committee was called for. Mr. Morthland proceeded to read the following printed resolutions drawn up by the committee.

[Resolved :

That this Convention, taking under consideration the insidious, wicked, and inflammatory artifices employed by the enemies of all reform to misrepresent and calumniate the Friends of the People as the promoters of public discord, and advocates for an unjust and absurd violation of private property by an equal division, think it incumbent upon them to declare that they hold all such designs in utter detestation and abhorrence, and that they will maintain the established constitution of Great Britain on its genuinely acknowledged principles, consisting of Three Estates—King, Lords, and Commons.

Resolved :

That the members of this Convention will, to the utmost of their power, concur in aiding and strengthening the hands of the civil magistrate throughout this kingdom to repress riot and tumult, and all attempts whatsoever to disturb the tranquillity, happiness, and good order of society.

Resolved :

That it appears to this Convention that very great abuses have arisen in the government of this country from a neglect of the genuine principles of the Constitution ; that these abuses have of late grown to an alarming height, and produced great discontents.

Resolved :

That the essential measures to be pursued in order to remove these abuses and effectually to do away with their mischievous consequences are :

First, to restore the freedom of election, and an equal representation of the people in Parliament.

Secondly, To secure to the people a frequent exercise of their right of electing their representatives.

Resolved :

That for the purpose of accomplishing these constitutional objects, the proper and legal method is that of applying by petition to Parliament.

Resolved :

That these resolutions be printed in the Scotch and English newspapers ; and also be printed in handbills for general distribution among the Associated Friends of the People in different parts of Scotland.] [1]

Mr. Morthland having read the first resolution, a country delegate objected to the words, " King, Lords, and Commons," and insisted that if they were retained, the word " Unanimously " should be deleted. He proposed the following addition by way of amendment : " That every organisation against the Friends of the People is malicious, and ill-founded." Seconded.

Mr. Drummond, printer, objected to the correction and amendment.

The former delegate rose. He said, " Our constituents will be disappointed by such resolutions. We came here to petition for redress of grievances, not to declare acknowledged principles."

A clergyman from the country wished that the resolution had not been moved, but as it was moved in its present form, he hoped

[1] The parts enclosed in square brackets are taken from the official minutes.

that the Convention would adopt it, as the rejection of the clause, " King, Lords, and Commons," would give wing to the malicious slanders of their enemies.

Mr. John Wilson, teacher, was for retaining the clause, and approved of the resolutions as printed. He objected to the amendment, particularly to the word " malicious." He even thought that the words " wicked " and " enemies of all reform " might be omitted.

Mr. Morthland vindicated the printed resolution as it stood, and said that the words were not too strong. They applied in their fullest extent to the whole junto of placemen and pensioners.

Mr. Bisset of Dundee objected to the word " sedition " as ambiguous.

One of the delegates from Pathhead moved to leave out the words " King, Lords, and Commons."

T. Muir, Esq., said, " Our great business is to reform not to alter, to hold up the Constitution to the people, to get it restored to its original purity." He vindicated the word " sedition," and proposed altering the arrangement of the sentence by placing the words " the established constitution of Great Britain " before " on its genuine acknowledged principles," which would prevent ambiguity.

Mr. Allen moved that the word " acknowledge " be inserted instead of " maintain."

Mr. Buchanan seconded this amendment.

Mr. Muir mentioned an anonymous letter he had received, which contained some impertinence which he despised.

Several speakers arising, Mr. Wm. Campbell moved that only one person be allowed to speak at once.

Mr. Clark moved that as Friends of the People were calumniated with entertaining notions of Liberty and Equality inimical to property that an addition should be made to the resolution explaining what was meant by the word " Equality "—that it was only *political* equality that was wanted.

Mr. Muir approved of the motion, but said it ought to form a separate resolution.

Mr. Morthland put the question, " Shall this resolution pass ? " Upon a show of hands it carried by a great majority.

Mr. Drummond then begged that the dissentient members

would allow it to be marked as printed " Unanimously." " By no means," replied many voices.

Mr. Morthland read the second resolution.

Captain Johnston moved to insert " violation " for " neglect."

Mr. Muir moved that " real " be inserted instead of " acknowledged."

Mr. Buchanan wished that the Convention would come forward and mention specific grievances in the present stage of the business.

Mr. Fowler approved of Captain Johnston's amendment, but thought that " neglect " should be retained. He proposed that the clause should be " neglect and violation." The question being put, it was passed unanimously.

The third resolution was then read.

A country delegate said that he was instructed by his constituents to *insist* that *annual* Parliaments should be demanded, and that political equality should be urged.

Mr. Morthland was against any specification of grievances in the present stage; that it would be time enough when Parliament allowed a Bill to be brought in for a reform to specify particulars; that it was proper to wait for the opinion of their friends in England, whether *annual* or *triennial* Parliaments should be insisted for.

Mr. Forsyth went over the same ground, and proposed the word " establish " instead of " restore."

Mr. Muir went largely into this argument, and said that he could prove that both England and Scotland were once possessed of a free Constitution, and that therefore it was only a restoration of old rights and not an establishment of new ones that was wanted. He said if he were to object to any part of this resolution, it would be the words " strike at the root of," as the enemies of reform might construe this clause into treason, for the *root* of these abuses was well known. The House of Commons had voted many years ago that the royal influence " had increased, was increasing, and ought to be diminished." (A laugh.) To put it out of the power of our enemies, therefore, to say we mean to strike at the royal power, he proposed to insert the words " in order to remove."

Mr. Skirving proposed to omit the word " restore " and insert " obtain."

A country delegate followed the same idea.

Mr. Aitchison insisted that no word in the English language was so proper as "restore"; that if any other word such as "obtain" or "establish" was adopted, we might justly be accused of *innovation*; but in fact we had nothing more to ask than to be "restored" to our original rights; that he was certain that by the English Constitution, so long ago as the days of King Alfred, every free man had a vote in choosing his representative, and that in those days Parliaments were annual; that in the time of Edward I. and Edward III. Parliaments were expressly ordered to be called twice a year or *oftener*, if there was occasion. He was happy to hear from Mr. Muir that the freedom of Scotland was equally ancient, but at any rate as one people we are entitled to the same privileges.

Mr. Muir perfectly agreed with the last speaker, and added that he could prove from ancient records that Parliaments were often called by Edward I. four times a year. He also repeated his assurances that Scotch freedom was as ancient as English.

Messrs. Wilson and Forsyth, however, still insisted for the word "obtain" instead of "restore."

A country delegate called for the question.

Mr. Aitchison replied to Messrs. Wilson and Forsyth.

Mr. Muir insisted that although in those days all were not equally free, owing to the abuses introduced by the Conquest, yet every man who was free had a right to sit in Parliament, either by himself or his representative; that in Scotland a free man was even more free than in England. He insisted that if any word was adopted instead of "restore," we were wrong in complimenting our Constitution. "Why praise, why flatter the British Constitution (said he), if it is radically wrong, if it never was right?" In those periods of freedom he mentioned, not only our Parliaments were held four times a year, but every freeman of the age of twenty-one had a vote in choosing his representative.

A country delegate observed that the debate had deviated from the original question. Another called for the question, and insisted for a specification of grievances.

Mr. Morthland insisted that they should stick by the general idea of a reform, without condescending upon particular grievances.

A country delegate proposed the word " remove " instead of " strike at the root of."

A plaudit following this, it appeared to be the sense of the house when

Mr. Morthland proposed an amendment by adding after " remove," " the source of these abuses."

Mr. Muir said that he was not willing to dispute about words, or to spend the time of the Convention in mere verbal criticism, although the metaphor of " removing a source " did not quite please him. But gentlemen would do well to attend to the inferences that might be drawn from such a mode of expression. " What is the source of these abuses ?—The royal influence. What ! Are you to remove the King ? Then, gentlemen, according to this, we shall find ourselves in the same predicament with those foolish fellows who got drunk with the soldiers in the Castle the other week, and drank, " George the Third and Last." (A universal laugh.)

Mr. Fowler proposed " sweep away " instead of " remove."

Mr. Morthland read the resolution as amended, and put the question. Carried.

The fourth resolution was then read.

A country delegate proposed that the Convention should recommend to their constituents to send up petitions to Parliament.

The Rev. Mr. Palmer complained that part of last night's resolution had been neglected, particularly the following words which he had moved, " and they do recommend to the associations to petition accordingly."

It was agreed that Mr. Palmer was right, and that the omission should be supplied.

Mr. Morthland said that he had written out a resolution, but the paper had gone to press in its present form.

A delegate from Dunfermline said that his constituents wished to petition Parliament, but laboured under the difficulty of not knowing how to do it.

Mr. Fowler said that petitions ought to be sent not only from particular societies, but from the General Convention.

Mr. Forsyth observed that Parliament did not know us, could not acknowledge us as delegates. We must therefore petition as individuals.

A reverend delegate (Wilson, I think), wished that the Association should be instructed to petition early, and that our friends everywhere should be requested to attend Mr. Grey's motion, whatever it might be. (A loud laugh.)

A country delegate moved to petition for a repeal of our four Acts of Parliaments, viz. Henry VIII., Charles II., Queen Anne, and George I.

Mr. Palmer repeated his question whether the Convention wished to petition. He said that it would give life to the cause.

Mr. Forsyth said, " Parliament knows no such people. We can only petition as inhabitants of such a place. Every district should petition Parliament."

Mr. Morthland went over the same ground. He said that an instance happened a few years ago when a petition was thrown over the Bar of the House of Commons though presented by the gentlemen of the County of Northumberland, because it was signed in their name by the sheriff-depute. The speaker on that occasion observed, " The petition is indeed subscribed by the sheriff-depute (for the clerk), but not one of the gentlemen of the county has subscribed it. We know nothing of it as theirs." He therefore insisted that all must subscribe as individuals.

The Rev. Mr. Palmer proposed that the Convention should recommend to the associations to send up petitions from their different districts, and that they should also send up a petition as individuals as soon as possible.

Mr. Muir cordially agreed with Mr. Palmer's idea. He added that though they could only petition as individuals, they would be known. It would be whispered, it would be spoken of, that they were a representative body from the different associations of Scotland. Mr. Grey would even tell the House, " Your forms will not admit of their taking the title of a Convention, but it is in fact the deed of the representatives of a great body of the people." He would move for a Committee of Inquiry upon the general propositions. " He will insist that the people are *firm, collected*, and *strong*; and he will give the petition, though only signed by the Convention as individuals, all the weight of a representative body."

Wednesday—Evening Sitting.

(Colonel Dalrymple in the chair.)

[The Secretary presented the Plan of Organisation for individual societies, district associations, and for general conventions, together with a written motion by Mr. Fowler for a Committee of Publications for the purpose of communicating instruction. The same were received, and Messrs. Wilson and Fowler were requested to bring them before the House at the proper opportunity.

Mr. Muir and others brought forward the following motions, which were unanimously adopted, namely :

Resolved :

That this Convention do address the Friends of the People at London.

Resolved :

That the thanks of the Convention be returned to Messrs. Grey, Erskine, the Earl of Lauderdale, Colonel Macleod, Lord Daer, and Colonel Dalrymple for their patriotic services in the cause of the people ; to J. H. Tooke, Esq., for his masterly support of freedom ; to the Hon. Major Maitland, Mr. Sheridan, Mr. Muir, Mr. Bell, and Captain Johnston for their important assistance to overturn corruption ; also to the Rt. Hon. Charles Fox for his determined speech in the last meeting of the Whig Club ; and lastly, to all those members of the House of Commons who have supported in Parliament the cause of the People.

Agreed to Captain Johnston's two resolutions of yesterday, which are as follows :

Resolved :

That it be recommended to each society of the Friends of the People to expunge from the roll of its members, the name or names of any individual or individuals who may have acted illegally, tumultuously, or in any way to the disturbance of the public peace.

Resolved :

That any individual or individuals of the societies of the Friends of the People, whose conduct may have been legal and orderly, and who may be prosecuted by the arm of Power for adhering to the cause of the People, be defended by the united strength of the Friends of the People.

The five following motions, which Mr. Skirving proposed, were ordered to lie on the table :

I. That the Friends of the People in Britain should unite in the application to Parliament both as to the extent of the reform to be demanded, and as to the manner of executing their petition for the same.

II. That therefore this Convention should send two or three deputies to London to concert a common plan with the Friends of the People there, advising always with the several committees of Edinburgh, Glasgow, etc.

III. That these committees, while the deputies remain at London, should meet weekly, in order to instruct the deputies from time to time.

IV. That when a common plan of operation is thus procured, a General Convention be called to approve or amend the same, and particularly to direct the manner in which the petitions shall be executed and presented to Parliament.

V. That the Convention recommend that the Friends of the Constitution and of the People be in the meantime diligent in forming themselves everywhere into societies, in order to give the greater energy to their petitions.]

Mr. M'Intyre delivered a long speech, seemingly studied, full of learning and liberty, but delivered in an awkward manner. It occasioned no small entertainment. He complimented the Convention on their spirit and firmness, and quoted many authors in favour of the value of freedom. He concluded with the words of the poet, whom he quoted from " Justum et tenacem propositi virum," down to " Impavidum ferient ruinae "—a passage which, he said, exceeded all power of translation, which nevertheless he would attempt. This he did accordingly. During the whole of this *outré* speech there was much noise and laughter, mingled with plaudits.

Mr. Malcolm interrupted it more than once as foreign to the business.

Mr. Drummond called him to order, and insisted that Mr. M'Intyre should be heard.

The President said that the utmost respect was due to the venerable old man, and the Convention approved, universally calling out " Hear him, hear him."

Mr. Allen made a motion, which he read in so low a voice

that we could not hear it. [That in order to supersede the necessity of constantly resorting to the aid of a military force, it be recommended by the Convention to the Associated Friends of the People, in the different parts of the country, to hold themselves in readiness to support the civil magistrate when required for the suppression of any popular tumults that may arise in their neighbourhood.]

Mr. Muir insisted that it should lie on the table. Agreed.

Mr. Morthland called to the order of the day, and read the resolutions as last corrected. The word "sedition" was still objected to as ambiguous. Ordered to be printed.

Mr. Muir moved that a permanent Committee of Finances be appointed to be held at Edinburgh, and that one delegate from each county should be sent to it.

Mr. Malcolm proposed that it should consist of twenty-five members.

Mr. Drummond said that was too large a number, and proposed eleven.

A country delegate proposed that one should be sent from each place.

Mr. Muir proposed that there should be four Committees of Finance, to hold their meetings at Glasgow, Stirling, Perth, and Dundee, who should correspond with the one at Edinburgh, and receive contributions from the associations in their respective neighbourhoods.

Mr. Skirving proposed a Committee of Finance in every county, to correspond with that of Edinburgh. Agreed.

Mr. Muir explained the nature of the plan.

Mr. Fowler moved for a Committee of Publications to select and publish such constitutional extracts from the most approved authors in favour of liberty, as would tend largely to promote the cause of the reform by enlightening the minds of the people.

Colonel Dalrymple disapproved of the measure. "Let individuals publish what they think most proper for the general cause, but let not the Convention dictate to the people."

Mr. Muir supported the measure, and showed the danger from a recent instance of individuals publishing their own unguarded thoughts on politics.

The delegate from Johnstone approved of the measure, and

said that his constituents wished for information. Another spoke against it.

Mr. Fowler withdrew his motion.

Mr. Muir moved that some proposition should be fixed to be transmitted by the different associations to the permanent Committee of Finances.

Mr. Fowler insisted that a certain sum in proportion to the numbers should be limited.

Mr. Bisset was for leaving it to the voluntary contributions of the different associations, and moved that a Committee of Correspondence should be appointed to that purpose.

Mr. Skirving, the Presidents and Secretaries of the different societies were already appointed a General Committee of Finances in Edinburgh.

[The motions finally agreed upon were as follows :

Resolved :

That each district association shall have a committee for regulation of their own respective finances ; that the several committees of finance shall correspond with the Edinburgh committee of finance as the committee of finance for the General Convention, and remit to this committee as such, their respective contributions for the public interest.

Resolved :

That this committee of general finance in Edinburgh shall lay before each Convention a state of receipt and expenditure.

Resolved :

That the Convention, on the first day of their sitting, appoint a Committee of Constraint for the purpose of inspecting the accounts of the Convention's committee of finance, and report the result of their examination to the Convention.]

Mr. Crawford moved that the Convention should proceed to the consideration of the Irish Address.

Mr. Aitchison seconded the motion.

Mr. Allan moved that it should be printed, and copies of it dispersed among the members.

A country delegate seconded the motion.

Mr. Drummond approved of it.

Colonel Dalrymple said that he had already entered his protest against it, and hoped that the Convention would have nothing to do with it. Individuals might print it if they pleased.

A country delegate observed that the printers might take their risk of it.

Mr. Aitchison recommended it to any printers who were present. It would certainly sell well.

A country delegate observed that the Irish Address ought to be smothered in its cradle.

The Rev. Mr. Palmer moved that the Convention draw up a petition to Parliament, and that a committee be appointed to draw it up.

Mr. Muir insisted on an uniformity in a matter of such importance, and thought that the Convention should wait the proceedings of the London Association, and adopt the forms of their petition.

Mr. Palmer said that his constituents in the country were anxious that no time should be lost in petitioning Parliament.

Mr. Skirving said that there was a great danger in being too rash in sending petitions in a premature state. The cause of patronage was lost by the variety of different petitions that were presented on that subject.

Mr. Drummond said that a committee on that business was superseded.

A country delegate wished that no time should be lost lest the zeal of the people should cool.

Mr. Muir was for appointing a committee immediately. "We must have petitions to Parliament. The first must be drawn up in general terms for a reform; the second may specify particulars. The great object we ought all to have in view is equal representation; that every man, who is twenty-one years of age, who is not insane, under influence, or a criminal, should have a voice in the election of his representatives." Here he used some strong expressions about "the Offspring of the Almighty," the beginning and conclusion of which was drowned amidst the voice of the plaudits it met with. He also adverted to the law of patronage alluded to above, and said that the Act of 1690, established at the Revolution, which was thought so friendly to the cause of the people, was a mere juggle, and had been a foundation of *eternal quibbles*.

Mr. Drummond called the attention of the House to a matter of importance. A gentleman near him, who was not a delegate, nor indeed a friend to the reform, had got in by some means or other. He therefore wished that the gentleman would withdraw and save trouble to the Convention.

Colonel Dalrymple proposed calling the roll and turning out all who were not delegates.

One gentleman went out ; but the one alluded to continuing, Mr. Drummond said that he would be more particular. He was a clerk in a public office, and he wished to know how he had got a ticket or from whom.

The gentleman at last came forward to the table and showed his ticket, but said that he had not got it from a delegate, but accidentally in a coffee house.

Mr. Muir said that the investigation of this trifling intrusion was unworthy the Convention and below their dignity. As their sole object was the public good, they ought not to regard who came in, whether friends or foes, as there was room to hold them.

Mr. Drummond called the attention of the House once more [to the Irish Address], and moved that it ought to be taken into immediate consideration.

Colonel Dalrymple thought that it would tend to divide the Friends of the People.

Mr. Muir was of a different opinion, and insisted that it should be answered.

Colonel Dalrymple, Mr. Fowler, Lord Daer, Mr. Forsyth, Mr. Morthland, and Mr. Bell were against meddling with it ; and Messrs. Muir, Drummond, Palmer, and Buchanan spoke in favour of it.

Mr. Fowler said that it contained high treason against the Union betwixt England and Scotland.

Mr. Forsyth moved that the Address be returned by Mr. Muir with a private letter of acknowledgment from himself.

Mr. Muir was clear that the Convention should answer it. He spoke largely in favour of the expression "*willing* a reform," and said that the whole nation willed it. The Lord Chief Baron and the gentlemen of the county *willed* it, the Royal Burghs *willed* reform, "and cursed be the man who wills it not." (Plaudits.)

Colonel Dalrymple repeated his protest against any answer being given by the Convention to such an illegal and treasonable paper.

Mr. Fowler complimented the Irish on their spirit, but said

that they were a foreign country, and we could not legally correspond with them.

Mr. Muir agreed to withdraw the Address, to remit it to Mr. Drennan, and to mention the passages objected to that they might be smoothed.

The Rev. Mr. Palmer insisted that a general petition to Parliament be drawn up this evening, and that a committee be appointed to do it. Agreed.

Mr. Fowler being appointed one of the committee, he said that he was too much exhausted to do anything this evening.

Colonel Dalrymple recommended to the Convention to send up a petition as soon as the form should be adopted.

Mr. Fowler moved that a committee be appointed to inquire into the state of the country—its population, commerce, taxation, revenue, exports, and imports, etc.

Mr. Aitchison remarked that the first of these inquiries was almost unnecessary, being already superseded by the exertions of the patriotic baronet, Sir John Sinclair, whose *Statistical Account of Scotland* is now publishing and nearly completed.

Colonel Dalrymple replied that the committee and the correspondents in the country could obtain information on that head without the least trouble by consulting his works.

A letter from the Association at Paisley was read, congratulating the Convention on the progress of Light and Liberty.

Adjourned till Thursday at 10 o'clock.

Thursday, 13th December, 1792.

(Colonel Dalrymple in the chair.)

The petition to Parliament was presented, read, and approved. The scroll of a circular letter to the associations was read and approved, ordered to be printed, and signed by the chairman.

Mr. Allan moved that we should hold ourselves in readiness to assist the civil magistrate in suppressing all riots and tumults, and that the associations should be properly provided with arms for that purpose.

A reverend delegate made a curious speech on this subject, and asked if it was necessary that he too should wield the sword and musket.

Mr. Drummond was clear that every associator should be provided with what is commonly called a "Brown Janet," with powder, ball, and bayonet, to be provided in quelling every appearance of riot and sedition.

Mr. Newton and several others spoke against the motion.

Mr. Allan withdrew it.

Mr. Drummond and a country delegate renewed the subject of the Irish Address.

Mr. Morthland spoke upon the impropriety of taking notice of it. He approved of the spirit, but disliked the letter of it. There was one expression which seemed to be borrowed from Lafayette's memorable speech made in time of actual rebellion.

Mr. Skirving spoke in favour of the Address.

Messrs. Fowler and Bisset went over the ground they had formerly used against it.

Mr. John Thomson, Mr. Wm. Campbell, and a country delegate were for the Convention answering it.

Colonel Dalrymple repeated his former arguments against it. He understood it to be withdrawn, and wished Mr. Muir had been present.

Mr. Wilson read the plan of organisation, paragraph by paragraph.

Mr. Wm. Campbell thought that Lord Daer's motion should be added to it.

Mr. John Wilson proposed a committee on the business.

[After reading over the whole of it, the Convention recognised the right of individual societies to regulate their own internal order, and resolved that these words should be inserted: "with power to any ten towns, in which there is a society of the Friends of the People, to call a General Convention."] [1]

(Captain Johnston in the chair.)

The minutes of the last sederunt were read by Mr. Skirving.

Mr. Morthland read a motion by Mr. Thomas Ritchie, a delegate from the country, and a member of the Royal Burghs, proposing "That the Convention should order their Secretary to send an address to them along with a few copies of the resolutions,

[1] Footnote in the official minutes: "The plan of organisation to be revised and published by the Edinburgh Association."

and to request them to co-operate with the Associations of the Friends of the People in promoting a Parliamentary Reform."

Mr. Bisset (from Perth and Dundee), who is also a member of the Convention of Royal Burghs,[1] seconded the motion, and assured the meeting that the measure would be very agreeable to the members of the Convention of Royal Burghs.

A country delegate objected to the motion as improper on various accounts, particularly as the Convention of Royal Burghs had refused to co-operate with the Friends of the People when applied to some time ago.

Mr. Wm. Campbell was for the motion, although he wished that all the petty distinctions between burgesses and non-burgesses were abolished.

Mr. Bisset replied to the accusation made against the Convention of Royal Burghs, and said that there were many among them that disapproved of co-operating with the Friends of the People in the beginning of the business, being afraid that it might impede the success of their plan of a Burgh Reform ; yet they all wished for a Parliamentary Reform, and he had reason to believe that all of them now wished to co-operate with the Friends of the People to obtain it. He added that the Dean of Faculty, who was at first against the measure, was now a friend to it.

Mr. Drummond confirmed this, and assured the Convention that the Dean of Faculty, upon seeing the resolutions just published, had expressed himself in terms of high approbation of their moderation and constitutional spirit, and he had said that now he saw that they did not aim at overturning the Constitution, he would heartily wish them success in their plan of a Parliamentary Reform.

A country delegate objected to the motion of a co-operation with a set of men who, though they had set out with expressing a wish for Parliamentary Reform, had since relinquished it, and confined their demands solely to a reform in the internal government of their burghs,—an object with which the people at large had little or no concern.

Mr. Aitchison saw no harm in the motion, if it went no further than empowering the Secretary to send a letter with copies of the resolutions to the Convention of Royal Burghs, declaring our

[1] *I.e.* the Convention of Burgh Reformers, which is here confused with the Convention of Royal Burghs. V. *ante*, ch. ii. p. 9, fn. 2.

sentiments, and inviting them to co-operate individually; but we surely could not invite them to join us as a body while their object was so very distinct.

Mr. Skirving was clear that, as a Convention of the Friends of the People, we could not with propriety join any class of men or body of burgesses whatever.

Mr. Drummond was of the same opinion, but thought that we should invite them to join us as individuals.

Colonel Dalrymple declared his determined zeal to support a Parliamentary Reform. He was always a friend to it. All the rhetoric of the Dean of Faculty, all the oratory of Cicero would never persuade him to desert it. No oratory whatever would influence him to desert the great object of an actual representation of the people and a short duration of Parliament. He therefore wished to invite the members of the Royal Burghs and all classes of men to co-operate with us in obtaining these great objects.

Mr. Bisset insisted on the propriety of Mr. Ritchie's motion, assured the Convention of the good-will of the burgesses at large to the cause of reform, and mentioned Mr. Sheridan and Mr. Fox as ready to support the objects of both Conventions in Parliament along with Mr. Grey. He said that the Royal Burghs deserved much praise from the Friends of the People. They were the first that lifted up the standard of reform in Scotland, and though they had been long trifled with by Parliament, and had never yet attained their objects, their money had been well laid out, and had excited a spirit of inquiry into public grievances that would not be speedily extinguished.

Mr. Skirving was sensible of the benefits that the Burgh Reform had already conferred on the cause of liberty, but was against Mr. Ritchie's motion of inviting them to co-operate as a body.

Mr. Aitchison was convinced by what he had heard that the motion was improper. "If we invite them to co-operate with us at all, we can only invite them to join us as individuals." He therefore moved that the Secretary be desired to write to the Convention in that style only.

Mr. John Thomson seconded the motion, and thought that any other measure would be absurd.

A Glasgow delegate deprecated the idea of inviting any class of men whatever to co-operate with us, and was particularly severe upon the rights of burgesses, chartered monopolies, and all those distinctions that tended to separate man from man.

An Aberdeen delegate took the same ground, and was against the motion for the various reasons already assigned.

Mr. Fowler argued strongly for the motion, and hoped the backwardness shown by some of the members of the Royal Burghs to co-operate with us when the measure was first stated would be forgiven. They were now sensible of their error. They were penitent, and, like the Prodigal Son returning to his father, they ought to be joyfully received. He hoped that the Convention of the Friends of the People would not act so *aristocratic* a part as to reject any class of men who were willing to co-operate with us.

Captain Johnston deprecated the idea of the Friends of the People acting an aristocratic part. He said that the Royal Burghs had done so at the beginning of this business in July last, in consequence of which the Friends of the People had associated for reform, and taken that business into their own hands. Therefore we had nothing to do with them as burgesses, and if we are to invite the Royal Burghs as a separate class to co-operate with us, we should also invite the gentlemen of the county, with the Lord Chief Baron at their head. Their professed object is the same—a Parliamentary Reform. After these, we must invite other classes for consistency's sake. But the fact is, we ought to invite none but the nation at large. Our principles are published. Our objects are known. Let people of all ranks who approve of them join us, but let us not invite any. It is below the dignity of a Convention of the Friends of the People to invite any particular class of men.

Mr. Fowler replied that he had no idea of the Friends of the People taking so much state upon them as to refuse to invite particular classes of men. His Majesty himself condescended to invite the lowest classes of the people. In his Royal Proclamation, read yesterday at the Cross, he invited the seamen and landsmen of whom none would rank among the higher classes.

Mr. Muir, who had been absent at the Court on a private cause, came in during Mr. Fowler's speech. He said that he did not know what had been said upon the motion, but from the little he had heard, he was clearly against the motion. The

Friends of the People could not with any consistency invite a particular class of men to co-operate with them. As to inviting the Royal Burghs, there was a peculiar impropriety in the measure. He then gave them a particular and uninteresting detail of the conduct of the Dean of Faculty and other leading men in the Convention of Royal Burghs, when the measure of co-operating with the Friends of the People was first started. He showed how their refusal had given birth to the Edinburgh Association in Fortune's, the first proposal of which he himself had had the honour to make. He congratulated the Convention on the rapid increase in the number and respectability of the associators since the 26th of July last, and expressed his hopes that now that our principles were declared, and our objects published, they would daily increase tenfold. He concluded by expressing his hearty disapprobation of the motion, though he had every reason to hope that the members of the Royal Burghs would join the associations, as many of them had done individually. (Plaudits.)

The question was now loudly called for, when

Mr. Aitchison said he had been up some time before, but had given place to better speakers. He would not now detain them, having but one observation to make, which perhaps might place the subject in a clear point of view. The whole argument might be comprehended in a nutshell. " We call ourselves the Friends of the People. Are the burgesses a part of the people, or are they a distinct class of men? If the former, we cannot address them separately from the people at large." He therefore agreed with Captain Johnston and Mr. Muir, that we ought to invite the whole nation, but no particular class of men. (An universal plaudit.)

The question was now put, but the House appearing nearly divided, a vote was called for. To save trouble, Colonel Dalrymple counted the number for and against the motion, when there appeared for the motion, 40; against, 42—majority, 2.

[In place of this motion, the following, submitted by Mr. Skirving and seconded by Captain Johnston and others, was adopted: " That if any members of the Association for Burgh Reform apply to the Friends of the People to be admitted, they will be received cordially. But the Convention can admit no societies but societies of the Friends of the People."]

Mr. Morthland then read two additional resolutions which he proposed to be added to those already published. Agreed.

[Resolved, That since a speedy and complete redress of our present grievances will be most effectually obtained by the joint co-operation of every Briton who yet retains the spirit and the wish to be free, this Convention will, as far as their principles and objects will allow them, co-operate with the Friends of the People in London.

Resolved, That this resolution, along with those voted at a former sitting of this Convention, be transmitted by their Chairman to the Society of the Friends of the People in London.]

Mr. Muir made a proposal that the whole minutes of the Convention should be printed for the information of the public. This was also agreed to, and the following gentlemen appointed a committee to assist the Secretary in drawing them up previous to their being put to press, viz. Mr. Hugh Bell (chairman), Colonel Dalrymple, Mr. Fowler, Mr. Aitchison, Lord Daer, Captain Johnston, Mr. Morthland, Mr. John Millar, Mr. Forsyth, Mr. Muir, Mr. Skirving, and Mr. Bisset.

It was agreed to print at least 15,000 copies of the minutes of Convention. The number was left to the determination of the committee.

Mr. Muir proposed that copies should be dispersed all over the kingdom. Agreed.

John Millar called the attention of the Convention to an advertisement, signed by Sir John Inglis, Mr. Wauchope of Niddry, and Mr. Bain Whyte, in the *Edinburgh Herald* of the day [of which the following is a copy :

" We, whose names are hereunto subscribed, being unanimously and decidedly of opinion, That for the security and happiness of all classes of our fellow-countrymen, for the maintenance of our rights and liberties, and for those of our posterity, it is, in the present moment, incumbent on us and all good subjects to give to the executive government an effectual support in counteracting the efforts of sedition, and in suppressing, in their beginnings, all tumults or riots on whatever pretence they may be excited ; do hereby publicly declare our determination to take all such steps for these purposes as are within the limits of our duty in the several stations in which the Constitution of our country has placed us, and to afford by our individual exertions that active assistance to the authority of the lawful magistrate, and to the maintenance of the Established Government which is at all times due from the subjects of this free and happy kingdom, but which we feel to be more peculiarly necessary at a time when insidious attempts have been made to deceive and mislead the unwary. With these sentiments, and to this intent, we are RESOLVED AND DO DECLARE that we will stand by the Constitution with our lives and fortunes.

" We will jointly and individually use our utmost endeavours to counteract all seditious attempts, and in particular, all associations for the publication or dispersion of seditious and inflammatory writings, or tending to excite disorders and tumults within this part of the kingdom.

" That we will on every occasion exert ourselves, on the first appearance of tumult or disorder, to maintain the public peace, and to act in support of the civil authority for suppressing all riots and tumults that may be excited.

"And whereas we are of opinion that it would greatly conduce to the maintenance of peace and good order, that means should be used to give such just and proper information to our fellow-subjects as may tend to remove the false and delusive opinions that have been industriously circulated amongst them, and to impress on their minds a proper sense of the invaluable blessings secured to this nation by our happy Constitution, we have agreed diligently to promote the circulation of such writings as may contribute to this important end."]

Mr. Millar said that this was evidently one of these insidious and malicious attempts of the enemies of reform alluded to in our resolutions to thwart the measures of the Friends of the People, and to bring the cause of reform into discredit with the public, as if the Friends of the People were the friends of riot and sedition. He therefore proposed that as the best method of counteracting this insidious attempt, the members of the Convention should go down in small parties and subscribe the declaration, which indeed contained nothing that any friend to reform could disapprove of.

Mr. Drummond seconded the motion, and begged to be the first to subscribe.

Captain Johnston (who was in the chair) said he hoped Mr. Drummond would yield the first place to him as Chairman of the Convention, and added that he heartily approved of the measure proposed by Mr. Millar as the best method of *springing the mine* laid by their enemies.

A country delegate expressed some doubts of the propriety of the measure, as the addition of their names would increase the number of the *apparent* enemies of reform.

Mr. Clark was of the same opinion, and added that by their subscribing the resolutions of their enemies it would appear as if they had deserted the cause of the people. If the Convention, however, thought that it would serve the cause of the people to subscribe, he had no further objection, provided every member should add to his subscription the designation, "A Friend of the People."

Captain Johnston seconded this, and said that he himself would subscribe as Chairman of the General Convention of the Friends of the People.

One gentleman only continued to object. He hoped that he would be excused in not signing a declaration which did not entirely meet his approbation. He was answered from the chair that there was no compulsion, every member of the Convention being at liberty to subscribe or not as he pleased.

Captain Johnston then went out with Messrs. Millar, Morthland, and several other gentlemen to subscribe the declaration at the Goldsmiths' Hall.

(Mr. Clark in the chair.)

No business was done. Conversation turned on the probable reception Captain Johnston and his friends might meet with. On their return, Captain Johnston informed the Convention of their having all subscribed, each adding after his name his proper designation as "Chairman of the Convention," "Delegate from such a Society of the Friends of the People," etc.

The second party now went out with Mr. Clark at their head, soon after which the Convention adjourned till 6 o'clock in the evening.

Evening Sitting.

(Mr. Bisset in the chair.)

[The Convention resolved, That a great number of their resolutions and minutes be printed, and sent to all the societies, and committed the same to the Committee of Finance at Edinburgh.

Mr. Muir moved, That the Secretary be enjoined to give a sufficient notice to the Edinburgh Committee of Finance that they were likewise appointed the Committee of Finance for the General Convention.

Upon the Secretary's motion, the following instructions, drawn up by Mr. Muir, were unanimously recommended to their observation:

"To the Committee of Finances of the Edinburgh Convention.

"The General Convention has instructed each particular society to form a Committee of Finance for managing their own private and public contributions. The Convention has requested you to take the management of the expenses which their sittings here may have incurred.

"In this department of their business, they consider you as their committee. The particular societies will transmit to you their respective proportions of the general expense. The first General Convention has left each particular society to the freedom of their own will in regard to the different assessments they may lay upon their members.

"You will keep a regular account of the public expenditure and outlay, which you will lay before each General Convention for their examination.

"As soon as you have collected the amount of the general expense, inform each particular society by a circular letter, in order that the societies may, without delay, transmit to you their respective proportions."]

Mr. Palmer again moved the question *when* the petition to Parliament was to be presented for subscription.

He was answered by Mr. Fowler and Mr. Morthland that it would be prudent to wait till the London Association sent us down a copy of theirs.

Mr. Morthland, in corroboration of his argument, said that though he was well acquainted with the law of Scotland, there were certain forms in the English law which he pretended to no knowledge of, and some of which might be necessary in presenting petitions to Parliament.

Mr. Palmer insisted that no time should be lost in preparing the petition. It would strengthen the cause of reform all over the country. It would show the people that we were in earnest. "There is a great deal of danger in letting the spirit of the people cool by procrastination."

A country delegate expressed the same sentiments, and said that his constituents were impatient for this measure.

Another country delegate was of the same opinion, and urged the danger of delay. Nothing would strengthen the cause more, except the *rejection* of their petition, *which he hoped would be the issue of the business.* (Plaudits.)

A third country delegate said that it would be the most fortunate circumstance the Friends of the People could meet with if Parliament in their great wisdom would reject their petitions. (Plaudits.) It would increase the number of the associations an hundred fold.

Another delegate moved that the Friends of the People should form a resolution to support each other in the course of their business in private life, as their zeal for reform might deprive them of the employment of the aristocracy.

Mr. Morthland answered that a general resolution of this kind would answer no purpose, as there were certain connections in every man's business which could not easily be dissolved.

Mr. Drummond agreed with the proposal, and as an evidence of the propriety and necessity of it, informed the Convention that one of the most amiable female characters in the whole aristocracy of Scotland, viz. the Duchess of Buccleuch, had the other week discharged her haberdasher, paid him his amount, and informed him that he would get no more of her employment because he had joined an association of the Friends of the People.

Mr. Fowler said that the Friends of the People ought to despise imitating such mean conduct as her Grace had been guilty of.

The proposal was dropped.

Mr. Morthland (or Mr. Muir) moved that the thanks of the Convention be given to Convener Lindsay for his spirited defence of the Friends of the People at the meeting of the fourteen Incorporations in the New Church Aisle.

Mr. Drummond moved that similar thanks should be returned to Mr. Mitchell Young for his spirited conduct on that occasion.

Both motions were agreed to and applauded.

Mr. Drummond gave a very humorous account of his going to the Goldsmiths' Hall accompanied by a great number of the associators intending to subscribe, but the members in his retinue or his own *Democratic face* had alarmed the town officials, and the young man who kept the book, so much, that he and his friends were not allowed to subscribe. They were indeed desired to wait till Mr. Bain Whyte should come in, but as it was dinner hour, they declined this.

Mr. Aitchison said that he was one of those who accompanied Mr. Drummond on that occasion, and had been refused. He therefore begged to know whether those who had been refused should make a second attempt, or whether a resolution should not be made that no more members of the Association should subscribe that paper.

Mr. Morthland and Mr. Fowler were of opinion that a second attempt should be made.

Mr. Aitchison then moved that a particular account of what had passed on this occasion, with the reason and mode of subscribing, and the circumstances of the refusal, should be recorded in the minutes of the Convention.

Mr. Thomson seconded the motion. Agreed.

Mr. Aitchison then started another difficulty, whether if upon making a second attempt the clerk or the officer should tell them that they were welcome to subscribe provided that they did not add the words "A Friend to the People," they should subscribe under that restriction or not.

Captain Johnston answered, "Certainly not." It was therefore unanimously agreed that no member of any association should subscribe these resolutions unless allowed to distinguish himself as a member of the association to which he belonged.

A country delegate proposed that Captain Johnston should take proper notice of the business in his *Gazette*.[1]

The Captain replied that the Convention might trust that to him.

Colonel Dalrymple read a very spirited address from the Associated Friends of the People in Glasgow, which met with much merited applause.

Mr. Aitchison moved that it should be printed, and dispersed among the Friends of the People.

Mr. Morthland said that, as Glasgow was his native town, he

[1] *I.e. Edinburgh Gazetteer.*

hoped that the Convention would allow him the honour to be at the expense of reprinting 1000 copies of it.

This proposal met with great applause, and Mr. Aitchison moved the thanks of the Convention to Mr. Morthland for his genteel offer. Seconded by Mr. Thomson, and applauded.

Mr. Fowler moved thanks to the Society for Preserving the Freedom of the Press. Agreed to with plaudits.

Mr. Muir congratulated the Convention on the propriety of their conduct and the happy result of their deliberations. He particularly complimented them upon the free spirit of inquiry and jealous attention which had pervaded all their debates. They had paid no respect to the authority of leaders. They had not assented to a single clause in their various resolutions in compliance to great names. They had entered into the *minutiae* of everything, and scrutinised every syllable before they gave it their consent, instead of tamely yielding their judgments to those of others. This was the true spirit of liberty which, now that it was fairly begun to be understood amongst his countrymen, he hoped would never cease till it became universal, and till every object they wished for was accomplished.

Mr. Fowler moved that all present should take the French oath, "*To live free or die.*" The whole Convention as one man rose, and, holding up their right hands, took the oath. (Reiterated plaudits.)

Colonel Dalrymple then rose and said that though he could not but be highly pleased with that spirit of freedom which pervaded all present, yet he would beg leave to caution them against yielding too much to the enthusiasm of the moment. They stood on perilous ground, and must therefore take care to give their enemies no just ground against them. The oath, or rather *vow*, just now made was in itself harmless, but might be magnified by their enemies as sowing the seeds of sedition. He therefore hoped that no notice would be taken of it in their minutes or in the newspapers.

Mr. Fowler acknowledged the justice of the Colonel's remarks, and said that he meant no more by the motion than simply to impress upon the minds of all present uniformity and steadiness in the cause of freedom and virtue.

The business of the Convention being now at an end, Mr. Muir moved the thanks of the meeting to Mr. Bisset, and expressed his hopes that on all future occasions virtue and patriotism, such as he possessed, would be the only recommendation to that chair.

Adjourned till April.

Before adjourning, a country delegate asked if the Convention would meet again before April, and was answered, " Not unless some extraordinary business rendered it necessary, but that any *ten* towns agreeing together might call a Convention."

APPENDIX B.

LIST OF SOCIETIES REPRESENTED AT THE SECOND GENERAL CONVENTION OF THE FRIENDS OF THE PEOPLE, 30th April to 3rd May, 1793.

As explained in the text, only part of the minutes of this Convention has been preserved. The following is a list of the Societies represented, according to the Spy's Report, P.R.O. London. *Home Office (Scotland) Correspondence*, vol. viii.

Kilwinning : Mr. Robert Barr.

Miltoun, Campsie : Mr. James M'Gibbon.

Galston, Newmills, etc. : John Wallace.

Dundee : James Peat (stocking-maker).

Strathaven : John Smith.

Dunfermline : James Masterton, James Boyd, Andrew Mercer.

Potterrow, Edinburgh : John Clark, And. Newton, Geo. Cotton (tobacconist), Adam Pringle, David Young, James Dun, Geo. M'Latchie, Geo. Freer, And. Paterson, Eben. Brown, Thos. M'Lash, James Tod, Geo. Innes.

Hawick : James Turnbull.

Operative Society, Edinburgh : John Thynne.

Glasgow Societies : Walter Hart, Henry Rose, John Sinclair.

Paisley Societies : Wm. Moodie, Wm. Mitchell, Jas. Kelly, Archd. Hastie, John Tayler, John Tannyhill, Wm. Wood.

Linlithgow : Stephen Gibson.

Newton : James Sommerville, Esq. of Holmes.

Whitburn : John Stark, Esq. of Gateside.

Selkirk : Alex. Dobson.

Dalkeith : Peter Lyden or Lyeten, Thos. Taylor, Wm. Howieson.

Canongate, No. 1 *and* 2, *Edinburgh :* Robert Yuill (?), Alex. Aitchison, Archd. Wright, John Thomson, John Stronach, Alex. Fortune, Alex. Carse, Alex. Miller, Wm. Simpson, Robert Ruthven.

New Town, Edinburgh: John Wilson, Walter Davidson, Robert Wright, David Bertie, John Reid, Alex. Ingram, Alex. Knox, John Bruce, Alex. Bremner.

Penicuik: Jas. Smith, Jas. Anderson.

Linktoun: Jas. Mather.

Auchterderran: Robert Wemyss (letter of apology).

Kilmaurs: James Lambroughton.

Cowgate Society, Edinburgh: Alex. Reid, Archd. Binny, John M'Intyre, John Gourlay, Geo. Callum, Mitchell Young (painter), Charles Salter, Isaac Salter.

Musselburgh: Wm. Wilson, Duncan Charles.

New Town and Calton, Edinburgh: James Muirhead, Jas. Smith, Wm. Philp, Robert Christie, Geo. Watt.

Water of Leith: John Rymer (?), Wm. Farquharson.

Fenwick: Jas. Fulton.

Cowgate No. 3, Edinburgh: John Laing, David Taylor, Wm. Robertson, Jas. Calder, Jas. Weir, Wm. Stark, John Tweedie, John Hamilton, John Spalding, Alex. Adams, Chas. Stirling, Peter Moffat, Neil Campbell.

Kilmarnock: Rev. Jas. Robertson.

Portsburgh, Edinburgh: Robert Jardine, John Thomson, Geo. Anderson, Jas. Tweedie, Peter Wood, Jas. Thomson, David Sinclair, Wm. Skirving, Esq., Wm. Moffat (writer).

Montrose: Rev. Mr. M'Farlane, Mr. James Glen.

Midcalder: Adam Wilson.

Anstruther: Mitchell Young.

Twelve United Societies in Perth: Robert Sands, Thos. Smith, David Jack, Wm. Thomson, Moses Wylie, And. Dott, David Johnston.

Pathhead: Geo. Drummond.

APPENDIX C.

Letter of Henry Dundas on the defence of Scotland, March 7, 1797, from the Edinburgh University Laing MSS., Division II., No. 500.

Somerset Place,
7th March [1797].

Dear Advocate,

Being at home this morning with a little of a headache, I have taken up my pen to put together in one letter what occurs to me respecting the extent and nature of the defence of Scotland. Perhaps I think it equally applicable to the defence of England; but as they have already a malitia upon their own construction, and certainly a most usefull and important body of troops, disciplined as well as troops can be who have never seen service, it is not my intention to extend my ideas at present beyond what relates more immediately to Scotland.

I have before me the Report of the Distribution of the Force now in North Britain, and so far as I am competent to judge, it is very judiciously distributed; but it is certainly too small a force, and I think there is this obvious defect in it, arising from the smallness of the force, that there is not placed any considerable collection of force in those few places where it may be supposed an enemy may be disposed to come in any force. With a view of remedying this defect to a certain extent, I have given it as my opinion to the Duke of York that the skeletons of regiments which have been on foreign service, and are now at home, consisting of little more than their commissioned and non-commissioned officers, should be distributed over England, Scotland, and Ireland, to be there recruited by every means possible; and altho it was out of common rotine of military detail, I was further of opinion, and gave it to His Royal Highness, that in order to recruit those regiments more rapidly, I would recruit on the condition of not serving out of the country, or for a longer period than three or five years. I am aware that this is in a manner for a time converting those Regular Regiments into the state of Fencible Corps. It is perfectly true; but as we have not more foreign conquests to aim at, and security at home during the ensuing campaign ought to be the chief object of attention, it did not occur to me that there was any solid objection against the measure. When peace arrived, His Royal Highness, with his usual care and attention, would find no difficulty to new model the regiments in any way more conducive to the general service. It is more than probable that, after serving some time, the very men recruited on those limitations, moved for a guinea more at the peace, would agree to re-enlist on the common terms of general service. I likewise gave it as my opinion that in order more rapidly to fill up those skeletons a portion of each of the Fencible Infantry Corps should be induced to enlist into them. If you ask me in what respects these Regular Regiments so modelled would be better than the other Fencible Corps, my answer is, that altho many of the Privates would be but raw men, still they would be serving under a set of Officers, all or most of whom had been on actual service; and I am sure, if we were to come to serious business at home, it is uncalculable what would be the advantage of even a small body of troops so circumstanced being mixt with troops of a different description. They would aid and support and give them confidence in a variety of different respects. I therefore do recommend it to your serious consideration to urge every man everywhere in Scotland, where your advice can extend, to contribute their utmost exertions to compleat to their full establishment those regiments of skeletons sent to Scotland. The use they will be of I will have occasion hereafter to refer to.

The next body of men now existing in Scotland to which I shall advert are the bodies of Volunteers formed and forming in different parts of Scotland. The objects of these are twofold, to preserve the *internal Tranquillity*, and to repell *foreign Invasion.* As to the first object, there can be but one opinion as to their utility, and it is unnecessary for me to dilate upon it. As to the other object of repelling foreign Invasion, I confess I see the subject in a different point of view, and must distinguish according to different local situations. In so far as Volunteer Corps are formed in towns on the sea coast, or in the neighbourhood of it so as to co-operate with them, they certainly may be of essential service to make countenance against any small predatory landings which may be attempted on any of the different extended coast of Scotland, and against which, if they escape the vigilance of our Navy, it is impossible to provide a defence by the regular force of the country, let it be on the most extended scale that any man could suggest, or that the revenues of the country could bear. I must confess that with regard to the same kind of force in the *interior* of the country, and from the nature of their institutions limited to very narrow districts, I am not satisfied that their utility is great, or that they can be considered as forming any rational system for the general defence of the country against any foreign enemy. At the same time I am very far from meaning in any respect to derogate from their merit. I pay the highest tribute of applause and justice to their zeal, and unless the requisite force can be made up in some other mode, they are the best that the nature of the case admits under the present deficiency of regular force.

This leads me to observe that in truth there is no solid resource in this point of view except by embodying a portion of the strength of the country, selected in the most impartial and equal way, for the defence of the remainder, and capable of being further augmented as circumstances may render necessary. You are already acquainted of my sentiments on this subject, by a letter which I had occasion to write to the Duke of Montrose last autumn. The more I think of it, I am the more satisfied of the propriety of my reasoning, and by the multitude of letters I have recently received from Scotland, I perceive that many are now converts to my opinion. In time of peace and for future security it may be sufficient annually to train all of the age of twenty, but for the immediate safety of the country it would be proper to ballot all those from twenty to thirty years of age inclusive, in order to ensure a certain supply of men to be embodied and regularly trained during the continuance of the war. Out of those so balloted, I should think it right, in the present moment, to embody under the King's authority to the amount of at least ten, but perhaps I would speak more wisely if I said at least twelve thousand men. If this was done, I would then wish the internal tranquillity of the country to rest on the Volunteer Corps, which have been incorporated for that purpose, aided by those local bodies of Horse Volunteers, which I understand have lately been established in some of the counties of Scotland, and which I would hope would become more general; for I look to the same good effects to arise from them which have flowed from the establishment of the Yeomanry Corps in England.

Supposing those measures to be followed out, I should then feel the country to be in a state of rational security; but with that view I would certainly remedy that defect which I have stated in the beginning of this letter, I mean the want of any efficient body of force being collected together in any place for the purpose of acting against any enemy meaning to take the chance of escaping our Fleet, and coming against any vulnerable part of the country.

I would propose to have 1500 regular force; 2000 or 2500 malitia force, with 3 or 400 cavalry and the due proportion of artillery, either encamped or cantoned at Dunbar or some other place about the mouth of the Firth of Forth, ready to move immediately if any hostile armament should appear with an intention to make a landing to attack Edinburgh, or any place within that side of the Firth; and it is clear that, if any considerable body of force should come to that quarter, the Metropolis or its neighbourhood must be the object, but it is obvious that by such a collected body of force, and in the position I have stated, any such attempt would unquestionably be frustrated.

Upon the same principle I would have a collected force of about the same extent, and formed of similar materials, somewhere on the coast of Montrose or Aberdeen (I don't pretend to fix upon the spot), for the protection of that North-East coast, and a third force of a similar nature still further north, probably at Fort George or thereabouts; but here again I leave to others better acquainted locally with that part of the country to point out the spot. I only desire to be understood as explaining the principle.

Another force of a similar nature, and certainly not inferior to any of the others, ought to be cantoned or encamped as far as convenient down the Firth of Clyde, in order to be on the watch to march in a moment for the protection of that important coast against any considerable force that may be sent against it.

I have not, you'll observe, in this discussion, taken any notice of that most recent and most valuable addition to the strength of the country, which has lately made its appearance in Scotland, in the shape of the various offers from the farmers in the country to transport from place to place the troops, ammunition, baggage, etc., of the army when called upon for that purpose. It is impossible to figure any system better calculated to answer the purposes of internal security, or more expressive of real usefull zeal and public spirit. It forms an essential part of all I have stated, as contributing to move with rapidity any part of the collected force that may be requisite to any point within the district where there are reasonable grounds to apprehend the attack is intended.

I think I have now stated what will be sufficient to convey to you a distinct view of my sentiments on this business, which of course you will communicate to Lord Adam Gordon, in case he should be of opinion that any part of what I have stated is worthy of consideration. If any such plan is adopted, or any one upon similar principles, it appears to me that all the security is afforded to the country that the nature of the case admits of; and such a force joined to the confidence we may justly repose on the superiority of our fleet, ought to keep the minds of the country quiet, and banish every unmanly gloom from our spirits. The Volunteer Corps on the coast would preserve it from any small predatory attempts, and if anything of more consequence should be attempted, the force which is collected in a body would be moved to their support and defence. Besides the Volunteer Corps on the coast, it will be observed that if there is such a force in the country as I have supposed, it would enable the Commander-in-Chief to add to the security of such intermediate places between the collected depots of force, as the danger or importance of any particular place might require. I send you along with this a paper the Duke of York put into my hands a few days ago. I believe His Royal Highness prepared it with the assistance of General David Dundas, and it will shew you in what way it is proposed to distribute the force in England, as well with a view to the strength of each district, as with a view to their mutually lending aid to each other, according to circumstances and the place of attack the enemy may chuse to fix upon.

Having wrote at so great length, I will not have occasion to trouble you much more on the same subject, unless perhaps from time to time on such points as may occasionally cast up.

I remain, My Dr Advocate,

Yours affectly,

HENRY DUNDAS.

BIBLIOGRAPHY.

(A) General.

1. France and Europe.
2. Great Britain and Ireland.
3. Scotland: (*a*) Histories, Biographical Dictionaries, etc.; (*b*) Modern Works dealing with Scotland and the French Revolution.

(B) Special.

1. Unpublished Material in Great Britain.
2. Hist. MSS. Com. Reports.
3. Parliamentary Debates and Acts of Parliament.
4. Periodical Publications: (*a*) Contemporary; (*b*) Review Articles.
5. Biographical: (*a*) Primary; (*b*) Secondary.
6. County and Burgh Reform.
7. Contemporary Books and Pamphlets dealing with the French Revolution and the Consequent Unrest in Great Britain: (*a*) Primary; (*b*) Secondary—mainly Scottish Pamphlets.
8. The British and Irish Political Societies and the State Trials.
9. Contemporary French Sources—MS. and Printed.
10. Ecclesiastical Affairs.
11. Local History.
12. Travels.
13. Poetry, Drama, and Fiction.

(A) General.

1. *France and Europe.*

Aulard, F. A. Études et Leçons sur la Révolution Française. Paris, 1892-1907.

Alison, A. History of Europe from the Commencement of the French Revolution to the Restoration of the Bourbons, 1774-1815. New edn. 14 vols. Lond. and Edin. 1849-50. Continued in the History of Europe, 1815-1852. 8 vols. and index. Lond. and Edin. 1852-9.

Carlyle, T. The French Revolution. Ed. C. R. L. Fletcher. 3 vols. Lond. 1902.

Cambridge Modern History. Vol. viii. The French Revolution; vol. ix. Napoleon. Camb. 1904 and 1906. Full Bibliographies.

Lavisse, E., and Rambaud, A. N. Histoire Générale. Vol. viii. Paris, 1896. Full Bibliographies.

Rose, J. Holland. The Revolutionary and Napoleonic Era. (Camb. Hist. Series.) Camb. 1901. Selected Bibliography.

Sorel, A. L'Europe et la Révolution Française. 6 vols. Paris, 1885-1903.

Stephens, H. M. European History, 1789-1815. ("Periods of European History" Series.) Lond. 1900.

Sybel, H. von. Geschichte der Revolutionzeit von 1789 bis 1800. Trans. W. C. Perry. 4 vols. Lond. 1867-9.

2. *Great Britain and Ireland.*

Adolphus, J. History of England from the Accession of George III. 8 vols. Lond. 1840-1845. Valuable references to contemporary pamphlets.

Brodick, G. C., and Fotheringham, J. K. History of England, 1801-1837. ("Political History of England" Series, vol. x.) Lond. 1906. Bibliography.

Cunningham, W. The Growth of English Industry and Commerce. Part ii. Camb. 1909. Full Bibliography.

Dictionary of National Biography. 69 vols. Lond. 1885-1901.

Hunt, W. History of England, 1760-1801. ("Political History of England" Series, vol. x.) Lond. 1905. Bibliography.

Lecky, W. E. H. History of England in the Eighteenth Century. 8 vols. Lond. 1879-1890.

Massey, W. History of England during the Reign of George III. 4 vols. Lond. 1855-1863.

May, T. E. The Constitutional History of England since the Accession of George III. 1760-1860. 3 vols. Lond. 1871.

3. *Scotland.*

(*a*) HISTORIES, BIOGRAPHICAL DICTIONARIES, ETC.

Anderson, W. The Scottish Nation. 3 vols. Edin. 1860-3.

Bremner, D. The Industries of Scotland. Edin. 1869.

Buckle, H. T. Introduction to the History of Civilisation in England. Ed. J. M. Robertson. n.d. Chaps. xviii.-xx. "The Material and Intellectual Condition of Scotland in the Eighteenth Century."

Brown, P. Hume. History of Scotland. Vol. iii. (1689-1843). (Camb. Hist. Series.) Camb. 1909. Illust. edn. (to 1910). Camb. 1911. Bibliography.

Caw, J. L. Scottish Painting Past and Present, 1603-1908. Edin. 1908.

Chambers, R. Biographical Dictionary of Eminent Scotsmen. New ed. 5 vols. Glas. 1853-5.

Craik, H. A Century of Scottish History (1745-1845). 2 vols. Edin. and Lond. 1901.

Foster, J. Members of Parliament, Scotland, 1357-1832. Priv. printed. Lond. and Aylesbury, 1882.

Graham, H. Grey. Scottish Men of Letters in the Eighteenth Century. Lond. 1901.

——— Social Life in Scotland in the Eighteenth Century. New edn. Lond. 1906.

M'Cosh, J. The Scottish Philosophy . . . from Hutcheson to Hamilton. Lond. 1875. Useful for biographical details.

Mackintosh, J. History of Civilisation in Scotland. 4 vols. New edn. Lond. and Paisley, 1896.

Mathieson, W. L. Scotland and The Union. A History of Scotland from 1695 to 1747. Glas. 1905.

——— The Awakening of Scotland. A History from 1747 to 1797. Glas. 1910.

Millar, J. H. A Literary History of Scotland. Lond. 1903.

Ramsay, Dean. Reminiscences of Scottish Life and Character. New edn. Edin. and Lond. 1908.

Rogers, C. Social Life in Scotland from Early to Recent Times. 3 vols. Edin. 1884.

Social England, ed. H. D. Traill and J. S. Mann. Illust. edn. 6 vols. Lond. 1901-4. Vol. v. chaps. xviii. and xix.

Young, T. P. Histoire de l'Enseignement primaire et secondaire en Écosse, plus spécialement de 1560 à 1872. Paris, 1907. Full Bibliography.

(*b*) MODERN WORKS DEALING WITH SCOTLAND AND THE FRENCH REVOLUTION.

W. L. Mathieson's *The Awakening of Scotland*, chap. iii., "The Political Awakening," is an admirable account, based almost wholly on printed material. P. Hume Brown's *History of Scotland*, vol. iii. chap. ix., "The Dundas Despotism and the French Revolution," is an excellent and suggestive outline. Sir H. Craik's *A Century of Scottish History*, vol. ii. chap. xvi., "The Tory and Whig Parties in Scotland," is less scientific in treatment, and biassed on the Tory side. The subject is also dealt with, somewhat incidentally, in G. W. T. Omond's *The Lord Advocates of Scotland*, 2 vols., Edin. 1883, vol. ii. (Henry and Robert Dundas); and in the same author's *The Arniston Memoirs, Three Centuries of a Scottish House*, Edin. 1887. Mr. Omond was the first to print extracts from the Scottish documents now preserved in the Public Record Office (P.R.O.), London, and he had also access to the Dundas papers in Arniston House.

(B) SPECIAL.

1. *Unpublished Material in Great Britain.*

The chief unpublished sources are the volumes of Home Office (Scotland) Correspondence in the P.R.O., cited in the text as *Scot. Corr.* As mentioned above, they were used by Mr. Omond, but he did not submit them to an exhaustive examination. They consist chiefly of the correspondence of the Home Secretary with the Lord Advocate of Scotland, arranged chronologically. Vol. 1 begins at 1782. The correspondence increases in bulk during the crisis of 1792-4, but thereafter resumes its normal proportion of one volume for one year. Vols.

1-41 (1781-1832) have been consulted, as well as supplementary vols. 59-63, and the Entry Books, Entry Book Warrants, Criminal Books, and Criminal Entry Books which relate to Scotland.

Of the P.R.O. Irish Correspondence, vols. 38-77 (1792-1798) have been used for the United Irishmen.

The Scottish documents in the P.R.O. are partly supplemented by those in the Laing MSS. in the University of Edinburgh. Nos. 500 and 501, Div. ii., and No. 294 consist of a large number of letters to and from R. Dundas while Lord Advocate; No. 295 of a smaller packet to H. Dundas while Lord Advocate and Home Secretary. In the same collection (No. 113, Div. ii.) there is a short contemporary memoir of Robert Macqueen of Braxfield, Lord Justice Clerk, by Alex. Young, W.S. Among the general MSS. of the same University is a volume of letters to Dr. Carlyle of Inveresk, the well-known Moderate divine, many of which deal with the ecclesiastical politics of the time. Numerous extracts are given in C. Rogers' *Social Life in Scotland*, vol. iii. chap. xvii. The British Museum MSS. cited in the text are: the Pelham Correspondence, Add. MSS., No. 33,049 (appointment of Lords-lieutenant in 1745), No. 33,108, f. 450 (letter of H. Dundas regarding patronage); the Auckland Papers, Add. MSS., No. 33,412, f. 352 (letter of H. Dundas regarding emigration); No. 34,416 ff. 470,472 (Correspondence of H. Dundas and Adam Smith regarding free trade between Britain and Ireland); Banks Correspondence, Add. MSS., No. 33,982, f. 294 (Memorial for Gillies, Historiographer Royal for Scotland); Parochial Statistics of Scotland, Add. MSS., No. 15,746, compiled by George Chalmers, the Scottish antiquarian, from Webster's and Sinclair's *Statistical Accounts of Scotland*. In the Place Collection, Add. MSS., Nos. 27,808–27,818, there is valuable material relating to the London Corresponding Society, including its Letter Books, Journal, and Correspondence, together with a large number of papers, printed and MS., referring to the State prosecutions in 1793, 1794, and 1798.

2. *Hist. MSS. Com. Reports.*

In connection with these, C. S. Terry's *Index to the Papers relating to Scotland in the Hist. MSS. Com. Reports*, Glas. 1908, is useful. The MSS. of Robert Dundas, Esq., at Arniston, described in the Third Report, were unfortunately not available for the present work. Mr. Omond in his *Arniston Memoirs* has published some extracts. The *Dropmore MSS.*, Thirteenth Report, Appends., contain some letters of, and numerous references to, H. Dundas, as well as some interesting " secret intelligence " papers relating to France. In the *Rutland MSS.*, Fourteenth Report, Append. I., there are a few references to H. Dundas.

3. *Parliamentary Debates and Acts of Parliament.*

The debates in Parliament are given in the *Parliamentary History of England,* from vol. xx. (1780), Lond. 1814-19. The Acts are published as *Statutes at Large* (vol. ix. 1780), Lond. 1786 *et seq.* *The History of Two Acts* (Treasonable Practices and Seditious Meetings), Anon., Lond. 1796, contains an account of the public meetings, petitions, and parliamentary debates connected with them.

4. *Periodical Publications.*

(*a*) CONTEMPORARY.

The only general guide to Scottish newspapers is J. Grant's *The Newspaper Press : Its Origin, Progress, and Present Condition,* 3 vols., Lond. 1871. An excellent account of Edinburgh periodicals is W. J. Couper's *The Edinburgh Periodical Press, being a Bibliographical Account of the Newspapers, Journals, and Magazines issued in Edinburgh from the Earliest Times to* 1800. 2 vols., Stirling, 1908. Vol. ii. covers the period. The history of each paper is given, as well as the names of the libraries where extant copies are to be found.

Leading articles were unknown in Scottish newspapers during the eighteenth century, and their political complexion is to be gauged by the manner in which the news is selected and reported. Much information regarding political movements may be gleaned from the advertisements inserted by the various reforming societies. After 1793, the leading newspapers became Ministerialist, few of the democratic periodical publications surviving the crisis in home affairs.

The files of the *Caledonian Mercury,* a moderate " Revolution Whig " newspaper, have been examined for the years 1750 to

1770, and from 1778 to 1798, and the *Scots Magazine* from 1780 to 1798. The others mentioned below have been consulted on important points. Those marked with an asterisk were anti-Ministerialist.

The Bee, or Literary Weekly Intelligencer, 18 vols., Edin. 1791-4.

The Edinburgh Evening Courant, files from 1792-6.

* *The Edinburgh Gazetteer* (1792-1793 ?). A few numbers in the Brit. Mus. and P.R.O., London. Of the * *Caledonian Chronicle* (1792-3), no copies have been discovered.

The Edinburgh Herald, files from 1791-2. Supported from the Secret Service Fund.

* *The Historical Register or Edinburgh Monthly Intelligencer,* July, August, October, December, 1791 ; January-July, 1792. Signet Library, Edinburgh.

* *The Historical Register or Universal Monthly Intelligencer,* April-September, 1792. Signet Library, Edinburgh.

* *The Political Review of Edinburgh Periodical Publications,* 1792.

The Scottish Register, 1794-5.

* *The Scots Chronicle,* 1796-1801.

* *The Glasgow Advertiser,* files for 1789 to June 28, 1790, 1793, and 1794 have been consulted. These, with later issues, are in the *Glasgow Herald* Office, Glasgow.

The Glasgow Courier, files for 1792-3. Stirling's Library, Glasgow.

The Glasgow Mercury, files for 1790.

The Anti-Jacobin Review, 1799.

For the period 1802-1832, the *Edinburgh Review, Blackwood's Magazine,* and the *Scotsman* newspaper, have been referred to.

In the British Museum Place Collection there are valuable cuttings from English newspapers from 1792 onwards. Vols. 36-40 are labelled " Libel and Sedition," " Politics," " Reform." W. T. Laprade in his *England and The French Revolution,* 1789-1797, Baltimore, the Johns Hopkins Press, 1909, quotes largely from contemporary English newspapers, of which he gives a list in his bibliography.

The columns of *La Gazette Universelle ou Le Moniteur Universel* (cited in the text as the *Moniteur*), reveal French interest in Scottish affairs. It is significant that, in a pamphlet entitled

A Few Thoughts on Political Subjects, Edin. 1792, the Scottish reformers were accused of " sending paragraphs to France."

(*b*) LATER REVIEW ARTICLES, ETC.

La Révolution Française, xiv. 1888 : " La Politique Étrangère du Comité du Salut Public," by F. A. Aulard.

The Scottish Historical Review, July, 1909 : " The King's Birthday Riot in Edinburgh, June, 1792 " ; April, 1910 : " The Learning of the Scots in the Eighteenth Century " ; January, 1911 : " Two Glasgow Merchants in the French Revolution "—Arts. by H. W. Meikle.

Transactions of the Franco-Scottish Society, Edin. 1912. " Glasgow and the French Revolution," by H. W. Meikle.

Others are mentioned under the special headings.

5. *Biographical.*

(*a*) PRIMARY.

The most important is Lord Cockburn's graphic *Memorials of His Times* (1779-1850), Edin. 1875, new edn., Edin. 1909—a unique record of the political and social history, primarily of Edinburgh, but also of Scotland as a whole. The same author's *Life of Jeffrey* (1773-1850), 2 vols., Edin. 1852, contains much autobiographical material. *Letters on the Affairs of Scotland from Henry Cockburn to Francis Kennedy . . . 1818 to 1852*, Lond. 1874, is also authoritative. Allowance must be made for Cockburn's strong Whig views. Another Whig account of the capital is to be found in the opening chapters of the *Autobiography of Mrs Fletcher* (1770-1858), Edin. 1876. T. Somerville's *My Own Life and Times* (1741-1814) is of great value, Somerville being a Moderate divine of the best type. For general purposes the *Autobiography of the Rev. Dr. Carlyle* (1722-1805), ed. J. Hill Burton, Edin. and Lond. 1860 (new edn., Edin. 1910), is more useful for the period preceding 1780 ; but as Carlyle was one of the leaders of the Moderate Party it is indispensable for later ecclesiastical affairs. *Scotland and Scotsmen in the Eighteenth Century, from the MSS. of John Ramsay, Esq. of Ochtertyre*, ed. A. Allardyce, 2 vols., Edin. and Lond. 1888, reflects the spirit of the Tory landed gentry of the time. There are some interesting notes in the early pages of *Reminiscences of a Scottish*

Gentleman, commencing in 1787, by Philo-Scotus, Lond. 1861, and of the *Life and Times of Henry Lord Brougham*, written by himself, 2 vols., Edin. and Lond. 1871, vol. i.

G. W. T. Omond's *The Lord Advocates of Scotland*, vol. ii., and his *Arniston Memoirs*, both already mentioned, are the main authorities for Henry and Robert Dundas. *The Correspondence of George III. with Lord North*, ed. W. A. Donne, 2 vols., Lond. 1867, vol. ii.; *Memorials and Correspondence of C. J. Fox*, ed. Lord J. Russell, 3 vols., Lond. 1853-4, vol. ii.; Wraxall's *Historical and Posthumous Memoirs*, ed. H. B. Wheatley, 5 vols., Lond. 1884, are sources for the early career of Henry Dundas. There are contemporary character sketches in Cockburn's *Memorials;* Somerville's *My Own Life;* Brougham's *Statesmen of the Time of George III.*, 3 vols., Lond. 1855, vol. i.; J. Sinclair's *Memoirs of . . . Sir John Sinclair*, 2 vols., Lond. 1837, vol. i.; and J. G. Lockhart's *Peter's Letters to his Kinsfolk*, 3 vols., 2nd edn., Edin. 1819, vol. ii. Other contemporary sources include *A Letter to the Lord Advocate of Scotland*, by Eugène, Edin. 1777; *Criticisms on the Rolliad*, Pt. I., 8th edn., Lond. 1788; *The Melviad, or the Birth, Parentage, Education, and Achievements of a Grete Mon*, by I-Spy-I, 3rd edn., Lond. 1805. Dundas's political life as the colleague of Pitt is traced in Lord Stanhope's *Life of Pitt*, 4 vols., 2nd edn., Lond. 1862; at greater length, being based on ampler material, in J. Holland Rose's *William Pitt and National Revival* and *William Pitt and the Great War*, Lond. 1911, and more briefly in Lord Rosebery's sketch of *Pitt* ("Twelve English Statesmen" Series), Lond. 1891.

A. Fergusson's *The Hon. Henry Erskine, Lord Advocate of Scotland, with notices of certain of His Kinsfolk and of His Time*, Edin. and Lond. 1882, is the standard life of the leader of the Scottish Whigs. Of the numerous works on Burns, the best for this subject are A. Angellier's *Robert Burns, Sa Vie et Ses Œuvres*, 2 vols., Paris, 1893, where the influence of the French Revolution on Burns is fully discussed; and *The Life and Works of Robert Burns*, ed. R. Chambers, revised by W. Wallace, 4 vols., Edin. and Lond. 1896. J. G. Lockhart's *Life of Sir Walter Scott*, numerous reprints, provides much material for the political history of the time from the Tory point of view. In J. Kay's *A Series of Original Portraits*, edited with good biographical notices by J. Paterson and J. Maidment, 2 vols., Edin. 1838, there is a unique collection of portraits and caricatures of almost every personage mentioned in the text, especially those connected with the State trials.

(*b*) SECONDARY.

The following are of secondary importance. As a rule, the references in the text exhaust the information they afford on the subject.

Alger, J. G. Englishmen in the French Revolution. Lond. 1889. His Paris in 1789-1794, Lond. 1902, contains references to the same subject.

Allen, J. Biographical notice in his Inquiry into the Rise and Growth of the Royal Prerogative in England. New edn. Lond. 1849.

Atkinson, R. H. M. B., and Jackson, G. A. Brougham and His Early Friends. Letters to James Loch, 1798-1809. 3 vols. priv. printed. Lond. 1908.

Beattie, W. Life and Letters of Thomas Campbell. 3 vols. Lond. 1849.

Benger, Miss. Memoirs of the Late Mrs. Elizabeth Hamilton. 2 vols. 2nd edn. Lond. 1819.

Campbell, Lord. Lives of the Lord Chancellors and Keepers of the Great Seal of England. 8 vols. and index. Lond. 1845-1869. Vols. v.-viii.: Loughborough, Erskine and Brougham.

Carlyle, E. I. Life of Cobbett. Lond. 1904.

Chevrillon, A. Sydney Smith et la Rennaissance des Idées Libérales en Angleterre au xixe Siècle. Paris, 1894.

Conway, M. D. Life of Thomas Paine. Ed. H. B. Bonner. Lond. 1909.

Craig, J. Life of John Millar, prefixed to his Origin of Ranks. 4th edn. Edin and Lond. 1806.

Forbes, M. Beattie and His Friends. Westminster, 1903.

Forbes, W. An Account of the Life and Writings of James Beattie, LL.D. 2 vols. Edin. 1806.

Fraser, A. C. Thomas Reid. (Famous Scots Series.) Edin. 1898.

Galt, John. Autobiography. 2 vols. Lond. 1833.

Grant, Mrs. Letters from the Mountains, being the Correspondence with her friends, between the years 1773 and 1803, of Mrs Grant of Laggan. Ed. J. P. Grant. 2 vols. 6th edn. Lond. 1845.

Haldane, A. Memoirs of the Lives of Robert Haldane of Airthrey, and of His Brother, James Alex. Haldane. Lond. 1852.

Hanna, W. Memoirs of Thomas Chalmers. 2 vols. Lond. 1863.

Hardcastle, Mrs. Life of John, Lord Campbell. 2 vols. Lond. 1881.

Holland, Lord. Memoirs of the Whig Party during My Time. Ed. Henry Edward, Lord Holland. 2 vols. Lond. 1852.

Horner, L. Memoirs and Correspondence of Francis Horner, M.P. 2 vols. Lond. 1843.

History of the Speculative Society of Edinburgh from Its Institution (1764). Edin. 1845. Contains biographical notices of the members.

Jardine, W. Life of Alex. Wilson, in American Ornithology. 3 vols. Edin. and Lond. 1832.

Lichtenberger, A. Le Socialisme Utopique. Paris, 1898. Chap. viii.: Jean Oswald, Écossais, Jacobin, et Socialiste.

Mackintosh, R. Life of Sir James Mackintosh. 2 vols. Lond. 1835.

Minto, Countess of. Life and Letters of Sir Gilbert Elliot. 3 vols. Lond. 1874.

Morley, J. Burke, a historical study. Lond. 1867.

——— Burke. (E.M.L. Series.) Lond. 1904.

Nicholson, A. Memoirs of Adam Black. Edin. 1885.

Rae, J. Life of Adam Smith. Lond. 1895.

Romilly, S. Memoirs. 3 vols. Lond. 1840.

Seward, Anna. Letters of Anna Seward written between the years 1784 and 1807. 6 vols. Edin. 1811.

Stewart, D. Biographical Memoirs of Adam Smith, William Robertson, and Thomas Reid, to which is prefixed a Memoir of Dugald Stewart by J. Veitch. Works of Dugald Stewart. Ed. W. Hamilton. Vol. x. Edin. 1858.

Welsh, D. An Account of the Life and Writings of Thomas Brown, M.D. Edin. 1835.

Younger, J. Autobiography of John Younger, Shoemaker, St. Boswells. Kelso, 1881.

6. *County and Burgh Reform.*

The best description of the Scottish burgh and county electorate before 1832 is E. and A. Porritt's *The Unreformed House of*

Commons, 2 vols. Camb. 1903, vol. ii. with bibliography. T. H. B. Oldfield in vol. vi. of his *Representative History of Great Britain*, Lond. 1816, reprints the *Report of the Committee of the* (*London*) *Friends of the People . . . appointed to examine into the State of the Representation of Scotland*, (1793). It is also given in *Political Papers, chiefly respecting . . . Reformation of the Parliament of Great Britain*, collected by the Rev. C. Wyvill, 6 vols., York, 1794-1802, which contain the correspondence of the Yorkshire Committee with sympathisers in Scotland.

There is no history of the county reform agitation, but the various test cases are discussed in W. Bell's *Treatise on the Election Laws*, Edin. 1812; A. Connell's *A Treatise on the Election Laws in Scotland, to which is added an Historical Enquiry concerning the Municipal Constitution of Towns and Burghs*, Edin. 1830. A report of much value is a *View of the Political State of Scotland in the Last Century*: *A Confidential Report on the Political Opinions, Family Connections, or Personal Circumstances of the* 2662 *County Voters in* 1788, ed. (with a good introduction) by C. E. Adam, Edin. 1887. Similar compilations of less value, being merely lists of voters without comment, are a *View of the Political State of Scotland at the Late General Election*, by Alex. Mackenzie (?), Edin. 1790, and J. Bridge's *View of the Political State of Scotland at Michaelmas* 1811, Edin. 1811.

The following are the most useful contemporary pamphlets relating to county reform:

Remarks on the Bill which was intended to be brought into Parliament in 1775 for annulling Nominal and Fictitious Qualifications. Edin. 1782.

Observations on the Laws of Elections of Members of Parliament. Edin. 1782.

An Address to the Landed Gentlemen of Scotland upon the Subject of Nominal and Fictitious Qualifications . . . with Observations upon Two Sketches of Bills presented to the Standing Committee upon Freehold Qualifications at Edinburgh. Edin. 1783.

R. Fergusson, The Proposed Reform of the Counties of Scotland impartially examined. Edin. 1792.

The story of the burgh reform movement is admirably told in A. Fletcher's *Memoir concerning the Origin and Progress of the*

Reform proposed in the internal government of the Royal Burghs of Scotland, Edin. 1819. He gives extracts from the reports, etc., of the early reformers. These and other relevant publications are included in the following list:

The Letters of Zeno to the Citizens of Edinburgh on the present mode of electing a Member of Parliament for that City (Edin.), 1783.

A Letter from a Member of the General Convention of Delegates of the Royal Burghs to the Citizens of the Royal Burghs which have not yet acceded to the Plan of Reform. Edin. 1784.

The Sett or Constitution of the Royal Burghs of Scotland as recorded in the Books of the Convention. Edin. 1787.

Bill proposed to be submitted to the Consideration . . . of Parliament for Correcting Abuses . . . in the Internal Government of the Royal Burghs in Scotland. Edin. 1787.

An Illustration of the Bill proposed to be submitted etc. Edin. 1787.

Historical Accounts of the Government and Grievances of the Royal Burghs transmitted by Different Burghs associated for the purpose of Reform. Edin. 1787.

Abstract of Facts respecting the Revenues of the Royal Burghs of Scotland. Lond., June 9, 1788. The reply of the anti-reformers.

Observations by the Delegates . . . on the case of the Town Councils stiling themselves the Royal Burghs of Scotland. Edin. (?), 1788.

Memorials for Burgesses and Inhabitants of the Royal Burghs associated for correcting abuses etc. Edin. (?), 1789 (?).

Substance of the Reports transmitted by the Committees of Burgesses of different boroughs etc. Edin. (?), 1789.

State of the Evidence contained in the Returns to the Orders of the House of Commons regarding the illegal exaction, within the Royal Burghs in Scotland, of a greater sum in the name of land tax than is paid Government. Lond. (?), 1791.

Report from the Committee to whom the several petitions presented to the House of Commons from the Royal Burghs of Scotland were referred. (1793.) Reprinted Glas. 1818.

Documents connected with the Question of Reform in the Royal Burghs of Scotland. 2nd edn. Edin. 1819.

A full study of the question should also include :

General Report of the Commissioners appointed to inquire into the state of Municipal Incorporations in Scotland, and Local Reports of the Commissioners, Municipal Corporations (Scotland), Parts i. and ii. London, H.M. Stationery Office, 1835.

7. *Contemporary Books and Pamphlets dealing with the French Revolution and the Consequent Unrest in Great Britain.*

(*a*) PRIMARY.

The following are fully discussed in Chapter iii. :

Burke, E. Reflections on the French Revolution. Ed. Payne. Oxford, 1886.

B——de, Mons. Reflections on the Causes and Probable Consequences of the Late Revolution in France with a View of the Ecclesiastical and Civil Constitution of Scotland (trans.). Edin. 1790.

Christie, T. Letters on the Revolution of France and on the New Constitution established by the National Assembly occasioned by the Writings of the Rt. Hon. Edmund Burke, M.P. and Alex. de Calonne, late Minister of State . . . with an Appendix containing original papers and authentic documents. . . . Part i. Lond. 1791.

Mackintosh, J. Vindiciae Gallicae. 4th edn. Lond. 1792.

Paine, T. The Rights of Man, etc. Works. Ed. M. D. Conway. Vols. ii.-iv. New York and Lond. 1894-6.

(*b*) SECONDARY—MAINLY SCOTTISH PAMPHLETS.

A full list of the Scottish pamphlets produced by the controversy could be drawn up from the advertisements in the *Scots Magazine* and other contemporary periodicals. Most of the following selection have been referred to in the text, and in the case of the others, even the titles are suggestive. Those marked with an asterisk were circulated by the Goldsmiths' Hall Association, and other "constitutional" societies. The majority of the pamphlets are in the Signet Library, Edinburgh, where they are conveniently catalogued.

A Few Thoughts on Political Subjects submitted to the Consideration of the Manufacturers and Others in the West of Scotland. Edin. 1792.

A Protest against T. Paine's "Rights of Man" addressed to the Members of a Book Society. 5th edn. Edin. 1792.

* A Word in Season to the Traders and Manufacturers of Great Britain. 6th edn. Edin (?), 1792.

An Address to the Associated Friends of the People by A Lover of His Country. Edin. 1792.

Ask and You Shall Have. Lond. 1795.

Asmodeus, or, Strictures on the Glasgow Democrats in a Series of Letters several of which were lately published in the Glasgow Courier. Glas. 1793.

Biographical Sketches of Some of the Leading Men at present at the Head of Affairs in France. Edin. 1792.

Callender, J. T. The Political Progress of Great Britain . . . tending to prove the Ruinous Consequences of the Popular System of Taxation, War, and Conquest. Edin. 1792. Pts. i. and ii. Philadelphia, 1795.

[Chalmers, G.] Francis Oldys. The Life of Thomas Paine with a Review of His Writings. Lond. 1792. Chalmers was the well-known Scottish antiquarian. This life is the source of the calumnies against Paine.

Christie, A. The Holy Scriptures, the Only Rule of Faith and Liberty, asserted and maintained in sundry letters to the Kirk Session of Montrose. Montrose, 1790.

——— Scripture Truths Humbly Addressed to All Christians, particularly such as are Candidates for a Seat in Parliament, and Their Electors, at the ensuing General Elections. Montrose, 1790.

Christie, W. An Essay on Ecclesiastical Establishments in Religion . . . to which are added Two Discourses by a Protestant Dissenter. Montrose, 1791.

Cobbett, W. A Bone to Gnaw for the Democrats, or, Observations on a Pamphlet entitled, "The Political Progress of Britain." 3rd edn. Phila. 1795.

——— Observations on the Emigration of Dr. Joseph Priestley. Phila. 1795.

Dalgleish, W. The Excellence of the British Constitution and the Evil of changing It, demonstrated in Two Sermons. Edin. 1793.

Douglas, N. A Monitory Address to Great Britain by Britannicus. (Poem.) Edin. 1792.

——— The African Slave Trade. Edin. 1792.

——— An Address to the Judges and Jury in a Case of Alleged Sedition on the 26th May, 1817. . . . Glas. 1817.

Dunn, W. A Sermon preached from Rev. xxi. 5. Glas. 1792.

Erskine, J. The Fatal Consequences and the General Sources of Anarchy. A Discourse on Isa. xxiv. 1-5. Edin. 1793.

Facts, Reflections, and Queries submitted to the Consideration of the Associated Friends of the People. Edin. 1792.

Free Communing . . . or, A Last Attempt to cure the Lunatics now labouring under French Disease. Edin. 1793.

Geddes, A. K. Carmen Seculare pro Gallica Gente Tyrrannidi Aristocraticae Erepta. A Secular Ode on the French Revolution translated from the original Latin. Lond. and Paris, 1790.

Hardie, T. * The Patriot, addressed to the people on the present state of affairs in Britain and in France, with observations on Republican Government and discussions of the principles advanced in the writings of Thomas Paine. Edin. 1793.

——— Fidelity to the British Constitution, the Duty and Interest of the People. Edin. 1794.

——— The Importance of Religion to National Prosperity. Edin. 1794.

Hill, G. The Present Happiness of Great Britain. A Sermon on Deut. xxxiii. 29. Edin. 1792.

Keith, S. S. A Caution against Irreligion and Anarchy. Edin. 1794.

* Letters from the Friends of the People, or, The Last Words of a Weaver to His Children. Glas. 1792.

Look before Ye Loup . . . by Tam Thrum, An Auld Weaver. Edin. 1792.

Look before Ye Loup. Pt. ii., or, Another Box of Healin' Sa' for Crackit Crowns of Country Politicians. Edin. 1794.

Macleod, N. Two Letters to the Chairman of the Friends of the People at Edinburgh. Edin. 1793.

Macleod, N. Considerations on False and Real Alarms, dedicated with sincere and affectionate respect to the Earl of Lauderdale. Lond. 1794.

Mealmaker, G. The Moral and Political Catechism of Man. To which is added a narrative of the examination and imprisonment of the author for treasonable practices. Edin. 1797.

Modern Politics. Edin. 1793.

Observations on Paine's "Rights of Man." Edin. 1791.

Pat-Riot, A New Song by Mr. Hewardine. Edin. 1794.

Patriotic Wolves, A Poem by A Scotch Episcopal Clergyman. Edin. 1794.

* Plain Questions to the Working People of Scotland. Edin. 1792.

Political Preaching. . . . A Letter addressed to the Rev. Wm. Dunn, Kirkintilloch. Glas. 1792.

Reform or Ruin. Edin. 1798.

Robison, J. Proofs of a Conspiracy against all the Religions and Governments of Europe carried on in the secret meetings of the Free Masons, Illuminati, and Reading Societies, collected from good authorities. Edin. 1797. 3rd edn., corrected, Edin. 1798.

Scott, A., Citizen and Hairdresser. Plain Reasons for adopting the Plan of the Societies calling themselves Friends of the People. Edin. 1792.

Sempill, Hugh, Lord. A Short Address to the Public on the Practice of Cashiering Military Officers without a Trial, and a Vindication of the Conduct and Political Opinions of the Author. . . . Lond. 1793.

Shanks, A. Peace and Order recommended to Society in an Address to the Associated Congregation of Jedburgh from Jer. xxix. 7. Edin. 1793.

Sketch of the Character of the Late Thomas Reid, D.D. . . . with Observations on the Danger of Political Innovation, from a Discourse delivered on the 29th November, 1794, by Dr. Reid before the Literary Society in Glasgow College. Glas. 1796.

Somerville, T. The Effects of the French Revolution with respect to the Interests of Humanity, Liberty, Religion, and Morality. Edin. 1793.

Somerville, T. Observations on the Constitution and Present State of Great Britain. Edin. 1793.

Taylor, W. An Address to the People of Scotland on French Irreligion and Impiety. Edin. 1794.

* Ten Minutes' Reflection on the Late Events in France recommended by a Plain Man to his Fellow Citizens. Edin. 1792.

The French Constitutional Code as Revised, Amended, and Finally Completed by the National Assembly. Edin. 1791.

The Interests of Man in opposition to the Rights of Man, dedicated to Sir John Inglis of Cramond, Bart., and the other Gentlemen of the County and City of Edinburgh associated for the purpose of suppressing Sedition. Edin. 1793.

The Philistines, or, The Scotch Tocsin Sounders. Edin. 1793.

The Reformers, A Satirical Poem. Edin. 1793.

The Rights of Asses. (Poem.) Edin. 1793.

The Rights and Powers of Juries . . . by A Member of the College of Justice. Edin. 1791.

* The Spirit of the Times. Glas. (?), 1793.

The Telegraph: A Consolatory Epistle from Thomas Muir of Botany Bay to the Hon. Henry Erskine. (Edin.), 1796.

The Telegraph Inverted; or, Lauderdale's Peep at the Author and Adherents of the Telegraph. Edin. 1796.

Thoughts on the Privileges and Powers of Juries suggested by the Case of James Robertson and Walter Berry, Printer and Bookseller. Edin. 1793.

Wilde, J. An Address to the lately formed Society of the Friends of the People. Edin. 1793.

——— Sequel to an Address to the lately formed Society of the Friends of the People. Edin. 1797.

Young, J. * Essays on the Following Interesting Subjects, viz.—I. Government. II. Revolutions. III. British Government. IV. Kingly Government. V. Parliamentary Representation. VI. Liberty and Equality. VII. The Present War and the Stagnation of Credit connected with it. Edin. 1794. Numerous reprints.

8. *The British and Irish Political Societies and The State Trials.*

There is no monograph on the Scottish societies: their activities must be studied in the documents of the P.R.O. *Scot. Corr.* and in the contemporary press. The minutes of the first Convention of the Friends of the People in Scotland will be found in Appendix A, and the names of the delegates to the second in Appendix B of this work. The official minutes of the first are printed in the *Report from the Committee of Secrecy of the House of Commons relative to the Proceedings of the Different Persons and Societies in Great Britain and Ireland engaged in a Treasonable Conspiracy,* March 15, 1797, *Parl. Hist.* xxxiv. 579 *et seq.* The minutes of the third, and of its successor, the British Convention, are given in the *Second Report from the Committee of Secrecy of the House of Commons respecting Seditious Practices,* May to June, 1794, *Parl. Hist.* xxxi. 844 *et seq.*, and more fully in the *State Trials,* xxiii. 391 *et seq.* These reports were also issued in pamphlet form at Edinburgh and London. See also *An Account of the Proceedings of the British Convention held in Edinburgh, the 19th of November,* 1793, by a Member, Lond. n.d.; *The Address of the British Convention assembled at Edinburgh, November* 19, 1793, *to the People of Great Britain,* Lond. n.d.; and J. Gerrald's *A Convention the Only Means of saving us from Ruin, in a Letter addressed to the People of England* (1793), new edn. Lond. 1796.

Most of the relevant literature centres round Muir and his fellow "martyrs." P. Mackenzie's *The Life and Trial of Thomas Muir,* Glas. 1831, and the same author's *Reminiscences of Glasgow and the West of Scotland,* 3 vols. Glas. 1865-1883, have hitherto been the main sources of information. Mackenzie was a noted Radical of his day and these books are more or less political pamphlets. Of the same nature are *Memoirs and Trials of The Political Martyrs of Scotland,* Edin. 1837; *The Trial of W. Skirving with an Original Memoir and Notes,* Glas. 1836; and *The Trial of J. Gerrald with an Original Memoir and Notes,* Glas. 1835. The last two are contained in the first. For Muir, see also the French sources mentioned below; *Histoire de la Tyrannie du Gouvernement Anglais exercée envers le Célèbre Thomas Muir, Écossais,* Paris, an vi. (Brit. Mus.); F. Michel's

Les Écossais en France et les Français en Écosse, 2 vols. Lond. 1862, vol. ii.; *Old and New,* vol. ix. 1894, Thomas Muir, art. by B. Drew (worthless for biographical purposes, but showing the interest excited in America by the trial); *Notes and Queries,* 4th series, vol. iii. 365, 389. There is an account of Margarot in the *Place Coll. Brit. Mus. Add. MSS. No.* 27816. G. Dyer's *Slave and Famine Punishments for Sedition,* 2nd edn. Lond. 1794, contains a sketch of Palmer. Further material will be found in *A Narrative of the Sufferings of T. F. Palmer and W. Skirving during a Voyage to New South Wales,* 1794, *on board the Surprize Transport,* by T. F. Palmer, Camb. 2nd edn. 1794; *The Monthly Magazine,* xvii. 83-5; *The Monthly Repository,* xii. 204, 261 *et seq.*; and the *Dict. Nat. Biog.*

The various *Reports of the Committees of Secrecy* are also the contemporary sources for the English societies. As indicated in the text, they must be used with caution. Of the numerous pamphlets of the time *The Proceedings of the Society of the Friends of the People associated for the purpose of obtaining a Parliamentary Reform in the year* 1792, Lond. 1793, and *A Collection of Addresses transmitted by certain English Clubs and Societies to the National Convention of France . . .* 2nd edn. Lond. 1793, may be noted.

For the United Scotsmen, see *Reports from the Committees of Secrecy,* 1797, and *State Trials,* xxvi. 1135-1179. For the United Irishmen the following works have also been consulted: The first and second *Reports from the Committee of Secrecy of the House of Lords* (Ireland), Dublin, 1798; *Report from the Committee of Secrecy of the House of Commons of Ireland, 10th May,* 1797, Lond. 1797; R. Madden, *The United Irishmen,* 7 vols. Lond. 1842-6; W. Wolfe Tone, *Life of Theobald Wolfe Tone,* 2 vols. Washington, 1826; W. J. Fitzpatrick, *Secret Service under Pitt,* Lond. 1892; E. Guillon, *La France et l'Irlande pendant La Révolution,* Paris, 1888; W. E. H. Lecky, *History of England,* vols. vii. and viii.

The *State Trials* were edited by T. B. and T. S. Howell, Lond. 1809-28. Vol. xxiii. begins with those of 1793. The Scottish trials are discussed from the Whig point of view in Lord Cockburn's *Examination of the Trials for Sedition in Scotland,* 2 vols. Edin. 1888; and in D. Hume's *Commentaries on the Law of Scotland respecting Crimes,* 2 vols. Edin. 1844, and J. Burnett's

A Treatise on Various Branches of the Criminal Law of Scotland, Edin. 1811, from the Tory standpoint.

The chief English biographies relating to the subject are: G. Wallas's *Life of Francis Place,* Lond. 1898; *Memoir of Thomas Hardy,* written by himself, Lond. 1832; C. Cestre's *John Thelwall, A Pioneer of Democracy and Social Reform in England during the French Revolution,* Lond. 1906; F. D. Cartwright's *Life and Correspondence of Major Cartwright,* 2 vols. Lond. 1826.

Of general works dealing with the political societies the following may be mentioned: J. B. Daly's *The Dawn of Radicalism,* Lond. 1892; C. Kent's *The English Radicals,* Lond. 1899; W. T. Laprade's *England and the French Revolution,* 1789-1797, Baltimore, 1909; E. Smith's *The Story of the English Jacobins* (based on the Place Collection), Lond. 1881; J. Holland Rose's *William Pitt and the Great War,* Lond. 1911, chap. vii., "The British Jacobins."

9. *Contemporary French Sources—MS. and Printed.*

The archives of the French Foreign Office throw a flood of light on the opinions regarding the political condition of Great Britain and Ireland which prevailed in official circles during the Revolutionary era, and on the schemes for invading the British Isles. Most of the documents relate to England or Ireland, but there are various reports of officials, spies, and refugees on the state of Scotland.

"Correspondance Politique" (Angleterre), tomes 584-602, and Supplé. 21, and "Mémoires et Documents" (Angleterre), tomes 2 and 53, have been examined. There is a descriptive index to each volume. Akin to these sources is F. A. Aulard's *La Société des Jacobins,* 6 vols. Paris, 1889-1897, vols. iii. and iv. of which have yielded a few references to Scotland.

The following pamphlets in the British Museum Collection relating to the French Revolution reveal the French attitude towards Scotland during this period:

Adresse des Anglois, des Écossois, et des Irlandois résidans et domiciliés à Paris à la Convention Nationale, séance du 28 nov. 1792. Imprimé par ordre de la Convention Nationale, Paris, 1792.

Brissot, J. P. Exposé de la Conduite de la Nation envers le Peuple Anglais. Paris, 1793.

Chas, J. Tableau Historique et Politique de la Dissolution et du Rétablissement de la Monarchie Anglaise depuis 1625 jusqu'en 1702. Paris, an viii.

Constant, B. Des Suites de la Contre Révolution de 1660 en Angleterre. Paris, an vii.

Diacon, J. Guerre à l'Angleterre. Paris, n.d.

Dillon, A. Progrès de la Révolution Française en Angleterre. Paris, ce 27 avril, 1792.

Dorat-Cubières. Prophétie Républicaine adressée à M. Pitt et à ses Complices . . . le 17 nivôse de l'an ii. Paris (?).

Gallet, P. A l'Europe et au Gouvernement Anglais, un Aperçu sur les Causes de la Guerre et sur les Résultats pour la Puissance Agressive. Paris, an xi.

Lachevardière, A. L. Discours sur la Constitution et le Gouvernement d'Angleterre, Prononcé à la Société des Jacobins à Paris. 1er pluviôse de l'an deux. Paris.

Mandar, Théo. Adresse au Roi de la Grande Bretagne sur . . . la Nécessité d'une Prompte Paix. 3e éd. Paris, an vii.

P—— C—— Ode aux Français sur leur Projet de Descente en Angleterre. Paris, an xii.

Peyrard, le c. Précis Historique des Principales Descentes qui ont été faites dans la Grande Bretagne. 2e éd. Paris, an vi.

——— Résponse à la Déclaration du Roi d'Angleterre relativement à ses Motifs pour continuer la Guerre actuelle. Paris, an ii.

10. *Ecclesiastical Affairs.*

The best general history is J. Cunningham's *Church History of Scotland*, 2 vols. Edin. 1859, written from the Presbyterian standpoint. An ultra-evangelical work is that of W. M. Hetherington, *History of the Church of Scotland*, Edin. 1843. G. Grub's *An Ecclesiastical History of Scotland*, 4 vols. Edin. 1861, treats the same subject from the Episcopalian point of view. The standard Roman Catholic history is A. Bellesheim's *History of the Catholic Church in Scotland* (trans. Hunter Blair), 4 vols. Edin. and Lond. 1887. For the Seceders, see G. Struthers' excellent *History of the Rise, Progress, and Principles of the Relief Church*, Glasgow, 1843; J. M'Kerrow's *History of the Secession*

Church, 2 vols. Edin. 1839; D. Scott's *Annals and Statistics of the Original Secession Church* (with lists of pamphlets), Edin. 1886. The fullest account of the Moderates will be found in W. L. Mathieson's *Scotland and the Union*, 1695-1747, Glas. 1905, chaps. vi. and vii., and the same author's *The Awakening of Scotland*, 1747-1797, Glas. 1910, chaps. iv. and v.

AUTOBIOGRAPHIES, BIOGRAPHIES, AND MEMOIRS.

A. Carlyle, *op. cit.*, and T. Somerville, *op. cit.*, are indispensable. There is a *Biographical Memoir of William Robertson*, the leader of the Moderates, in D. Stewart's Works, vol. x., ed. W. Hamilton, Edin. 1858. Robertson's successor was Dr. Hill, whose biography was written by G. Cook—*Life of George Hill*, Edin. 1850. H. Moncreiff Wellwood's *Account of the Life and Writings of John Erskine, D.D.*, Edin. 1818, describes the policy of the Popular Party, especially regarding Patronage. J. F. Gordon's Life of Bishop Hay in his *Journal and Appendix to Scotichronicon and Monasticon*, Glas. 1867, traces the history of Roman Catholicism in Scotland during this period. A. Haldane's *Memoirs of the Lives of Robert Haldane of Airthrey and of his brother James Alexander Haldane*, Lond. 3rd edn. 1853, gives a too sympathetic account of these lay preachers. W. Hanna's *Life of Dr Chalmers*, 2 vols. Edin. and Lond. 1863, is useful for later ecclesiastical and social affairs.

PAMPHLETS AND MINOR AUTHORITIES.

Patronage:

Hardie, T. The Principles of Moderation addressed to the Clergy of the Popular Interest in the Church of Scotland. Edin. 1782.

An Address to the People of Scotland on Ecclesiastical and Civil Liberty. Edin. 1782.

An Inquiry into the Principles of Ecclesiastical Patronage and Presentation in which are contained Views of the influence of this Species of Patronage on the Manners and Character of the People. Edin. 1783.

A Speech addressed to the Synod of Glasgow and Ayr, April, 1784. Glas. 1784.

Missions and Lay Preaching:

Warneck, G. Outline of a History of Christian Missions. 8th edn. Trans. by G. Robson. 3rd edn. Edin. and Lond. 1906.

Account of the Proceedings and Debate in the General Assembly of the Church of Scotland, May 27, 1796. Edin. 1796.

An Account of the Proceedings of the Society for Propagating the Gospel at Home. Edin. 1799.

Douglas, N. Journal of a Mission to Parts of the Highlands of Scotland in 1797. Edin. 1799. The best of its kind.

Haldane, J. Journal of a Tour through the Northern Counties of Scotland and the Orkneys in the Autumn of 1797. Edin. 1798.

Haldane, R. Address to the Public concerning Politics and Plans lately adopted to promote Religion in Scotland. Edin. 1800.

Hill, Rowland. Journal of a Tour through . . . Parts of Scotland etc. Lond. 1799.

——— A Series of Letters occasioned by the Late Pastoral Admonition. Lond. 1799.

——— Extracts of a Second Tour through Scotland. Lond. 1800.

Jones, W. Memoirs . . . of the Rev. Rowland Hill. Lond. 1834.

Philip, M. J. Hans Neilsen Hauge, art. in *Missionary Record of the United Free Church of Scotland*, April, 1911.

Wilberforce, R. J. and S. Life of W. Wilberforce. 5 vols. Lond. 1838.

Seceders and Sedition:

Porteous, W. The New Light Examined. Glas. 1800.

Peddie, J. A Defence of the Associate Synod against the Charge of Sedition addressed to Wm. Porteous, D.D. Edin. 1800.

11. *Local History.*

The Statistical Account of Scotland drawn up from Communications of the Ministers of the Different Parishes, ed. Sir J. Sinclair, 21 vols. Edin. 1791-99, is an original authority of great importance for the social condition of Scotland at the close of the eighteenth century. In not a few cases the writers touch on current political affairs, especially the influence of Paine's works on their parishioners.

Most of the local histories of Scotland are antiquarian rather than political. The following have been found useful:

Chambers, W. A History of Peeblesshire. Edin. and Lond. 1864.

Cowan, S. The Ancient Capital of Scotland (Perth). 2 vols. Lond. 1904.

Craig-Brown, T. A History of Selkirkshire. 2 vols. Edin. 1886.

Creech, W. Edinburgh Fugitive Pieces. Edin. 1815.

Henderson, E. The Annals of Dunfermline. Glas. 1879.

M'Dowall, W. History of Dumfries. Edin. 1867.

Metcalfe, W. M. A History of Paisley. Paisley, 1909.

Miller, J. The Lamp of Lothian (Haddington). Haddington. New edn. 1900.

Wilson, J. Annals of Hawick, 1214-1814. Edin. 1850.

Wilson, R. History of Hawick. 2nd edn. Edin. and Hawick, 1841.

12. *Travels.*

For a full list of travellers in Scotland during this period, see A. Mitchell's *List of Travels and Tours in Scotland* (1296-1900), reprinted from the *Proceedings of the Society of Antiquaries of Scotland*, vol. xxxv., Edin. 1902, and continued in vol. xxxix.

Cobbett, W. Tour in Scotland and in the Four Northern English Counties in the Autumn of the Year 1832. Lond. 1833.

Heron, R. Observations made in a Journey through the Western Counties of Scotland in the Autumn of 1792. 2 vols. 2nd edn. Perth, 1799.

Latocnaye, M. de. Promenade d'un Français dans l'Irlande. Dublin, 1797.

Lettice, I. Letters on a Tour through Various Parts of Scotland in the Year 1792. Lond. 1794.

Moore, J. A Journal of a Residence in France from the beginning of August to the middle of December, 1792, to which is added an Account of the most remarkable events that happened at Paris from that time to the death of the late King of France. 2 vols. Lond. 1793.

Pichot, A. Historical and Literary Tour of a Foreigner in England and Scotland. 2 vols. Lond. 1825; also 3 tomes, Paris, 1825.

13. *Poetry, Drama, and Fiction.*

Burns, R. Life and Works, ed. R. Chambers. New edn. ed. W. Wallace. 4 vols. Edin. and Lond. 1896.

Campbell, T. Poetical Works, with biographical sketch, ed. W. A. Hill. Lond. 1851.

Wilson, A. Poetical Works, also his Miscellaneous Prose Writings, Journals, Letters, Essays, etc. Belfast, 1844.

Fyfe, A. The Royal Martyr, King Charles I. A Tragedy. Lond. 1709.

Logan, J. Poems and Runnamede, A Tragedy. New edn. with life of the author. Edin. 1805.

The historical novels of John Galt are of great value. Having lived during the period, he described the changes which he himself had witnessed, and in his *Annals of the Parish* (1760-1810) he gives a realistic picture of the social and political condition of Scotland during the second half of the eighteenth century. *The Provost* depicts municipal affairs before 1833. Scott being a more imaginative writer, is of less importance in this connection; but in *The Antiquary* ("Border Edition," ed. A. Lang, Lond. 1898) he draws largely upon his own experiences for the description of the "False Alarm" and the politics of "Fairport." *St. Ronan's Well* deals with certain aspects of Scottish society about 1823. The hero of E. H. Strain's *A Prophet's Reward*, Edin. and Lond. 1908, is Thomas Muir, the historical details being reproduced from contemporary sources.

INDEX.